Prenatal Genetic Testing, Abortion, and Disability Justice

Prenatal Genetic Testing, Abortion, and Disability Justice

Amber Knight
and
Joshua Miller

OXFORD
UNIVERSITY PRESS

Great Clarendon Street, Oxford, Ox2 6DP,
United Kingdom

Oxford University Press is a department of the University of Oxford.
It furthers the University's objective of excellence in research, scholarship,
and education by publishing worldwide. Oxford is a registered trade mark of
Oxford University Press in the UK and in certain other countries

© Amber Knight and Joshua Miller 2023

The moral rights of the authors have been asserted

All rights reserved. No part of this publication may be reproduced, stored in
a retrieval system, or transmitted, in any form or by any means, without the
prior permission in writing of Oxford University Press, or as expressly permitted
by law, by licence or under terms agreed with the appropriate reprographics
rights organization. Enquiries concerning reproduction outside the scope of the
above should be sent to the Rights Department, Oxford University Press, at the
address above

You must not circulate this work in any other form
and you must impose this same condition on any acquirer

Published in the United States of America by Oxford University Press
198 Madison Avenue, New York, NY 10016, United States of America

British Library Cataloguing in Publication Data

Data available

Library of Congress Control Number: 2022949314

ISBN 978–0–19–287095–7

DOI: 10.1093/oso/9780192870957.001.0001

Printed and bound in the UK by
Clays Ltd, Elcograf S.p.A.

Links to third party websites are provided by Oxford in good faith and
for information only. Oxford disclaims any responsibility for the materials
contained in any third party website referenced in this work.

In honor of our parents

Todd and Juliette Knight

and

Paula and Julian Miller

Acknowledgments

We have many people to thank for their support and feedback on this book. First and foremost, we owe a debt of gratitude to Michael Lienesch, a man who continues to mentor and advise us despite the fact that we finished graduate school many years ago. We intend to leave him in peace to enjoy his well-earned retirement now that the book is finished, but we make no promises. In addition, we are grateful to Daniel Engster and Nancy Hirschmann for providing input on early chapter drafts and helping to steer the project in the right direction from the start. Many individuals took the time and energy to provide detailed and insightful comments on the book as it took shape, including Jennifer Denbow, Claire McKinney, Maggie Quinlan, Monica Schneider, Jeff Spinner-Halev, Katie Turner, Penny Weiss, and Jason Windett. In addition, Mel Atkinson, Susan Bickford, Gordon Hull, and Jim Walsh commented on drafts of our book proposal and provided helpful advice about the publication process. We also thank the anonymous reviewers at Oxford University Press for their generous comments and constructive criticism. Sincere thanks are also due to our editors, Dominic Wyatt and Jade Dixon, for their much-needed guidance and encouragement. Finally, here at UNC Charlotte, we are grateful for the enduring support of our wonderful colleagues and students.

We were also fortunate enough to receive feedback on the book at several workshops, colloquia, and conferences. In 2019, the "Theorizing the Politics of Disability Research Workshop" (funded by the American Political Science Association's Edward Artinian Fund) gave us the opportunity to receive input on the project while it was still in its infancy. Likewise, participants in the Western Political Science Association's Critical Disability Studies virtual community have helped us to improve our arguments over time. This community of political theorists, who all share an interest in disability justice, is filled with some of the most supportive, kind, and brilliant scholars in academia, and we are truly grateful for their camaraderie. In addition, chapters benefited from feedback that we received at the University of Minnesota Political Theory Colloquium and The Ohio State University Political Theory Workshop. Comments and questions from discussants and audience members at conferences—including the Association for Political Theory, the

viii Acknowledgments

American Political Science Association, the Western Political Science Association, and the Southern Political Science Association—also improved the book along the way.

Finally, we would like to thank Cambridge University Press for giving us permission to use revised portions of a published article. Portions of an earlier version of Chapter 3 appeared as "Prenatal Genetic Screening, Epistemic Justice, and Reproductive Autonomy" in *Hypatia: A Journal of Feminist Philosophy*, volume 36, issue 1, pp. 1–21.

A personalized note from Amber. This book makes the case that individuals, and their capacities and opportunities in life, flourish within relationships of support and care. Thus, it is only fitting that I acknowledge the various networks that have made my academic career and the completion of this book possible. I am grateful beyond measure to my immediate biological family and the various extended "friendship families" that I have joined all over the country, including friends and colleagues from Georgetown, Santa Cruz, Chapel Hill, Saint Louis, and Charlotte. In addition, I appreciate Josh and his willingness to share the book-writing journey with me. Moreover, I could not have written this book without my life partner, Jason Windett. His meal preparation, technological support, and feminist commitment to equal co-parenting made it possible for me to write a book during a global pandemic with limited access to childcare. Choosing him as my life partner was the best decision that I have ever made. Finally, I am indebted to Logan, my loving child, for his patience and understanding. I have no doubt that he will work to make the world a more inclusive, caring place for the next generation.

A personalized note from Josh. Much of this work demonstrates how our decisions are shaped by the options we see before us. In that spirit, I would like to thank my mentors at Stetson University—especially Gary Maris, John Pearson, Bill Nylen, and Gene Huskey—for making a life in political theory seem like a viable option. I would also like to thank my students at UNC Charlotte for making that life richer by the day. Thanks to Amber for transforming the usually solitary work of scholarship into a collaborative practice of friendship. Most of all, thanks to Katie Turner, who has both deepened and expanded my thinking over thrown-together dinners, meandering dog walks, and twenty years' worth of lunch dates. This book and I are better because of her.

Contents

Abbreviations	xi
Introduction	**1**
Scope	4
Contributions to the Literature	9
Political Theory	9
Feminist Theory	12
Disability Studies	16
Chapter Summaries	21
References	26

PART I.   THEORY

1. Autonomy in Political Theory	**35**
Why Autonomy?	36
Meaning	39
Value	47
Politics	51
Conclusion	55
References	55
2. Reproductive Autonomy and Genomic Medicine	**61**
Meaning	63
Value	68
Politics	74
Conclusion	81
References	82

PART II. APPLICATIONS

3. The Healthcare System	**89**
Informed Consent and Physician Authority	93
(Mis)Informed Choice from Biased and Limited Information	97
Testimonial Injustice and Its Harm	103
"Pro-Choice" Defense of Government Regulation	106
Conclusion	114
References	115

x   Contents

4. The Neoliberal Welfare State   **121**
Neoliberal Policy and Disability   125
Pregnant Women as Neoliberal Biocitizens   133
From the Limited Neoliberal State to the Supportive State   138
Policy Implications   143
Conclusion   146
References   147

5. Ableist and Sexist Social Norms   **155**
The Sexual Division of Labor and the Costs of Lifelong Motherhood   158
Pernicious Cultural Constructions   161
   Ableist Prejudice   161
   "Good Moms" and "Perfect Babies"   164
   The Idealized Nuclear Family   167
Social and Cultural Change   169
Conclusion   176
References   176

6. Conclusion: The Coronavirus Pandemic and Its Implications   **183**
References   189

Afterword: Prenatal Genetic Testing and Abortion after *Dobbs*   **193**
References   198

Index   199

Abbreviations

AAMC	Association of American Medical Colleges
ABLE	Achieving Better Life Experience
ACMG	American College of Medical Genetics and Genomics
ACOG	American Congress of Obstetricians and Gynecologists
ADLs	activities of daily living
AFP	alpha-fetoprotein
CAPS	Coalition for Access to Prenatal Screening
CDC	Centers for Disease Control
CLASS	Community Living Assistance Services and Supports
CMS	Centers for Medicare and Medicaid Services
CVS	chorionic villus sampling
FDA	Food and Drug Administration
FINDS	Family and Individual Needs for Disability Supports
FLSA	Fair Labor Standards Act
hCG	human chorionic gonadotropin
HDI	Human Development Index
IADLs	instrumental activities of daily living
IDEA	Individuals with Disabilities Education Act
IEP	Individualized Education Program
LDT	laboratory-developed test
NDAC	National Down syndrome Advocacy Coalition
NDSS	National Down Syndrome Society
NIPT	non-invasive prenatal testing
NSGC	National Society of Genetic Counselors
OECD	Organization for Economic Cooperation and Development
PGD	preimplantation genetic diagnosis
SCD	stem cell-derived
SMFM	Society for Maternal Fetal Medicine
SNT	special needs trust
SSI	Supplemental Security Income
WHO	World Health Organization

Introduction

The rapid adoption and proliferation of prenatal genetic testing has placed disability front and center in the decades-long culture war over abortion and women's reproductive rights in the United States.[1] Various technologies for prenatal screening and diagnosis have been used since the late 1960s, but non-invasive prenatal testing (NIPT), which was developed in the wake of the human genome project, has only recently become a part of mainstream prenatal care. First introduced for clinical practice in Hong Kong in 2011, NIPT detects various chromosomal atypicalities—including Down syndrome (trisomy 21), Edwards syndrome (trisomy 18), and Patau syndrome (trisomy 13)—from cell-free fetal DNA in the mother's bloodstream.[2] The screening procedure is remarkably accurate and carries no risk of miscarriage, since it requires a simple blood draw (Norton et al. 2015; Taylor-Phillips et al. 2016).[3] The procedure is also relatively low cost, and major private insurance plans began to cover it in 2013.[4] NIPT is performed earlier in pregnancy than standard tests, which gives women more time to make an informed decision about how to move forward with their pregnancy.[5] The shortened timeline between screening, diagnosis, and selective termination matters, since abortion is illegal in most states after at least twenty-four weeks.

The procedure has become increasingly popular among patients and healthcare providers alike, and it has been widely adopted as a routine part

---

[1] The terms "screening" and "testing" connote different types of procedures. Screening procedures estimate the likelihood or risk that a fetus has a genetic impairment. Prenatal genetic tests more conclusively diagnose whether a fetus actually has a specific disorder.

[2] NIPT can also screen for sex chromosome atypicalities, including monosomy X (Turner Syndrome), XXY (Klinefelter's Syndrome) and XXX (Triple X).

[3] Although NIPT is a screening procedure that allows for remarkably accurate early detection of Down syndrome, positive results still require diagnostic confirmation via amniocentesis or chorionic villus sampling (CVS). Only approximately 6% of American women whose NIPT results indicate a high probability of fetal chromosomal anomaly elected to abort without further verification (Taneja et al. 2016). Ilana Löwy (2020: 4) suspects some of them may decide to terminate a pregnancy on the basis of NIPT results alone because "they preferred not to wait until it was possible to confirm those results with amniocentesis and risk facing a more complicated second-trimester abortion."

[4] In the US, nearly all major commercial health insurance companies cover NIPT for "high-risk" patients of advanced maternal age, as do most state-sponsored Medicaid programs. Medicaid programs also cover NIPT for average risk women in several states (Gadsboll et al. 2020).

[5] NIPT is usually offered ten weeks into the pregnancy. Its early administration gives prospective parents the option to learn the sex of the fetus much earlier than a second trimester ultrasound.

Prenatal Genetic Testing, Abortion, and Disability Justice. Amber Knight and Joshua Miller, Oxford University Press.
© Amber Knight and Joshua Miller (2023). DOI: 10.1093/oso/9780192870957.003.0001

2 Prenatal Genetic Testing, Abortion, and Disability Justice

of prenatal care in many advanced industrialized societies (Hui and Bianchi 2017). In 2012, a year after the first test hit the market, four companies manufactured NIPT. In 2022 more than forty commercial biotech labs offer the procedure. The increase in supply has been matched by an increase in demand. Earlier prenatal screening technologies were offered to women of "advanced maternal age" who were at higher risk of giving birth to a child with Down syndrome. By the end of 2016, several North American professional societies—including the Society for Maternal Fetal Medicine (SMFM), the American Congress of Obstetricians and Gynecologists (ACOG), and the American College of Medical Genetics and Genomics (ACMG)—altered their position to recommend that NIPT be made available to all pregnant women. The pool of patients grew considerably as a result. At an international meeting of reproductive scientists in 2019, the inventor of NIPT, Dennis Lo, told the audience that six million women from ninety countries had so far been screened. According to economic forecasts, global revenues for the industry are expected to exceed $2.5 billion by 2025 (Molteni 2019).

Despite their routinized use, prenatal genetic screening and testing technologies have ignited their fair share of political controversy. In a 2012 interview on CBS's *Face the Nation*, then Republican presidential candidate and former Senator Rick Santorum (R-PA) sharply criticized the Affordable Care Act for requiring health-insurance companies to cover certain prenatal tests. Santorum argued that insurance companies should not be required to pay for prenatal genetic testing, because the procedure is a gateway to abortion. In Santorum's words, "the bottom line is that a lot of prenatal tests are done to identify deformities in utero and the customary procedure is to encourage abortions" (quoted in DeLong 2012). In his book *Bella's Gift* (2015), which centers around Santorum's experience parenting his daughter Bella, who was born with trisomy 18, he further criticized the federal government for allowing prospective parents "to kill their children once they find out their babies aren't perfect" (Santorum 2015: 49).

National debate over prenatal screening and selective abortion has also made headlines in the US media. In 2015, The *New York Times* published an op-ed asking, "Does Down Syndrome Justify Abortion?" (Schrad 2015). The topic re-emerged in 2017 after *CBS News* had published a controversial article, titled "'What Kind of World do you Want to Live In?' Inside the Country where Down Syndrome is Disappearing." The piece investigated the rise of prenatal screening across Europe and the United States to examine the potential effect on termination rates for fetuses with Down syndrome. The article, which claims that "few countries have come as close to eradicating Down syndrome births as Iceland," set off a media firestorm in several countries (Quinones and Lajka 2017). In the US, conservative columnist George Will (2018) responded by claiming that Iceland "is close to success in its program of genocide" and that America "is playing catch-up in the Down syndrome elimination sweepstakes."

This framing of prenatal screening as a conduit to selective abortion has helped pro-life organizations successfully leverage the rhetoric of disability rights to advance an anti-abortion agenda. Several states have recently proposed or passed "prenatal non-discrimination acts," which criminalize abortion in cases of fetal genetic impairment. In 2013, one year before NIPT was introduced in the United States, North Dakota became the first state to prohibit abortion in cases where there is "genetic abnormality or a potential for a genetic abnormality." Louisiana and Indiana enacted prenatal disability non-discrimination acts in 2016. In 2017, Ohio passed its version banning abortion if a "pregnant woman is seeking the abortion, in whole or in part, because of ... a test result indicating Down syndrome in an unborn child." Kentucky's legislation was enacted in 2019. Most recently, Missouri, Arizona, and South Dakota have signed such bills into law.[6] The exact terms of these statutes differ, but all prohibit abortions in cases of potential fetal impairment.

Although these legislative acts regulating reproductive decisions claim to protect individuals with disabilities and their families, critics have argued that their primary goal is to prohibit abortion and eventually overturn *Roe v. Wade* (Piepmeier 2013; Denbow 2015; Giric 2016). These critics argue that, if the primary goal of these measures really was to promote disability rights, they would have been accompanied by public policies to expand resources that improve the social situation of people living with disabilities. As Sujatha Jesudason and Julia Epstein (2011: 542) observe, this has not been the case in most states:

> Anti-choice advocates tend to idealize disability while opposing the entitlement programs and government funding of social services, such as state developmental disability programs, funding for the Individuals with Disabilities Education Act, and the access mandates of the Americans with Disabilities Act that would make raising a child with a disability more possible.

---

[6] As of 2021, nineteen states have introduced bills that prohibit abortion based on a fetus's diagnosis or potential diagnosis of Down syndrome, and six of those states have enacted the statues (Guttmacher Institute 2021). Many of these laws are currently making their way through the court system, and some courts have ordered temporary injunctions on the legislation, pending litigation. As of 2021 the only state to have a prenatal non-discrimination act overruled is Indiana. In 2017, the Indiana Southern District Court held the state's disability abortion ban unconstitutional under *Casey's* undue burden standard.

4 Prenatal Genetic Testing, Abortion, and Disability Justice

It follows that prenatal non-discrimination acts should therefore be understood as pro-life Trojan horses, in which their proponents use the rhetoric of disability rights to advance an anti-abortion agenda. Put simply, prenatal non-discrimination acts strip women of reproductive decision-making power under the thinly veiled guise of caring about and protecting future people with disabilities.

The ongoing political battles about prenatal testing, selective abortion, disability, and governmental regulation raise various questions at the heart of this book. What is the normative aim of prenatal genetic screening? Is it a means of enhancing women's reproductive autonomy, a contemporary tool of eugenics, or perhaps both? Who stands to benefit from the use of these technologies, and who may be harmed by their routinization? And, what, if anything, is the role of government in regulating prenatal screening technologies and/or selective termination? Grounding our inquiry in the wider literatures on liberal political thought, feminist theory, and critical disability studies, we grapple with these questions in an effort to defend women's reproductive rights *and* promote disability justice.

Scope

This book analyzes women's reproductive autonomy in the age of genomic medicine, at a time when prenatal genetic screening is the new normal in obstetric practice. Why women's reproductive autonomy? Throughout the writing process, we have debated which language to use in the book. "Expectant mothers" or "prospective parents"? "Pregnant women," "pregnant persons," or "gestating persons"? After all, it is not just cisgendered women who experience pregnancy, since transmen and non-binary individuals also give birth and raise children. The transgender rights movement has urged the use of gender-neutral language, such as "pregnant people" and "parent."[7] Although there are inclusionary benefits to speaking about parenting in gender-neutral terms, such language also masks the ways in which reproduction and parenthood are deeply *gendered* experiences. A binary understanding of gender is an indispensable part of the infrastructure of the public policy, political economy, and social norms that inform contemporary reproductive politics. To avoid the risk of making sexism and the specific oppressions of women invisible, we frequently employ the terms "woman" and "mother," although we do so with the recognition that

---

[7] For a compelling argument in favor of gender-neutral language, see Jack Halberstam (2018).

the boundaries of these terms are socially contingent, fluid, and open to contestation and revision. Moreover, our focus on women's reproductive autonomy has obvious limitations, since the book says little about how reproductive decision-making might play out for cismen, transmen, or non-binary individuals.

As a normatively based and empirically informed work of political theory, our focus is primarily on the United States and its particular medical practices, public policies, and cultural norms. Our goal is to provide an in-depth illustration of the various structural power relations that circumscribe American women's decisions about whether to use reprogenetic technologies and to what end. The United States is an interesting case because, as Nancy Hirchmann (2016: 43–4) has pointed out: "In a country that claims to provide among the strongest disability rights in the world, we find a reality that disabled persons are still often treated as second-class citizens." Moreover, with its privatized medical system, neoliberal welfare state, and privileging of the nuclear family as the primary site of care work, the United States also provides a stark example of a society that funnels primary responsibility for meeting children's disability-related dependency needs on mothers' shoulders while at the same time eroding women's capacities to obtain abortion services and opt out of motherhood.

Moreover, our analysis of reprogenetics is limited to a focus on prenatal genetic screening and selective abortion.[8] Broadly speaking, the term "reprogenetics" refers to the ways in which reproductive and genetic technologies converge to influence the particular genetic makeup of a child. More specifically, reprogenetics connotes biotechnologies that involve the creation, use, manipulation, selection, or storage of gametes or embryos (Jesudason 2009: 901). The expanded repertoire of technologies is quickly developing and evolving. In addition to prenatal genetic screening and diagnosis, some current reprogenetic procedures include: the use of donated gametes, *in vitro* fertilization and preimplantation genetic diagnosis (PGD), carrier screening, and the creation of stem-cell-derived (SCD) gametes. Regardless of the specific technology, the fact that parents can influence the genome of their children raises a whole host of complex ethical, philosophical, and political questions. However, each technology is different and must be considered on

---

[8] Although this book questions the potential repercussions of widespread use of NIPT on women's reproductive decision-making, we are not exclusively interested in NIPT since: (1) other types of screening procedures—including chromosome microarrays, biochemical marker screening, and ultrasound and nuchal translucency screening—are still commonly used; and (2) NIPT has actually lead to an increased usage of traditional diagnostic tests—including amniocentesis and chorionic villus sampling (CVS)—since positive screening results still require diagnostic confirmation.

6 Prenatal Genetic Testing, Abortion, and Disability Justice

its own terms, since there may be salient normative differences between selection and enhancement techniques, for example, or between technologies that enable conception and technologies that bring about pregnancy termination.

Reprogenetics is both a scientific and a commercial enterprise, and business is booming. Many of the biotechnology companies that manufacture NIPTs and profit from their use—including Sequenom and Quest Diagnostics—are publicly traded companies that operate in a highly competitive business landscape. These corporations face market pressures to expand operations and make money for their shareholders.[9] Because biotechnology companies are profit driven and have a vested interest in expanding the pool of consumers and the menu of tests to increase revenue, they have heavily promoted the routinization of NIPT in the US. This book considers both the economic and the scientific dimensions at play in reprogenetic medicine.

Our investigation into the impact that prenatal genetic screening has had on women's reproductive autonomy is guided by a sustained focus on fetal diagnoses of Down syndrome. Many of our analyses and insights are widely applicable to other conditions, but terms such as "people with disabilities" and "fetuses with impairments" obscure the complexity of different and distinctive impairments. The Down syndrome community is already diverse, because symptoms and prognoses vary in each case. As Michael Bérubé (1996: 20–1) observes: "Down's doesn't cut all children to one mold; the relationship between … genotype and phenotype [is] lacy and intricate." For the sake of clarity and specificity, therefore, the empirical realities of Down syndrome serve as a prism through which we gain a broader understanding of the nexus between prenatal testing and reproductive politics.

Down syndrome is the most common chromosomal disorder in the United States, occurring in approximately one of every 733 live births (Skotko, Capone, and Kishnani 2009).[10] While people usually have forty-six chromosomes that are grouped together in twenty-three pairs, individuals with Down syndrome have extra genetic material relating to the twenty-first chromosome. There are actually three different types of Down syndrome, which are differentiated by the way that the person receives the extra chromosome: trisomy (which accounts for 95 percent of all cases), translocation, and mosaicism (Wright 2011). The most common symptom associated with

---

[9] For example, Sequenom, which now offers the MaterniT21 screening procedure, was one of the highest performing stocks before the product even hit the market—the stock price increased from $4.70 on opening day in 2007 to $22.76 by September 2008 (Washburn 2009).

[10] Maternal age is known to increase the chance of having a baby with Down syndrome, since more babies with the condition are born to mothers aged 35 and above. However, the reason for the relationship between maternal age and Down syndrome remains unclear (Thomas 2017: 41).

all three types is cognitive and intellectual impairment, although the mental capacities of people with Down syndrome vary significantly. There is also a long list of potential medical complications attributed to the extra genetic material, with congenital and developmental cardiovascular problems being among the more common severe health problems. Individuals with Down syndrome are also at an increased risk of leukemia, thyroid problems, and Alzheimer's disease, as well as some minor illnesses and disorders such as sleep apnea, gastrointestinal blockages, hearing loss, seizures, poor vision, and skeletal problems. Although there is a wide range of phenotypic variation, Down syndrome is also associated with a specific set of physical characteristics. Common characteristics associated with Down syndrome include low muscle tone, short stature, almond-shaped eyes, low set ears, a relatively flat nose, a large protruding tongue, and a head that is flattened in the back (Wright 2011).

Not only is Down syndrome prevalent within the population, but screening for it has a relatively long clinical history. Scientists developed prenatal genetic testing technologies to detect Down syndrome over fifty years ago. As early as the 1960s, the use of amniocentesis made it possible for prospective parents to test for aneuploidy and make a decision whether they want to terminate the affected fetus (Wright 2011).[11] Maternal serum screening and an ultrasound exam (nuchal translucency screening) were developed in the 1980s to estimate the risk that a pregnancy might be affected by Down syndrome, although those deemed high risk are still required to receive diagnostic confirmation via amniocentesis or chorionic villus sampling (CVS).[12] What is now known as non-invasive prenatal testing (NIPT), or cfDNA screening, uses the small amount of placental DNA present in the mother's blood to estimate the likelihood that a fetus carries a given chromosomal marker. Regardless of the specific method, Down syndrome has become the main target of prenatal testing over time and is now subjected to what Gareth Thomas (2017: 25) describes as "the pervasive reproductive gaze."[13]

---

[11] Aneuploidy is defined as a deviation from the standard number of chromosomes.

[12] Maternal serum screening refers to the triple-test used to detect alpha-fetoprotein (AFP), human chorionic gonadotropin (hCG), and estriol. Abnormal levels of these substances in a pregnant woman's blood can indicate the possibility of Down syndrome. Nuchal translucency screening examines a small, clear space at the back of a growing fetus's neck called the nuchal fold, since fetuses with increased fluid at the base of their necks are at a statistically increased risk of having a chromosomal atypicality, such as Down syndrome. Maternal serum and nuchal translucency screening procedures are still widely used, since they can also detect neural tube defects, heart defects, and other rare genetic disorders.

[13] Many biotech companies that manufacture NIPTs are starting to expand their menus of tests to screen for rarer conditions like DiGeorge syndrome in an effort to gain a competitive advantage in the market. However, recent studies have found that NIPTs currently do not provide accurate results for rarer chromosomal atypicalities (Kliff and Bhatia 2021).

8　Prenatal Genetic Testing, Abortion, and Disability Justice

For our purposes, there are a few elements that make Down syndrome distinctive from other conditions for which embryos and fetuses are commonly tested. First, chromosomal atypicalities like Down syndrome cannot be "fixed" *in utero*. Prenatal surgical repair is possible for a neural tube impairment like spina bifida, for example, but there is no medical procedure that could cure a fetus of Down syndrome before the child is born. Abortion is the only medical intervention on the table if a fetus is prenatally diagnosed. Studies that have explored the decision-making process of prospective parents—and why they do or do not participate in screening—have found that parents-to-be are not always aware of or prepared to face the difficult decisions about termination associated with a positive result for Down syndrome (Baillie et al. 2000; Piepmeier 2015). In any case, the strong linkage between selective abortion and Down syndrome warrants sustained attention.

Second, the lived experience of Down syndrome is qualitatively different from other prenatally diagnosed conditions. For example, Tay-Sachs or anencephaly often cause a great deal of pain, physical suffering, and/or a remarkably short life span for the affected fetus. In contrast, Down syndrome does not necessarily hamper the ability of the affected child to lead a happy, fulfilling life. Knowledgeable medical care has helped raise the average life expectancy for people with Down syndrome to roughly sixty years— a dramatic increase from a twelve-year life expectancy in 1949 (Wright 2011). Not only has life expectancy increased, but, following anti-discrimination legislation and shifting social norms, the quality of life for most people with Down syndrome in many advanced industrialized societies has improved dramatically over the past few decades as well. More people with Down syndrome have access to education, gainful employment, and rewarding social relationships than ever before (Buckley and Buckley 2008). A recent survey questioned people ages 12 and older with Down syndrome about their self-perception and quality of life (Skotko, Levine, and Goldstein 2011). The overwhelming majority of respondents indicated that they were living happy and fulfilling lives (though, to be sure, not every person with Down syndrome is a happy person leading a rewarding life, just like the general population). Very few respondents considered their Down syndrome diagnosis a source of suffering in itself, although many acknowledged the medical challenges that accompany their prognosis. Indeed, respondents identified socially constructed phenomena—including loneliness and social isolation in group homes—as factors that negatively affected their quality of life, rather than the condition itself. In this way, Down syndrome offers a unique case study into the role that ableism plays in quality of life.

Last, we focus on Down syndrome because it is politically salient and occupies a central position in reproductive politics. It became a flashpoint in the national abortion debate after Republican vice-presidential nominee Governor Sarah Palin (R-AK), whose son Trig has Down syndrome, drew enormous public attention to the issue on the campaign trail in 2008. Supreme Court Justice Amy Coney Barrett garnered similar attention during her 2020 confirmation hearing when she described her youngest son Benjamin, who has Down syndrome, as the family's favorite. Noting that Barrett continued her pregnancy despite Benjamin's prenatal Down syndrome diagnosis, many supporters have used her case as proof that women really can "have it all." In addition, advocacy groups for and by people with Down syndrome and their family members (that is, the National Down Syndrome Congress and the National Down Syndrome Society) have been particularly active in advocating for reforms to prenatal testing practices.

Contributions to the Literature

Political Theory

We believe that this book's primary contribution to the scholarship on prenatal genetic testing and selective abortion is to shift our collective focus from ethics to politics. There is a great deal of overlap between these disciplines, especially within the subfield of political theory. However, even though the disciplines of political theory and ethics cover much of the same ground, the subtle distinctions between them distinguish our inquiry from much of the existing literature. Ethics involves the philosophical study of the moral values that should guide human conduct. As a field of inquiry, ethics makes critical judgments about right and wrong—or "good" and "bad"—moral conduct. Students of ethics ask questions about what constitutes the good life, the nature and origins of good persons, and which personal dispositions and virtues should guide moral behavior. Although not always the case, ethical analyses tend to focus a great deal on evaluating individual moral behavior.[14]

By contrast, political theory is more concerned with the organization and management of society. It focuses most directly on understanding ways in which collective life is governed. Students of politics are concerned with the relationship between citizens and society, as represented in its laws and policies. They ask questions about power, and how it operates in the lives

[14] Many feminist bioethicists have adopted a more contextual and relational (rather than individualistic) approach. For examples, see Susan Sherwin (1998), Anita Ho (2008), and Erin Nelson (2013).

10   Prenatal Genetic Testing, Abortion, and Disability Justice

of people. While ethicists aim to make positive change by providing a set of guidelines for personal or professional conduct, political theorists are typically more interested in proposing enforceable policy changes.[15]

The topic of prenatal genetic testing and the selective abortion of impaired fetuses has generated a spirited debate among moral philosophers and ethicists (Buchanan et al. 2000; Reinders 2000; Wasserman 2005; Sandel 2007; Davis 2010; Wilkinson 2015; Kaposy 2018; Garland-Thomson 2019). Most of the discussion has centered around two concerns. The first concern is with the moral status of prenatal genetic testing and selective abortion on the grounds of fetal impairment. Some moral philosophers have argued that prospective parents actually have a moral responsibility to select against disability owing to the harm that impairment may impose on the future child or others (Brock 1995; Buchanan et al. 2000; Savulescu 2001; Savulescu and Kahane 2009; Douglas and Devolder 2013). By contrast, another camp has suggested that prenatal screening and selective abortion are morally problematic, because these practices are based on stigmatizing misinformation about disability or because they distort the parent–child relationship by making certain genetic traits a precondition for family membership (Asch and Wasserman 2005; Rothchild 2005; Kaposy 2013, 2018). A second concern is ethical, with many scholars discussing the virtues that should guide these decisions. These virtues include an ethos of personal responsibility for private choices (Rakowski 2002), an ethic of unconditional welcome toward prospective children (Asch and Wasserman 2005: 202–3; Kaposy 2018), an acknowledgment of the giftedness of life (Sandel 2007: 27), and an attitude of humility and openness to the unexpected (Garland-Thomson 2019: 25).

This book shifts the analytic lens from ethics to politics in order to examine prenatal testing and selective abortion as issues of public debate and policy rather than exclusively personal decision-making. In our view, there is no single "right" answer to the moral quandary of whether to use prenatal screening technologies or to terminate a pregnancy affected by impairment. As Tom Shakespeare (2005: 234) has convincingly argued, "bioethics cannot generate an objective or universal 'right decision'" when it comes to choices regarding prenatal testing and selective abortion since every impairment is different and every woman who makes these choices has a different conception of the good life and what it entails. Moral theories that postulate one "correct" course of action violate principles of value neutrality in a diverse, secular, and liberal democracy. We bracket the issue of whether or not the personal

---

[15] For a more detailed discussion of the difference between (bio)ethics and (bio)politics, see Peter Kakuk's edited volume *Bioethics and Biopolitics: Theories, Applications, and Connections* (2017).

decision to use prenatal genetic testing technologies and selectively terminate a pregnancy is ethical, and instead highlight how at present they are part of an ableist power/knowledge system that pushes women to undergo testing and seek selective abortions following a positive result. Our objective, therefore, is similar to that of Dorothy Roberts (2009). Following Roberts's lead (2009: 795), we aim critically to "evaluate the social, political, and legal incentives for genetic testing as well as the consequences of genetic testing for people with disabilities ... without judging the morality of individual women's decisions."

Another reason for our focus on the politics of prenatal genetic testing and selective abortion is that it allows us to probe more deeply into questions of power better to understand how economic, social, and political forces create incentive structures for women to make certain reproductive choices over others. While the literature in moral philosophy sometimes acknowledges the wider forces that influence ethical decision-making, the disciplinary emphasis tends to be on evaluating individual decisions by isolated actors (that is, physicians, researchers, and patients) to determine their moral legitimacy. Consider Chris Kaposy's insightful book *Choosing Down Syndrome: Ethics and New Prenatal Testing Technologies* (2018). Grounded in disability studies scholarship and attuned to the lived experiences of people with Down syndrome and their families, Kaposy's compelling book offers a much-needed intervention into the bioethical literature on prenatal genetic testing and selective abortion. However, even though he touches on political and economic factors that sway women's reproductive decisions toward termination following a positive Down syndrome diagnosis, Kaposy's book— which develops a pro-choice argument "in favor of choosing to bring a child with Down syndrome into the world"—is ultimately concerned with questions of morality, virtue, and values (Kaposy 2018: p. xv). For example, his concluding chapter takes on the negative influence of capitalism on women's reproductive decisions. Yet, Kaposy's analysis decries the pernicious influence of *capitalist values* on reproduction, such as the commercialization of pregnancy and the commodification of children. He has comparatively little to say about the concrete material conditions of global capitalism and their effect on women's reproductive options. Relatedly, his recommendations for change aim radically to reorient our values to welcome children as complex and imperfect people rather than as perfect commodities, but his analysis falls short of offering specific recommendations for policy change.

Ultimately, research developed within ethics covers different terrain and should be seen as complementary, rather than contradictory, to our book project. We hope that our distinctly political analysis can fill in some of the gaps in the vast literature on the topic. Focusing on the role of politics

12 Prenatal Genetic Testing, Abortion, and Disability Justice

reorients the discussion toward the constitutive role that public policies, legal constraints, socioeconomic conditions, and interpersonal relationships play in the adoption of prenatal genetic screening and rates of selective abortion. The need for a more robust political discussion about this emerging technology is more urgent than ever, as lawmakers debate issues such as whether Medicaid monies should cover prenatal screening technologies, whether these technologies should be regulated by the Food and Drug Administration, or whether states can justifiably prohibit selective termination following a diagnosis of fetal impairment.[16]

The principal question of the book is: what kinds of institutional arrangements would enable prospective parents more autonomously to decide whether they want to undergo prenatal testing, terminate a pregnancy following a positive result, carry the fetus to term, raise a child with a disability, or choose adoption? The method we use to answer this question is indebted to feminist political theorists, who advance a non-ideal approach to theorizing and demand a closer link between philosophical conceptualizations of autonomy and the empirical observation of the everyday lives of those who exercise it.[17] In an effort to bridge the theory–praxis divide, we think about autonomy as a practical political ideal, one that is best understood in reference to the daily lived experiences of prospective and current parents of children with genetic impairments. Examining how pregnant women make complex reproductive choices embedded in specific contexts—medical institutions, welfare states, and cultural contexts—allows us to determine the specific social factors that shape our internal capacities to make and execute choices, as well as the way in which certain choices are made available or unavailable to us by virtue of the way that our external environments are designed. Hence, a major motivation behind the book is a desire to imagine how we might better enable women to have more options and control over their reproductive lives by changing oppressive political structures and sociocultural conditions.

Feminist Theory

Another objective of the book is to provide a feminist analysis of reproductive choice that builds from and refines ideas about autonomy. Autonomy

---

[16] NIPTs are not currently regulated by the Food and Drug Administration (FDA) or other government agencies. NIPTs are currently sold in the US by biotech companies that advertise and classify them as "laboratory-developed tests" (LDTs). Because of this loophole, the FDA is not technically required to regulate LDTs. However, the FDA has indicated that they are reconsidering their position as the debate surrounding these screening procedures continues to intensify (Allyse et al. 2015).

[17] For more on the difference between ideal and non-ideal theory, see Amber Knight (2020).

occupies an ambivalent status for contemporary feminist theorists. This ambivalence at least partly stems from the fact that feminists often face a dilemma about "choice" in a context of structural inequality. On the one hand, women need to feel empowered if feminists are to engage in a political struggle against sexism and other forms of oppression. In this regard, theoretical analyses must be able to comprehend women as autonomous agents who can make individual and collective choices about how to lead their lives and bring about social change, rather than as passive victims of oppression who are completely determined by power relations that precede and restrict them. On the other hand, feminist theorists also have to identify and illuminate the insidious structural forces that women are struggling against to determine how women's experiences of desire, choice, and autonomy are socially constructed and profoundly constrained by hierarchical power relations beyond their immediate control. This dilemma has created some tension within the discipline of feminist theory, with champions of autonomy charged with overlooking the complexities of power and the social construction of the self, while those concerned with oppressive power relations and socialization are accused of denying or undermining the possibility of agency and autonomy.[18]

Our goal is to forge a middle path by analyzing women's reproductive choices under structural constraints. Instead of seeing these feminist projects as oppositional, we envision them as complementary and even productive. Specifically, we believe that feminist theory will be incapable of developing strategies for resistance and social transformation that empower women to take more control over their reproductive lives in the absence of a satisfactory account of autonomy and agency. Yet, at the same time, we contend that feminist theory cannot fully illuminate the operations of insidious real-world operations of power that occur along the lines of gender, race, class, sexuality, and disability without a detailed account of oppression and its manifestations. To overcome the impasse between full autonomy and complete determinism, our goal is to offer an account of autonomy that describes and respects the socially constructed individual's capacity for some degree of self-determination *and* an analysis of oppression that examines how power operates relationally to shape and constitute who we are, what we desire, and what we are capable of doing. Our analysis of prenatal genetic testing and selective abortion thus simultaneously shows respect for the individual's avowed reproductive preferences while also critically interrogating social

---

[18] Amy Allen (2008) and Clare Chambers (2008) also identify and attempt to resolve this tension in feminist political thought.

14   Prenatal Genetic Testing, Abortion, and Disability Justice

context with the aim of opening up more significant options and reproductive possibilities in the future.

How do we chart this path? To begin, we examine how the twin forces of ableism and sexism combine severely to restrict women's reproductive options in the United States. We argue that prospective mothers who are currently weighing their options following a positive diagnosis of fetal genetic impairment do so in a context that devalues their prospective children and fails to provide adequate financial and social support for them to thrive. Widespread ableist attitudes in medical institutions, the privatization of care work, biased cultural norms, and the sexual division of labor ensnare prospective mothers in a web of tough choices. By emphasizing this structural inequality, we intend to reveal the inadequacies of conceiving reproductive autonomy exclusively in terms of the negative right to be left alone.

At the same time, we also consider women to be autonomous actors, and we value women's rights to make their own choices about their own bodies and fates, even if those choices are formed and made in a context never wholly of their own making.[19] Although we intend to bring into sharp focus the social forces that might sway women's reproductive decisions toward one outcome over another, we nevertheless take a firm "pro-choice" position (one that moves beyond a hyper-individualized notion of choice) and defend women's rights to access genetic services and choose selective termination within a legally protected sphere of privacy, should they so choose. We assert that there should be no legal limits on access to prenatal genetic screening technologies or selective abortion. Women must have the right to determine for themselves what is best for their own reproductive lives for whatever reasons they see fit. No one should usurp this power or manipulate them into a particular choice; such decisions are rightly their own.

We acknowledge that various moral, social, financial, and religious factors will influence whether a woman will choose to undergo prenatal testing and what decision she will make based on the genetic information she learns from the results. In a diverse society characterized by a variety of lived experiences, values, and preferences, we expect that pregnant women in similar situations will inevitably make different choices. Moreover, pregnant women also make reproductive decisions with some consideration for the best interests

---

[19] As we explain in more detail in Chapter 1, none of us can choose some of the crucial determinants of our values and belief systems, such as our parents, nationality, education, or religious upbringing. But just because we cannot choose who we are from scratch does not necessarily mean that we cannot reflect critically on those factors and make thoughtful decisions about what we want to do with our lives. As Nancy Hirschmann (2014: 74–5) explains, personal autonomy "does not require an essential core self, but it does require an *identifiable* self who is the final arbiter of her own choices."

of their families and their prospective children.[20] We expect women to make different judgments about how fetal diagnoses might impact on their own life prospects, the lives of their other family members, and the well-being of their prospective children. Given the unique circumstances surrounding every case, therefore, individual women themselves (not their partners, doctors, or the state) must determine whether they want to undergo prenatal testing, terminate a pregnancy following a positive result, carry the fetus to term, raise a child with a disability, or choose adoption. Consistent with the principle of individual autonomy, we argue that pregnant women must be the final decision-makers about whether they want to use this technology and for what purpose. The state can facilitate reproductive decision-making, but it cannot legitimately substitute its judgment and strip women of decision-making power "for their own good."

This is all to say that we are staunch proponents of women's reproductive rights, yet also deeply unsettled by what we perceive as a stacked deck against bringing a disabled child into the world. Understandably, many feminist theorists have opted to sideline or downplay the political and social pressures that influence women to end their pregnancies. The reality is that genetic testing technology has been widely adopted in prenatal care at the very same time that access to abortion has eroded. Hence, women find themselves in what Katharina Heyer (2018: 111) describes as "the position to receive more genetic information about their fetuses that force them to make reproductive choices in a setting where these choices are rapidly declining." In a political landscape hostile to women's abortion rights, therefore, feminists may reasonably fear the repercussions of admitting that some women are unfairly nudged toward aborting certain types of fetuses or judged when they decline to do so. Such an admission could set a dangerous precedent of "second guessing" all women's reproductive choices and become weaponized by anti-choice activists.

We readily acknowledge that feminist fears of co-optation are well founded, given the proliferation of prenatal non-discrimination acts, and we admittedly find it a bit unnerving to provide a critique of prenatal testing and selective abortion in a context in which disability is too frequently deployed to undermine abortion rights. Alison Kafer (2013: 164) rightly notes that in the current political climate even self-avowed feminists who express concerns

---

[20] Alison Piepmeier (2013) interviews women who have been confronted with the decision either to continue or to terminate a pregnancy following a positive Down syndrome diagnosis. She identifies similarities in their decision-making process. Nearly all women—whether they choose to terminate or not—reported agonizing over the decision as they tried to balance what was right for the fetus with what they perceived to be best for themselves and their family (Piepmeier 2013: 13).

16   Prenatal Genetic Testing, Abortion, and Disability Justice

about particular abortion practices can be too easily labeled enemies of the women's movement. Yet, despite the looming risks of co-optation, we think it unwise for feminist theorists to shy away from a critical interrogation of the ableist underpinnings and implications of prenatal genetic testing. If "our society profoundly limits the 'choice' to love and care for a baby with a disability," as Marsha Saxton (2013: 96) argues, it is particularly incumbent upon those committed to a pro-choice position to take this claim seriously. Critically examining the reasons why women disproportionately choose to terminate pregnancies based on disability *need not* and *should not* translate into denying women legal access to abortion. This book therefore follows in the footsteps (or along the wheelchair tracks) of feminist disability theorists—including Adrienne Asch and Michelle Fine (1988), Rayna Rapp (1999), Dorothy Roberts (2009), Sujatha Jesudason (2009), Ruth Hubbard (2013), Alison Kafer (2013), Marsha Saxton (2013), Alison Piepmeier (2013), Michelle Jarman (2015), and Eva Kittay (2019)— who share a joint allegiance to the movements for reproductive justice and disability rights. Building on this pioneering line of research, we aim to connect an analysis of reproductive autonomy to an intersectional social justice agenda.

Disability Studies

Finally, this book also contributes to ongoing debates about prenatal screening and selective abortion in disability studies (Parens and Asch 2000; Asch and Wasserman 2005; Hubbard 2013; Miller and Levine 2013; Saxton 2013). Although disability studies scholars do not think alike or speak in one voice on these issues, many have been worried about the potentially harmful impact these technologies may have on the disability community. One long-standing concern is what has come to be known as the "expressivist objection" (Asch and Wasserman 2005; Hall 2013; Saxton 2013). This objection holds that the decision to use prenatal screening and selectively abort expresses a negative or disrespectful message about the lives of people with disabilities, including the idea that a disabled life is not worth living and that people with disabilities are not welcome in the world.

We occupy a slightly different vantage point. Rather than worry about the symbolic messages that may (or may not) be sent by women employing these technologies, we focus on the concrete socioeconomic realities that lie behind women's reproductive decisions.[21] By turning our attention to the

---

[21] Claire McKinney (2016) also urges disability studies scholars to move beyond thinking about prenatal genetic diagnosis as some sort of attitudinal and/or ethical failure, arguing instead that questions of politics and sociology should be at the forefront of our analyses.

decisions and priorities of government officials and medical researchers, we critique the ways in which public research dollars have been allocated to improve and implement genetic tests instead of investing in care services and public accommodations for people with disabilities. As Tobin Siebers (2008: 66) bluntly explains, it seems that the American government "would rather eradicate people with disabilities than assist them." In this way, our analysis dovetails with disability studies scholarship on the so-called medical and social models of disability, since we are concerned with the way in which these technologies are used politically in applying medical means to solve social problems.

To clarify, disability studies scholars have identified two dominant paradigms for thinking about disability: the medical model and the social model (Shakespeare 2010). Proponents of the medical model see disability as an individual condition arising from a flawed or broken body or mind. Through this prism, disability is viewed as a pathology or tragedy that can be overcome through a medical cure. In contrast to the medical model, advocates of the social model of disability suggest that *impairment* and *disability* are distinct: the former is a biological condition, and the latter is a relational phenomenon that is socially constructed through exclusionary policies and practices. For example, one may have impaired mobility owing to the physical reality of paralysis. However, the inability to use one's legs and walk does not in-and-of-itself constitute a disability. Rather, if a person who uses a wheelchair wants to attend a meeting in a building that does not have ramps or elevators, then that person is consequently disabled insofar as he or she cannot access the meeting.

Ultimately, the social model recognizes that a primary source of disability-related disadvantage is rooted in the way society is structured without an impaired individual's needs in mind. From this perspective, impairment is not necessarily what needs fixing, since biodiversity is inevitable, and not all impairment leads to pain and suffering. Instead, change should be directed at ableist institutional arrangements. As applied to prenatal screening and selective abortion, the paradigm of the medical model is clearly dominant, since these practices were at least partly designed to fix social problems by curing or preventing impairment.[22] As Erik Parens and Adrienne Asch (2000: 13) explain, "rather than improving the medical or social situation of today's or tomorrow's disabled citizens, prenatal diagnosis reinforces the

---

[22] Screening technologies have other potential uses other than preventing the birth of children with genetic impairments, including giving prospective parents time to prepare for possible early therapeutic interventions.

18 Prenatal Genetic Testing, Abortion, and Disability Justice

medical model that disability itself, not societal discrimination against people with disabilities, is the problem to be solved." This medicalized approach assumes that the disadvantages experienced by people with disabilities are the direct result of physiological limitations that prevent them from functioning in society, rather than of the architectural, socioeconomic, and attitudinal limitations put on individuals with disabilities in an ableist context.

We argue that women are socially pressured to reinforce the medical model of disability, since they are often expected to manage medical risk and use medical means (that is, abortion) to prevent the birth of people with genetic impairments.[23] That is, prenatal screening actually generates greater surveillance of women's reproductive decisions, since abortion is often the only medical intervention available for most prenatally diagnosed genetic conditions. Prior to the advent of prenatal genetic testing, giving birth to a child with a genetic impairment was considered a matter of chance. However, with the proliferation and routinization of this technology, the likelihood of having a child with a genetic impairment has moved from the domain of chance to one of choice. The shift from chance to choice has changed the way in which people think about birthing and raising a child with a genetic impairment. Over three decades ago, Ruth Hubbard (1988: 230) presciently forewarned,

> If a [prenatal] test is available and a woman doesn't use it, or completes the pregnancy although she has been told that her child will have a disability, the child's disability is no longer an act of fate. She is now responsible; it has become her fault.

Put differently, the shift from chance to choice has been accompanied by the expectation of an individualization of responsibility, in which prospective parents can either choose to abort a disabled fetus or knowingly decide to incur the costs of caring for a disabled child on their own. According to this logic, the decision deliberately to move forward with a pregnancy affected by genetic impairment—which may cause the future child to need costly health care, education, and transportation services to flourish in a society that was not designed with her needs in mind in the first place—is either an irresponsible decision or an expensive lifestyle choice.

---

[23] The gendered nature of prenatal genetic testing is similar to other reproductive technologies. For example, Krystale Littlejohn (2021) demonstrates how women are socialized to take primary responsibility for preventing unwanted pregnancies by "just getting on the pill," whether they want to or not, thereby letting men off the hook for contraceptive use. Just as pregnancy prevention is seen as a woman's responsibility, and an unintended pregnancy is considered a woman's fault, women are expected to use prenatal testing to prevent fetal impairment. There is considerably less discussion about men's or society's responsibility to prevent congenital impairments (e.g. by ensuring that drinking water is safe and lead-free, for example, or by ensuring that all pregnant women have access to affordable, high-quality medical care).

In short, the rhetoric of personal choice and private responsibility surrounding prenatal screening has placed women's reproductive decisions under social scrutiny and eroded a sense of solidarity in creating a more disability-friendly world. Consider the response that Alison Peipmeier received when she wrote a post in the *New York Times* explaining her decision to forgo amniocentesis, carry her fetus to term, and raise her child regardless of whether she had Down syndrome or not. One commentator remarked, "I resent having to pay for children who are going to be a huge drain on society, financially and resource wise, if the parents knew in advance that they were going to have a special needs child" (quoted in Piepmeier 2013: 160). This sentiment can be found within liberal philosophy and bioethics as well. For instance, M. A. Roberts (2009: 3) suggests that parents alone should pay for the costs of raising and caring for disabled children, since they deliberately chose to have them "when they had the alternative of producing a healthier ... child instead." If children with disabilities are expected to cost more than they benefit economically, parents cannot, in Roberts's view, be entitled to state subsidies designed to offset the costs of meeting their "special needs," since doing so would burden others. This line of thought positions prospective parents as consumers who voluntarily select a certain type of baby but cannot ask society to help foot the bill if they have "buyer's remorse" after their decision has been made.[24]

This individualized ethos of personal responsibility is conducive to neoliberal policy goals. For the purposes of this book, neoliberal policies privatize social programs traditionally provided by government by transferring service delivery from the state to the private entities of market and family. Neoliberalism, with its attendant logic of consumer choice and market efficiency, turns to parents of children with disabilities to provide both income and care while absolving the state of any responsibilities. As we demonstrate in more detail later, public services for people with disabilities have been shrinking as prenatal genetic technologies have been expanding. These trends are not coincidental or independent of one another. As Dorothy Roberts and Sujatha Jesudason (2013: 317) make clear, prenatal genetic screening technologies "reinforce biological explanations for social problems and place reproductive duties on women that privatize remedies for illness and social inequities." One of our aims, therefore, is to illustrate how the shift from chance to

---

[24] Shortly after the advent of amniocentesis, Barbara Katz Rothman (1986) forewarned the consequences of infusing pregnancy with a commercial ethos. She cautioned against an assembly line approach to reproduction—the sorting out of "products" we wish to develop from those we wish to discontinue—out of concern that mothers-to-be would be expected to see their future children as commodities that needed to be carefully examined for quality control before leaving "the factory."

choice has subsumed reproductive decisions under a neoliberal logic that avoids collective responsibility for disability accommodations and services. When considered as a private pursuit, the financial hardships that result from meeting a disabled child's care needs are considered politically unimportant, because women presumably volunteered for these struggles when they voluntarily chose to move forward with their pregnancies. The economic rationale underpinning prenatal screening practices in a neoliberal society intent on slashing social services is all too real—disability-related expenditures decrease if most diagnoses of fetal impairment lead to abortion. In this way, a neoliberal political society reluctant or unwilling collectively to support people with disabilities and their family members can indirectly pressure women to terminate.

Prenatal screening has been touted as a means of enhancing women's autonomy by giving prospective parents more information and increased control over their reproductive lives, but we wonder whether current prenatal screening practices are about enhancing women's reproductive autonomy as much as they are about what Gareth Thomas and Barbara Katz Rothman (2016: 406) describe as "keeping the backdoor to eugenics ajar." If the neoliberal state relies on the expectation that all pregnant women will undergo genetic testing and prevent impairment through abortion, it can refuse to address social problems facing people with disabilities or publicly support initiatives such as universal design or increased funding for special education. Society does not have to pay the price of disability justice if women are pressured prenatally to reduce the number of otherwise costly people in society. In sum, we argue that prenatal genetic testing can benefit neoliberal cost containment efforts in health care and social welfare, diverting attention away from the need for disability-friendly public policies. Such measures act to the detriment of women's reproductive autonomy. Relying on women to "fix" the problems associated with disability unfairly infringes on their reproductive autonomy and may even perpetuate a form of eugenics driven by market forces and regulated by the laws of supply and demand.[25]

Ultimately, we are concerned with how women experience prenatal genetic screening in a neoliberal regime that foists responsibility for finding the "solution" to disability onto pregnant women, who are expected to make the "right" reproductive and medical decisions in a world of scarce resources. As Dorothy Roberts (2005: 1353) insightfully observes, "genetic screening

---

[25] We follow Dorothy Roberts's characterization (2009: 796) of eugenics as "the belief that reproductive strategies can improve society by reducing the births of socially marginalized people. The eugenic approach to social problems locates them in reproduction rather than social structure and therefore seeks to solve them by eliminating disfavored people instead of social inequities."

Introduction   **21**

programs, even if they are supposed to be voluntary, create the expectation that women will act on the results. Communities can put pressure on parents, especially mothers, to produce perfect babies for the sake of the whole." Hence, our policy analysis problematizes the notion that increased access to prenatal testing necessarily translates directly into an increase in women's reproductive liberation. Ultimately, women make these increasingly complex reproductive decisions by balancing a complicated array of needs and factors, including the familial, social, and financial support they reasonably expect to receive if they choose to carry a disabled fetus to term and raise her after birth. It is perhaps not so surprising that many women "choose" termination when confronted with the daunting prospect of raising a disabled child in a society that is not welcoming of people with disabilities and only grudgingly provides minimal financial support and services to families with children with intellectual and developmental disabilities.

The wider implication of our analysis is that, if the intent of prenatal screening is genuinely about enhancing women's reproductive autonomy, it must be administered alongside medical practices, social welfare policies, cultural norms, and family living arrangements that advance disability justice. In the absence of these measures, the rhetoric of reproductive autonomy may be reduced to a false pretense or may even serve as a smokescreen for a eugenic agenda.

Chapter Summaries

Feminist theorist Catherine Mills (2015: 83) argues that "reproductive autonomy is not exercised in a social vacuum; it is exercised only within the parameters set not only by law but also by social norms—the *habitus* in which any particular person lives." Turning our attention to specific parameters, this book is organized to illustrate how the reproductive options of prospective mothers of children with disabilities are currently constrained by three structural sociocultural factors: (1) an ableist medical profession that dissuades women from carrying their pregnancies to term; (2) neoliberal economic policies that refuse to take collective financial responsibility for disabled children's needs; and (3) oppressive social norms, including the sexual division of labor, ableist bias, and cultural tropes about "good moms" and "perfect babies." We intend to demonstrate how these factors impose restrictive social expectations on women to use technological and medical remedies for problems that are predominately social in origin. Each chapter envisions how to move beyond the status quo toward a more emancipatory future.

22 Prenatal Genetic Testing, Abortion, and Disability Justice

The book contains two theoretical chapters, followed by three applied ones. Chapter 1 provides the normative grounding of the book and explains why we have chosen to take autonomy as a theoretical focal point. Classically defined as self-rule, autonomy is generally characterized as the ability to make choices and shape the direction of one's own life, rather than being excessively controlled by outside forces. Within Western political thought, there is considerable disagreement over how the concept is defined, on what grounds it should be normatively valued, and what it entails in political practice. By engaging with a range of contemporary writers in the Western canon—including John Rawls, Joseph Raz, and Natalie Stoljar and Catriona Mackenzie—Chapter 1 offers a brief survey of different strands of thinking on the meaning, normative value, and political implications of the concept in order to illustrate how some conceptions of autonomy are better than others in accommodating the political interests of both feminists and those concerned with disability rights. The chapter has two core objectives, one descriptive and the other prescriptive. Descriptively, we break with traditional masculinist and ableist conceptions of autonomy to endorse a more realistic conception of relational autonomy that captures how vulnerable and interdependent beings actually go about making decisions. The distinctly political (rather than metaphysical or ethical) notion of autonomy that we endorse takes stock of how oppressive political relations negatively impact on the exercise of autonomy in practice. Prescriptively, we defend the normative value of giving people as much control as possible over their own life paths and advocate for autonomy as a useful ideal, perhaps especially for disadvantaged or subordinated persons. The conception of autonomy we describe and defend here favors a perfectionist liberal framework and requires an active politics of care to cultivate in citizens the capacities and opportunities necessary for the exercise of self-government.

Building from the political philosophy of relational autonomy and perfectionist liberalism we develop in the preceding chapter, Chapter 2 more concretely dives into the meaning and value of reproductive autonomy in the age of reprogenetics. Many people assume that the existence of prenatal genetic screening automatically increases women's reproductive autonomy, since it gives them more information with which to make pregnancy decisions. In this chapter, we complicate that claim by arguing that the extent to which prenatal genetic screening technologies and selective abortion enhance women's autonomy is dependent on the medical, social, and economic context within which these technologies are used. That is, these technologies operate differently for different women in different contexts. Our claim hinges on a critique of the privacy framework found in constitutional law and mainstream liberal thinking. Drawing from feminist legal theorists and reproductive justice scholars—including Robin West, Dorothy Roberts and Sujatha Jesudason, and Loretta Ross and Rickie Solinger, among others—we show how liberal ideas of privacy allow many women to opt out of mothering a child with a genetic impairment, but this line of thinking does not sit comfortably with notions of reproductive justice that would provide mothers with the resources needed to parent a disabled child with dignity. We make the case that the state should not be understood merely as a repressive force that robs women of authorial control over decisions about whether to use these technologies and to what effect. Rather, we suggest that certain types of legislation can harness the productive power of the state by shifting resources to those who lack the information and means to achieve self-determination in reproduction. Genuine reproductive autonomy requires both governmental restraint and active governmental support. Restraint and active support can work hand in hand to enlarge women's reproductive options.

The first two theoretical chapters are interrelated yet sufficiently distinct from one another. Our hope is that reproductive justice scholars who are unfamiliar with the history of Western political thought will benefit from a deeper consideration of the philosophical foundations of their positions as they read Chapter 1. Conversely, political philosophers who think about autonomy in abstraction might reconsider some of their philosophical commitments in light of the insights gleaned from Chapter 2, which features the lived experiences of pregnant women who are making difficult decisions in the era of genomic medicine. All in all, the distinctly political understanding of autonomy that we develop in the first two theorical chapters guides the subsequent analysis in the applied chapters.

Beginning with Chapter 3, we switch gears and get specific about the barriers that women face as they make reproductive decisions within the medical–industrial complex. Working from Miranda Fricker's notion of testimonial injustice, Chapter 3 examines how medical professionals who dismiss or discredit positive testimony about the value of disabled living can limit women's reproductive options. Healthcare professionals have a responsibility to provide patients with accurate and comprehensive information—in a clear and non-directive manner—so that patients themselves can make decisions about how to move forward with their pregnancies based on the information they receive. Many physicians attempt to live up to this responsibility, but some fail to do so, drawing prominently upon their own values when giving counsel on genetic testing. This is especially problematic given that several studies have shown that physicians and genetic counselors often harbor ableist biases by assuming that Down syndrome is inevitably undesirable or

24 Prenatal Genetic Testing, Abortion, and Disability Justice

tragic, and/or necessarily leads to a diminished quality of life. Such biases are at odds with the overwhelming positive testimony on the lived experience of living with Down syndrome or raising a child with the condition. Not only do physicians offer subjective advice colored by ableist biases, but they also face tremendous pressures to offer screening to patients and emphasize the benefits of termination to mitigate the risk of wrongful birth litigation. Ultimately, we argue that medical professionals undermine reproductive autonomy when they offer their patients information that is distorted (that is, information that is out of date or prejudicial) or limited (that is, information that fails to convey all of a patient's options following a positive diagnosis, including information about termination, adoption, and what it might be like to raise a child with a disability). Pregnant women cannot make truly informed and voluntary choices if they are not getting "the whole story" or if information is steeped in ableist or pro-life ideology. In order to prevent medical professionals from putting their thumbs on the scale (*without* excessively interfering in the private physician–patient relationship), we recommend federal oversight of the acquisition and dissemination of information that prospective parents receive following a positive diagnosis of Down syndrome to ensure that it is comprehensive and up to date. Chapter 3 includes several additional policy recommendations for improving genetic counseling services.

Next, Chapter 4 analyzes financial barriers to reproductive autonomy. Without sufficient income support or funding for long-term supports and services, the financial cost of raising children with disabilities can be immense. Many parents of children with Down syndrome are unable to keep a full work schedule in order to meet their children's heightened care needs in the absence of affordable and accessible childcare. In addition, families of children with disabilities face outrageous out-of-pocket expenses associated with medical care, therapeutic and educational services, special transportation needs, housing modifications, accommodating clothing, and so on. Costs not covered by insurance can quickly absorb every spare dollar in a household income. We argue that our social failure to provide reliable financial assistance to parents who care for their children with disabilities in a home setting may cause many pregnant women to see termination as their only realistic option. Drawing from Maxine Eichner's call for a "supportive state," this chapter makes the case that it is unjust for the neoliberal state to expect that all pregnant women will undergo genetic testing and selective abortion in order to legitimize its refusal publicly to support the care of disabled children. It concludes by proposing that we change America's current long-term care system for home- and community-based services from a means-tested public assistance program to a universal social insurance program. This change would better support people with disabilities and their families, and it would ensure that pregnant women's choices about pregnancy are less likely to be constrained by financial fears.

Chapter 5 examines how oppressive cultural norms shape women's reproductive desires and horizons. This chapter builds on various threads from the feminist literature on care and motherhood—and Eva Kittay's work, in particular—to identify pernicious cultural norms that shape women's reproductive preferences. For instance, many prospective parents who receive a positive fetal diagnosis of Down syndrome must grapple with their own ableist attitudes and internalized cultural expectations about "normalcy" and "perfect babies." Even prospective parents who themselves reject ableist social messaging must consider whether they can withstand the potential challenges of raising a child with Down syndrome in a society where it is still socially acceptable to ridicule, exclude, and disparage people with intellectual and developmental impairments. Another cultural obstacle is the feminization of care and the dominant idea that "good mothers" are self-sacrificial and totally absorbed in their children's lives. These expectations can be amplified when mothering a child with Down syndrome. Hence, fears of having to "go it alone" and step into the role of a "saint" who is completely devoted to her disabled child can also adversely impact women's reproductive options. In response, we call for several cultural changes—to language use, the media landscape, the sexual division of labor, and kinship patterns—to tackle ableist biases and gendered socialization patterns. Our goal is to think about how to bring about a society that welcomes people with disabilities and supports mothers.

In the conclusion, we discuss how the Covid-19 pandemic has exposed and accelerated problems with the existing infrastructure for people with intellectual and developmental disabilities that we have identified throughout this book. In the starkest terms, the pandemic revealed the dangers of congregate care settings, the shortcomings of America's privatized healthcare insurance and long-term care systems, and the depths of ableist attitudes regarding the value of disabled lives. This unprecedented crisis has been harrowing for the disability community and their families in many ways. Yet, despite the ongoing challenges, we are hopeful that the pandemic will become a watershed moment for lasting change. The crisis has the potential to be a wakeup call, one that presents us with the opportunity to "build back better," reimagine care work, and design a more disability-friendly world hospitable to the vulnerable beings that all humans truly are. The current groundswell of momentum among social justice organizations—including those working on behalf of care workers, the disability community, and feminist groups

26 Prenatal Genetic Testing, Abortion, and Disability Justice

committed to work–family balance—gives us hope that we can build a more just society where the choice to bring a child with Down syndrome into the world, and parent her with dignity, is no longer considered "crazy" but is instead respected and supported by the political community at large.[26]

We close the book with reflections on how the Supreme Court's decision in *Dobbs* v. *Jackson Women's Health Organization* (2022) disrupts the landscape of abortion access throughout the United States. The effects of this decision are still rippling through American political life. The Afterword provides our initial reflections on the decision and offers some tentative predictions about how states will regulate reproductive decision-making in the context of repro-genetics following the end of constitutional abortion rights. We anticipate that the *Dobbs* decision will have disparate effects on women depending on their place of residence and financial resources. NIPT may become more popular than ever for pregnant women from privileged backgrounds since it can provide results in a timeframe that would allow those who live in states with restrictions on abortion access to order abortifacient medications or travel to states with more open abortion policies should they want to terminate a pregnancy affected by genetic impairment. By contrast, women with limited means—who lack cash, reliable transportation, guaranteed time off work, and childcare—will face greater difficulties working around abortion bans. Given the *Dobbs* decision's negative fallout for members of socially marginalized groups, we argue that the need for coalition politics and intersectional solidarity within the reproductive justice movement has never been more urgent.

References

Allen, Amy (2008). *The Politics of our Selves: Power, Autonomy, and Gender in Contemporary Critical Theory*. New York: Columbia University Press.

Allyse, Megan, et al. (2015). "Non-Invasive Prenatal Testing: A Review of International Implementation and Challenges," *International Journal of Women's Health*, 16/7: 113–26.

Asch, Adrienne, and Michelle Fine (1988). "Shared Dreams: A Left Perspective on Disability Rights and Reproductive Rights," in Michelle Fine and Adrienne

---

[26] The word "crazy" is used in reference to James Watson (a geneticist involved in the discovery of DNA and the development of the Human Genome Project) and his controversial claim that "most couples don't want a Down child ... [and] you would have to be crazy to say that you wanted one, because the child has no future" (quoted in Kafer 2013: 3).

Asch (eds), *Women with Disabilities: Essays in Psychology, Culture, and Politics*. Philadelphia: Temple University Press, 297–305.

Asch, Adrienne, and David Wasserman (2005). "Where Is the Sin in Synecdoche? Prenatal Testing and the Parent–Child Relationship," in David Wasserman, Jerome Bickenbach, and Robert Wachbroit (eds), *Quality of Life and Human Difference: Genetic Testing, Health Care, and Disability*. Cambridge: Cambridge University Press, 172–216.

Baillie, Catherine, et al. (2000). "Ultrasound Screening for Chromosomal Abnormality: Women's Reactions to False Positive Results," *British Journal of Health Psychology*, 5/4: 377–94.

Bérubé, Michael (1996). *Life as We Know It: A Father, a Family, and an Exceptional Child*. New York: Vintage Books.

Brock, Daniel (1995). "The Non-Identity Problem and Genetic Harms: The Case of Wrongful Handicaps," *Bioethics*, 9/3–4: 269–75.

Buchanan, Allen, et al. (2000). *From Chance to Choice: Genetics and Justice*. Cambridge: Cambridge University Press.

Buckley, Frank and Sue Buckley (2008). "Wrongful Deaths and Rightful Lives: Screening for Down syndrome." Down syndrome Research and Practice 12(2): 79–86.

Chambers, Clare (2008). *Sex, Culture, and Justice: The Limits of Choice*. University Park, PA: Penn State University Press.

Davis, Dena (2010). *Genetic Dilemmas: Reproductive Technology, Parental Choices, and Children's Futures*. 2nd edn. Oxford: Oxford University Press.

DeLong, Matt (2012). "Rick Santorum: Prenatal Testing Encourages Abortions," *Washington Post*, February 19, https://www.washingtonpost.com/blogs/election-2012/post/rick-santorum-prenatal-testing-encourages-abortions/2012/02/19/gIQAvmZeNR_blog.html.

Denbow, Jennifer (2015). *Governed through Choice: Autonomy, Technology, and the Politics of Reproduction*. New York: New York University Press.

Douglas, Thomas, and Katrien Devolder (2013). "Procreative Altruism: Beyond Individualism in Reproductive Selection," *Journal of Medicine and Philosophy*, 38/4: 400–19.

Gadsboll, Kasper, et al. (2020). "Current Use of Noninvasive Prenatal Testing in Europe, Australia, and the USA: A Graphical Presentation," *Acta Obstetricia et Gynecologica Scandinavica*, 99/6: 722–30.

Garland-Thomson, Rosemarie (2019). "Welcoming the Unexpected," in Erik Parens and Josephine Johnston (eds), *Human Flourishing in an Age of Gene Editing*. Oxford: Oxford University Press, 15–28.

Giric, Stefanija (2016). "Strange Bedfellows: Anti-Abortion and Disability Rights Advocacy," *Journal of Law and Biosciences*, 3/3: 736–42.

Guttmacher Institute (2021). *Banning Abortions in Cases of Race or Sex Selection or Fetal Anomaly*. New York: Guttmacher Institute, https://www.guttmacher.org/evidence-you-can-use/banning-abortions-cases-race-or-sex-selection-or-fetal-anomaly.

Halberstam, Jack (2018). *Trans: A Quick and Quirky Account of Gender Variability*. Oakland, CA: University of California Press.

Hall, Melinda (2013). "Reconciling the Disability Critique and Reproductive Liberty: The Case of Negative Genetic Selection," *International Journal of Feminist Approaches to Bioethics*, 6/1: 121–43.

Heyer, Katharin (2018). "Prenatal Testing and Disability Rights: Challenging 'Genetic Genocide'," *Studies in Law, Politics, and Society*, 76: 101–29.

Hirschmann, Nancy (2014). "Autonomy? Or Freedom? A Return to Psychoanalytic Theory," in Andrea Veltman and Mark Piper (eds), *Autonomy, Oppression, and Gender*. Oxford: Oxford University Press, 61–84.

Hirchmann, Nancy (2016). "Disability Rights, Social Rights, and Freedom," *Journal of International Political Theory*, 12/1: 42–57.

Ho, Anita (2008). "The Individualist Model of Autonomy and the Challenge of Disability," *Bioethical Inquiry*, 5/2–3: 193–207.

Hubbard, Ruth (1988). "Eugenics: New Tools, Old Ideas," *Women & Health*, 13/1–2: 225–35.

Hubbard, Ruth (2013). "Abortion and Disability: Who should and should not Inhabit the World?," in Lennard Davis (ed.), *The Disability Studies Reader*. 4th edn. New York: Routledge, 74–86.

Hui, Lisa, and Diana Bianchi (2017). "Noninvasive Prenatal DNA Testing: The Vanguard of Genomic Medicine," *Annual Review of Medicine*, 68: 459–72.

Jarman, Michelle (2015). "Relations of Abortion: Crip Approaches to Reproductive Justice," *Feminist Formations*, 27/1: 46–66.

Jesudason, Sujatha (2009). "In the Hot Tub: The Praxis of Building New Alliances for Reprogenetics," *Signs: Journal of Women in Culture and Society*, 34/4: 901–24.

Jesudason, Sujatha, and Julia Epstein (2011). "The Paradox of Disability in Abortion Debates: Bringing the Pro-Choice and Disability Rights Communities Together," *Contraception*, 84/6: 541–3.

Kafer, Alison (2013). *Feminist, Queer, Crip*. Indianapolis, IN: Indiana University Press.

Kakuk, Peter (2017) (ed.). *Bioethics and Biopolitics: Theories, Applications, and Connections*. Cham, Switzerland: Springer International Publishing.

Kaposy, Chris (2013). "A Disability Critique of the New Prenatal Test for Down Syndrome," *Kennedy Institute of Ethics Journal*, 23/4: 299–324.

Kaposy, Chris (2018). *Choosing Down Syndrome: Ethics and New Prenatal Testing Technologies*. Cambridge, MA: MIT Press.

Kittay, Eva Feder (2019). *Learning from my Daughter: The Value and Care of Disabled Minds*. Oxford: Oxford University Press.

Kliff, Sarah, and Aatish Bhatia (2021). "When they Warn of Rare Disorders, these Prenatal Tests Are Usually Wrong," *New York Times*, January 1, https://www.nytimes.com/2022/01/01/upshot/pregnancy–birth–genetic–testing.html.

Knight, Amber (2020). "Disabling Ideal Theory," *Politics, Groups, and Identities*, 8/2: 373–89.

Littlejohn, Krystale (2021.) *Just Get on the Pill: The Uneven Burden of Reproductive Politics*. Oakland, CA: University of California Press.

Löwy, Ilana (2020). "Non-Invasive Prenatal Testing: A Diagnostic Innovation Shaped by Commercial Interests and the Regulation Conundrum," *Social Science and Medicine*, https://doi.org/10.1016/j.socscimed.2020.113064.

McKinney, Claire (2016). "Selective Abortion as Moral Failure? Reevaluation of the Feminist Case for Reproductive Rights in a Disability Context," *Disability Studies Quarterly*, 36/1.

Miller, Paul, and Rebecca Levine (2013). "Avoiding Genetic Genocide: Understanding Good Intentions and Eugenics in the Complex Dialogue between the Medical and Disability Communities," *Genetics in Medicine* 15/2: 95–102.

Mills, Catherine (2015). "The Case of the Missing Hand: Gender, Disability, and Bodily Norms in Selective Termination," *Hypatia: A Journal of Feminist Philosophy*, 30/1: 82–96.

Molteni, Megan (2019). "How Much Prenatal Genetic Information do you Want?," *Wired*, March 27, https://www.wired.com/story/how–we–reproduce–testing/.

Nelson, Erin (2013). *Law, Policy and Reproductive Autonomy*. Oxford: Hart Publishing.

Norton, Mary E., et al. (2015). "Cell-Free DNA Analysis for Noninvasive Examination of Trisomy," *New England Journal of Medicine*, 372: 1589–1597.

Parens, Erik, and Adrienne Asch (2000). *Prenatal Testing and Disability Rights*. Washington: Georgetown University Press.

Piepmeier, Alison (2013). "The Inadequacy of 'Choice': Disability and what's Wrong with Feminist Framings of Reproduction," *Feminist Studies*, 39/1: 159–86.

Piepmeier, Alison (2015). "Would it Be Better for her not to Be Born? Down Syndrome, Prenatal Testing, and Reproductive Decision-Making," *Feminist Formations*, 27/1: 1–24.

Quinones, Julia, and Arijeta Lajka (2017). "'What Kind of World do you Want to Live In?' Inside the Country where Down Syndrome is Disappearing," *CBS News*, August 15, https://www.cbsnews.com/news/down–syndrome–iceland/.

Rakowski, Eric (2002). "Who should Pay for Bad Genes?," *California Law Review*, 90/5: 1345–1413.

30 Prenatal Genetic Testing, Abortion, and Disability Justice

Rapp, Rayna (1999). *Testing Women, Testing the Fetus: The Social Impact of Amniocentesis in America*. New York: Routledge.

Reinders, Hans (2000). *The Future of the Disabled in Liberal Society: An Ethical Analysis*. Notre Dame, IN: University of Notre Dame Press.

Roberts, Dorothy (2005). "Privatization and Punishment in the New Age of Reprogenetics," *Emory Law Journal*, 54/3: 1343–60.

Roberts, Dorothy (2009). "Race, Gender, and Genetic Technologies: A New Reproductive Dystopia?," *Signs: Journal of Women in Culture and Society*, 34/4: 783–804.

Roberts, Dorothy, and Sujatha Jesudason (2013). "Movement Intersectionality: The Case of Race, Gender, Disability, and Genetic Technologies," *Du Bois Review: Social Science Research on Race*, 10/2: 313–38.

Roberts, M. A. (2009). "What Is the Wrong of Wrongful Disability? From Chance to Choice to Harms to Persons," *Law and Philosophy*, 28: 1–57.

Romano, Neil, et al. (2019) (chairman). *Genetic Testing and the Rush to Perfection: Part of the Bioethics and Disability Series*. Washington: National Council on Disability, https://ncd.gov/sites/default/files/NCD_Genetic_Testing_Report_508.pdf.

Rothchild, Joan (2005). *The Dream of the Perfect Child*. Bloomington, IN: Indiana University Press.

Rothman, Barbara Katz (1986). *The Tentative Pregnancy: How Amniocentesis Changes the Experience of Motherhood*. New York: W. W. Norton & Company.

Sandel, Michael (2007). *The Case against Perfection: Ethics in the Age of Genetic Engineering*. Cambridge, MA: Harvard University Press.

Santorum, Rick (2015). *Bella's Gift: How One Little Girl Transformed our Family and Inspired a Nation*. Nashville: Nelson Press.

Savulescu, Julian (2001). "Procreative Beneficence: Why we should Select the Best Children," *Bioethics*, 15/5–6: 413–26.

Savulescu, Julian, and Guy Kahane (2009). "The Moral Obligation to Create Children with the Best Chance in Life," *Bioethics*, 23/5: 274–90.

Saxton, Marsha (2013). "Disability Rights and Selective Abortion," in Lennard Davis (ed.), *The Disability Studies Reader*. 4th edn. New York: Routledge, 87–99.

Schrad, Mark Lawrence (2015). "Does Down Syndrome Justify Abortion?," *New York Times*, September 4, https://www.nytimes.com/2015/09/04/opinion/does–down–syndrome–justify–abortion.html.

Shakespeare, Tom (2005). "The Social Context of Individual Choice," in David Wasserman, Jerome Bickenbach, and Robert Wachbriot (eds), *Quality of Life and Human Difference: Genetic Testing, Healthcare, and Disability*. New York: Cambridge University Press, 217–36.

Shakespeare, Tom (2010). "The Social Model of Disability," in Lennard Davis (ed.), *The Disability Studies Reader*. 3rd edn. New York: Routledge, 266–73.

Sherwin, Susan (1998). "A Relational Approach to Autonomy in Healthcare," in Susan Sherwin et al. (eds), *The Politics of Women's Health: Exploring Agency and Autonomy*. Philadelphia: Temple University Press, 19–47.

Siebers, Tobin (2008). *Disability Theory*. Ann Arbor, MI: University of Michigan Press.

Skotko, Brian, George Capone, and Priya Kishnani (2009). "Postnatal Diagnosis of Down Syndrome: Synthesis of the Evidence on How Best to Deliver the News," *Pediatrics*, 124/4: 751–8.

Skotko, Brian, Susan Levine, and Richard Goldstein (2011). "Self-Perceptions from People with Down syndrome." American Journal of Medical Genetics Part A (155): 2360–69.

Taneja, Patricia, et al. (2016). "Noninvasive Prenatal Testing in the General Obstetric Population: Clinical Performance and Counseling Considerations in over 85,000 Cases," *Prenatal Diagnosis*, 36: 237–43.

Taylor-Phillips, Sian, et al. (2016). "Accuracy of Non-Invasive Prenatal Testing Using Cell-Free DNA for Detection of Down, Edwards and Patau Syndromes: A Systematic Review and Meta Analysis," *BMJ* 6, https://bmjopen.bmj.com/content/bmjopen/6/1/e010002.full.pdf.

Thomas, Gareth (2017). *Down's Syndrome Screening and Reproductive Politics: Care, Choice, and Disability in the Prenatal Clinic*. London: Routledge.

Thomas, Gareth, and Barbara Katz Rothman (2016). "Keeping the Backdoor to Eugenics Ajar?: Disability and the Future of Prenatal Screening," *American Medical Association Journal of Ethics*, 18/4: 406–15.

Washburn, David (2009). "The Fallout from Sequenom's Big Blunder," *Voice of San Diego*, May 12, https://www.voiceofsandiego.org/topics/science–environment/the–fallout–from–sequenoms–big–blunder.

Wilkinson, Stephen (2015). "Prenatal Screening, Reproductive Choice, and Public Health," *Bioethics*, 29/1: 25–35.

Will, George (2018). "The Real Down Syndrome Problem: Accepting Genocide," *Washington Post*, March 14, https://www.washingtonpost.com/opinions/whats–the–real–down–syndrome–problem–the–genocide/2018/03/14/3c4f8ab8–26ee–11e8–b79d–f3d931db7f68_story.html.

Wright, David (2011). *Downs: The History of a Disability*. Oxford: Oxford University Press.

PART I
THEORY

PART I

THEORY

1
Autonomy in Political Theory

Before we turn to an analysis of women's reproductive choices in the age of genomic medicine, we must begin with an examination of the theoretical foundations of our book. We start with a review of different strands of thinking about the meaning, normative value, and political implications of the concept of autonomy. At the most basic level, this chapter illustrates how some conceptions of autonomy are better than others in accommodating the interests of both feminists and those concerned with disability rights.

Our primary objective is to defend a theory of autonomy that combines respect for individual choice with a critical interrogation of the social forces that produce that "self" who makes choices and "self-governs." For some of its harshest critics, autonomy is an unrealistic and unhelpful relic of the Enlightenment that should be abandoned altogether. Rather than dismiss the value of autonomy outright, this chapter responds to poignant critiques developed by feminist theorists and critical disability studies scholars in an attempt to salvage a modified theory of autonomy that can serve the political interests of women and people with disabilities. Ultimately, we favor a relational conception of autonomy developed within a perfectionist liberal framework that can operate as both a normative standard of emancipation and a standard against which to judge the legitimacy of governmental interventions. Our analysis here provides the philosophical groundwork for Chapter 2, where we make the case that respect for autonomy is especially crucial in the context of reproduction to help combat the ongoing control and surveillance of women's reproductive choices.

A second aim of this chapter is to reassure disability studies scholars that our promotion and valorization of autonomy will not be weaponized against people with disabilities, especially those with severe cognitive impairments who lack the capacities necessary for autonomous decision-making. Understandably, many contemporary disability studies scholars approach autonomy with a great deal of suspicion, since the concept has been repeatedly leveraged against people with disabilities. Indeed, some philosophers have gone so far as to write individuals who do not measure up as autonomous

Prenatal Genetic Testing, Abortion, and Disability Justice. Amber Knight and Joshua Miller, Oxford University Press.
© Amber Knight and Joshua Miller (2023). DOI: 10.1093/oso/9780192870957.003.0002

36 Prenatal Genetic Testing, Abortion, and Disability Justice

individuals out of the human community altogether. We assert the possibility of simultaneously upholding self-governance as a normative value without dehumanizing those who lack the capacities to make autonomous decisions. In our view, autonomy should not specify the boundaries of the moral or political community. Alternatively, we argue that the basis for dignified treatment resides in our species membership rather than in any single capacity.

The chapter proceeds in four parts. The first section explains why autonomy warrants attention as a theoretical focal point and organizing political principle of this book, especially in contrast to related ideals such as agency and liberty. The next section explores some ways in which autonomy has been theoretically conceptualized by different schools of thought in the contemporary Western canon. Here the primary goal is to think critically about what constitutes an autonomous "choice" worthy of the name. In the following section we evaluate the normative significance of autonomy, envisioning it as a form of dignified treatment that can offer a corrective to oppressive social and political systems. Finally, we discuss what respect for autonomy entails in political practice in a liberal democracy, making the case that we have a positive social obligation to bring about an autonomy-enhancing social structure. Ultimately, we endorse a relational understanding of reproductive autonomy that embeds individual choice in its wider social context. What we hope to show is that a relational autonomy framework committed to perfectionist liberal politics is descriptively accurate, is normatively desirable, and has more political purchase than its mainstream liberal predecessor.

Why Autonomy?

Within political theory, the terms *autonomy*, *agency*, and *liberty* are often used interchangeably. While there is certainly a great deal of conceptual overlap, the subtle distinctions between them require differentiation. Some feminist theorists have recommended eschewing the language of autonomy in favor of a notion of agency to show that women are not merely passive victims, even when entrenched in oppressive circumstances (Abrams 1999; Showden 2011). We prefer to use the term autonomy over agency, because theories of agency have a tendency to cast their nets too widely for our purposes. As Jennifer Denbow (2015) points out, agency is often understood so broadly that a range of highly constrained, passive activities are considered agentic. For instance, Denbow (2015: 9) describes a woman who goes limp during a beating by her intimate partner in order to mitigate her injuries

Autonomy in Political Theory   37

as an illustrative example of agency. Although there is value in bringing attention to this kind of resistance, Denbow's example illustrates that the term agency does not go far enough in providing a foundation for women's empowerment. To be an agent is simply to initiate one's behavior—even if this behavior is impulsive, reactionary, or spontaneous—while a person who acts autonomously does so deliberately and for her own reasons.

We also favor the term autonomy over liberty, because liberty is too often used as a shorthand for "negative liberty." Building from Isaiah Berlin's well-known characterization ([1958] 1969), political theorists generally define negative liberty as freedom from restrictions on doing what you want to do or from being forced into a choice that you do not want to make. It is "negative" in the sense that it requires the absence of external obstacles, which are usually depicted as acts of coercion or interference from others, including legal restrictions. In our view, negative liberty is not opposed to autonomy. However, on its own, it lacks the resources to ground a more robust theory of freedom, which we embrace in this book. By contrast, autonomy, or what Berlin refers to as "positive liberty," connotes self-governance and indicates the possibility of making choices to take control of one's life and chart one's own path. To be autonomous is to "wish, above all," Berlin ([1958] 1969: 131) writes, "to be conscious of myself as a thinking, willing, active being, bearing responsibility for my choices and able to explain them by reference to my own ideas and purposes." It is "positive" in the sense that it often requires the presence of something for its realization, such as a minimal threshold of economic security or education.

Another reason we prefer to emphasize the discourse of autonomy over liberty is because the notion of self-governance invites us to delve deeper into the context in which the self exists and is formed. Autonomy offers a richer vision of freedom by encouraging us to move beyond a narrow concern with the protection of a sphere of privacy also to question (and potentially to revise or reject) traditions, norms, and social contexts that stifle individuality and eccentricity. To put it differently, negative liberty can exist without autonomy, but its practical value is greatly diminished unless individuals make self-directing choices, and those choices should reflect as much as possible individuals' authentic and deliberate desires. This point matters, because negative liberty can sit quite comfortably alongside oppressive conditions and pernicious forms of social conditioning. Daniel Engster (2021: 108) gets to the heart of the matter when he notes that "a person who mindlessly does whatever others suggest might enjoy negative liberty if no obstacles are placed in the way of their choices but hardly represents an inspiring vision of what it means to be free." We therefore envision autonomy and liberty as complementary and interconnected concepts: autonomy requires negative liberty but moves beyond it to enrich our notion of what makes choices truly free.[1]

Another advantage of subsuming negative liberty within our notion of relational autonomy is that it enables autonomy simultaneously to perform two vital political functions. Autonomy can serve as both (1) an aspirational ideal, and (2) a standard against which to judge the legitimacy of governmental interventions. The aspirational theory of relational autonomy that we develop in the following pages demands a great deal from the political environment. We plan to argue that oppression restricts and constrains autonomy, and we call on political communities actively to dismantle structural inequalities in order to foster individual capacities and opportunities for self-governance in the realm of reproduction. This aspirational function is integral to feminism, because it enlists autonomy as a tool in the fight against social oppression.

That said, there are serious political and legal consequences that follow from being deemed autonomous (or not), since the assignment of non-autonomy to individuals often justifies paternalistic interventions into their lives. Feminists have good reason to be wary of excessive paternalism, since women have historically been treated as though they are less able to direct their own lives. Contemporary reproductive regulations tend to feed into dominant gender assumptions that women are somehow unfit (that is, too irrational, fickle, or selfish) to make their own decisions about their own bodies and reproductive futures.[2] Therefore, a political theory of autonomy must also do the political work of identifying jurisdictional parameters of legal intervention. By making negative liberty part and parcel of our theory of autonomy, we sidestep the perils of paternalistic governance that might result from "second guessing" women's choices. Hence, we can simultaneously claim that some oppressed individuals fall short of achieving our aspirational vision of relational autonomy while still maintaining, in congruence with our commitment to negative liberty, that women must have *de jure* autonomy over their own bodies. Even if women live in an oppressive context mired in ableist and sexist social norms, their stated reproductive choices cannot be forcibly overridden by the government. Ultimately, reproductive choices around disability and selective abortion need to remain, like all reproductive decisions, in the hands of the woman who carries the fetus rather than in the hands of their partners, doctors, or government officials.

---

[1] Our analysis follows the lead of scholars such as Dorothy Roberts (1997), Nancy Hirschmann (2003, 2014), and Daniel Engster (2021) in this regard.

[2] Jennifer Denbow (2015: 25) offers a lengthier discussion of the various rationales underpinning the denial of women's capacities for autonomy.

Finally, we choose to examine prenatal genetic screening through the lens of autonomy to signal that reproductive autonomy should be understood to be the chief purpose and benefit of prenatal genetic screening technologies. By making reproductive autonomy central to our analysis, we distance ourselves from neo-eugenic rationales that defend prenatal genetic technologies as a means systematically to screen out disability, reduce the "burden of disease," save scare resources, and/or improve the human gene pool.[3] Put simply, the ability to access prenatal genetic technologies and select the genetic traits of one's children must be defended as an aspect of reproductive autonomy or risk allowing prenatal screening technologies to be turned into instruments of eugenic goals, such as reducing healthcare costs by preventing people who may require lifelong and costly medical treatment from coming into the world.

Meaning

We prefer the language of autonomy over related concepts, but what does the term autonomy actually mean? Autonomy has been construed in different ways throughout the Western canon. As its etymology suggests, autonomy refers to one's capacity to self-govern (the word is derived from the Greek *auto*—"self"—and *nomos*—"rule" or "law"). An autonomous person makes choices and takes actions to shape the direction of his or her life, free from excessive control by outside forces. By contrast, heteronomy indicates being dominated by outside factors in a direction not necessarily willed by the agent. Beyond this general characterization, however, what it really means to be self-governing is a vexed question. There are many ways to understand the phenomenon of self-governance, so the term has subsequently developed a broad and multidimensional character. As legal theorist Gerald Dworkin (1988: 6) observes:

> [Autonomy] is used sometimes as an equivalent of liberty (positive or negative in Berlin's terminology), sometimes as equivalent to self-rule or sovereignty, sometimes as identical with freedom of the will. It is equated with dignity, integrity, individuality, independence, responsibility, and self-knowledge. It is identified with qualities of self-assertion, with critical reflection, with freedom from obligation, with absence of external causation, with knowledge of one's own interests.

---

[3] The term "eugenic" broadly refers to the idea that social improvement can be brought about by controlling procreation and altering the human gene pool. For a recent overview of eugenics-based arguments in bioethics debates on reproductive technologies, see Giulia Cavalieri (2018).

40 Prenatal Genetic Testing, Abortion, and Disability Justice

It is beyond the reach of this book to provide a lengthy genealogy of the term or a detailed account of its link to the historical progression toward liberal democracy—that project would take volumes. However, it is worth noting that, while autonomy originally referred to a community's collective governance of itself, it has subsequently been used to refer to an individual right or capacity that determines the parameters of legitimate political authority. *Autonomia* first came into usage among the ancient Greeks during the fifth century BCE to describe a political community's capacity for self-determination. The term implied more than mere freedom from external constraints (*eleutheria*); it also carried connotations of self-regulation and willful, efficacious decision-making, and obedience to self-prescribed laws (Farrar 1988). Importantly, *autonomia* was a communal quality. Citizens enjoyed it only to the extent that they shared in the collective practices of political life, such as voting in the Athenian assembly. The term's first known appearance, in Sophocles' *Antigone* (441 BCE), suggests that, while it was always central to demands on others for moral and political recognition, such demands were also contested. There, the chorus explains that Antigone will die as a consequence of asserting her own "self-law" against the civil law set forth by her tyrannical uncle, Creon (Sophocles ([441 BCE] 1991: 811). Antigone asserts her autonomy, but Creon denies her claim.

The concept has evolved extensively since the time of the ancient Greeks. The modern notion of individual autonomy—and its linkage to negative liberty—began taking shape in the seventeenth century, first theorized in the wake of the English Civil War through works such as Thomas Hobbes's *Leviathan* ([1651] 1994: II. 21) and John Locke's *Second Treatise of Government* ([1690] 1980: §4). The emergence of modern liberalism changed ideas about citizenship and its associated definition of autonomy. Unlike the ancient republicans, who prized collective political self-governance, modern liberals generally exalt the personal autonomy of the individual, focusing on individual rights to make freely determined decisions beyond the reach of majority rule. Personal autonomy is an ideal in which individuals act as authors of their own lives. To possess authorial control over one's life includes setting goals, choosing the means of pursuing those goals, and determining how one's values will shape one's choices. Theories of autonomy inspired by the liberal tradition typically portray self-governance as an inherent characteristic of the person, a trait that one either possesses or lacks. The autonomous person is considered a self-determining agent who stands apart from environmental influences, including other human beings, and rationally chooses according to his or her own personal preferences.

Working from this starting point, liberals argued that autonomy required a field of privacy in which the state could not legitimately operate upon individuals. This field typically included private commerce, some matters of religious observance, and family affairs, which were understood as "pre-political" in nature.[4] Within the realm of private associations and attachments, rational and independent individuals were considered to be the best judges of their own needs and interests. As such, they were assumed to be best equipped to direct their own lives as they saw fit, free from unwarranted paternalistic interference. For example, John Stuart Mill ([1859] 2008) begins from the premise that individuals know what is best for themselves, especially in matters that pertain to their own private affairs. Insofar as the state has the power to encroach on the individual's sphere of autonomous decision-making, Mill portrays it as a threat to self-governance. As he writes: "Over himself, over his body and mind, the individual is sovereign" (Mill [1859] 2008: 13). What follows is that individuals have a right to self-governance and are entitled to follow their own life plans in line with their own beliefs and convictions, provided they do no harm to others.[5] "The only freedom which deserves the name," Mill ([1859] 2008: 16) concludes, "is that of pursuing our own good in our own way, so long as we do not attempt to deprive others of theirs, or impede their efforts to obtain it."

Although liberalism may be the dominant political ideology of the last few centuries, contemporary critical theorists—including feminist theorists and disability studies scholars—have exposed how the lived experiences of privileged persons have been overrepresented in liberal accounts of what autonomy means and how it operates in practice. Critics charge that the supposedly independent and autonomous liberal subject is an illusory ideal that excludes ways of being in the world that do not conform to dominant norms of propertied, white, prime-of-life, able-bodied, heterosexual, male subjects.

In developing critiques of liberalism, feminist theorists have led the way by demonstrating how traditional theories of autonomy have glorified masculine traits and behaviors, including self-sufficiency and independence (Pateman 1988; Young 1990; Fraser 1997).[6] Much mainstream liberal theory has

---

[4] The assumption of pre-political individual self-constitution and self-ownership motivates a great deal of contemporary libertarian political thought, which would militate against the policies we advocate in this book. According to the libertarian account, individuals enjoy rights to property in themselves, the violation of which is prohibited by moral precepts—or "side constraints"—derived from Kant's categorical imperative. See Robert Nozick (1974: 33) and Loren Lomasky (1987: 54).

[5] For most mainstream liberals, individual autonomy ought to be limited only where its exercise might result in harm to others. That is, limits are determined in accordance with John Stuart Mill's harm principle ([1859] 2008: 14). See also Joel Feinberg (1984).

[6] For a comprehensive yet succinct overview of these familiar criticisms, see chapter 2 of Marilyn Friedman's book *Autonomy, Gender, and Politics* (2003).

42 Prenatal Genetic Testing, Abortion, and Disability Justice

conceptualized human beings as essentially solitary and disconnected from one another, as lone "atomistic individuals" who are independent and self-made. According to many feminist theorists, this hyper-individualistic liberal self is an illusion. As Jennifer Nedelsky (1989: 12) explains, "relatedness is not, as our [liberal] tradition teaches, the antithesis of autonomy, but a literal precondition of autonomy." That is to say, human beings do not just spring up like mushrooms as fully formed autonomous beings, in the way that liberal theorists like Thomas Hobbes would have us believe. Rather, we learn to make choices through our relationships with parents, teachers, friends, and other loved ones who, according to Nedelsky (1989: 12), "provide the support and guidance necessary for the development and experience of autonomy." The reality is that all human beings are raised and sustained through a lengthy socialization process that takes years of time and effort, and the human capacity for autonomy, like other capacities, requires care and cultivation. Interdependence is a condition that governs all human beings, whether they openly acknowledge this reality or not. One becomes autonomous only through relationships, not apart from them.

Another traditionally masculine trait that has taken pride of place in mainstream liberal thinking is rationality, which is often juxtaposed with emotion. When Rousseau ([1755] 2008: 45) declared, "Man [*L'homme*] was born free, and everywhere he is in chains," he meant *man*. His subsequent examination of autonomy within society concentrates on a distinctly masculine subject capable of the rational will formation and moral discipline that Kant and later liberal thinkers adopt as their model of the ideal subject. Feminist critics have roundly criticized Kant for excluding women from the realm of active citizenship, because, in Sally Sedgewick's words (1997), "he finds them lacking that quality which constitutes human dignity" (quoted in Hirschmann 2008: 195).

According to feminist scholars, not only is this individuated and rationalistic notion of autonomy a fiction; it has served an exclusionary function as well. The veneer of the rational and independent liberal self, Susan Moller Okin (1989) argues, was made possible only by the exploitation of the liberal subject's dependants in the private sphere (that is, the servants and women who did the work of caring for the liberal subject's physical and emotional needs so he could "independently" go about taking care of his personal and public affairs). In turn, those who registered in the popular imaginary as dependants—including women, servants, people of color, and people with disabilities—were understood as lacking self-governance and requiring the rule of others. That is, those deemed non-autonomous were disqualified from being rights-bearing political subjects.

Autonomy in Political Theory   **43**

In a similar vein, disability studies scholars have also demonstrated how liberal theories of autonomy presume an able-bodied citizenry. Like feminists, disability studies scholars are concerned with the liberal linkage between independence and autonomy, arguing that self-sufficiency is an unrealistic and elusive ideal. As Susan Wendell (1996) and Simo Vehmas (1999) argue, most non-disabled people believe themselves to be independent because they are able to perform activities of daily living (such as washing, dressing, cooking, cleaning, and so on) by and for themselves. However, non-disabled people tend to forget their own dependence on many socially provided services—including clean water from the tap, electricity that powers their home, and safe food and clothing bought in markets but produced by others—to lead their allegedly "independent" lives. Moreover, everyone will eventually become disabled if they live long enough. Non-disabled people may take naive comfort in their own illusory self-sufficiency, but in truth no one exercises autonomy without the assistance of a supportive environment. The fact of the matter is that few human beings could survive, let alone exercise any degree of self-determination, if they were disassociated from our many social dependencies and had to do absolutely everything by and for themselves. Hence, critical disability theorist Laura Davy (2015) insists that autonomy is not about doing everything for oneself; it is about having a large degree of control over how services are provided and how care relationships are structured. As she explains, people with disabilities "are often able to make decisions *for themselves*, but not necessarily on their *own*" (Davy 2015: 140). Even those whom we consider able-bodied adults are connected through complex social ties to friends, family, and colleagues. To some extent we all formulate and express our choices interactively by collaborating with others, relying on their input, and soliciting their advice. In this way, autonomy emerges from collaborative social interactions that provide individuals with the capacities and opportunities needed for self-direction.

Disability studies scholars have also challenged what Stacy Clifford Simplican (2015) refers to as the "capacity presumption" for its exclusionary function. In much mainstream liberal theory, one must be in possession of a particular threshold of capacities to enjoy the status of an autonomous individual. Liberal autonomy presupposes certain interpretative, deliberative, critical, and executive capacities, even if there is little agreement about which skills and capacities in particular enable a person to form and execute choices as an autonomous political actor.[7] Too often, excessively stringent

---

[7] There continues to be a great deal of debate over which mental and psychological skills and capacities are essential for leading a life of one's own. Some of the capacities identified include: rationality

44   Prenatal Genetic Testing, Abortion, and Disability Justice

or singular competency conditions marginalize people with cognitive and intellectual impairments if they fall short of modeling how able-bodied people make and execute choices. Michael Bérubé (2009: 355) spells out the exclusionary implications, writing that "any performance criterion—independence, rationality, capacity for mutual cooperation, even capacity for mutual recognition—will leave some mother's child behind ... [and create] a fraction of the human family that is to be left out of the accounting." In order to appreciate biodiversity, therefore, capacity criteria need to be loosened and pluralized. People with mild cognitive impairments may lack the full range of capacities necessary to manage all of their financial affairs on their own, for example, but they may nevertheless have the capacities to make decisions about other important aspects of their own lives, such as where they want to live or with whom they would like to spend their time.

In response to these criticisms, critical theorists have developed a cluster of loosely related formulations on "relational autonomy," which think about autonomy as a socially constructed capacity (see Nedelsky 1989; Mackenzie and Stoljar 2000; Friedman 2003; Westlund 2009). Although we do not want to gloss over important differences amongst various authors, proponents of relational autonomy generally start from a shared conviction that persons are socially embedded and that individual identities, desires, and capacities are invariably formed within (rather than apart from) social relationships. As Catriona Mackenzie and Natalie Stoljar (2000: 4) explain, "the focus of relational approaches is to analyze the implications of the intersubjective and social dimensions of selfhood and identity for conceptions of individual autonomy and moral and political agency." By bringing the interplay between self and society into full focus, the scope of inquiry is broadened critically to analyze social context. In contrast to the atomistic liberal individual, therefore, the relational self who self-governs is not disconnected from social influence or free of relationships with others but is instead envisioned as socially constituted and situated.

We are mainly attracted to the idea of relational autonomy because it foregrounds socialization and takes stock of how oppressive social relations negatively impact on the exercise of autonomy. In Marilyn Frye's groundbreaking analysis (1983: 10), she characterizes oppression as "an enclosing structure of forces and barriers which tends to the immobilization or reduction of a group or category of people." Frye (1983: 2) argues that oppressed people often experience "situations in which *options are reduced to a very few and*

(Young 1986: 13); competence (Haworth 1986: 3), critical reflection (Meyers 1989: 81); self-trust (Govier 1993); introspection (Meyers 1989: 55); emotional attunement to self and others (Christman 1991: 16); communication skills (Meyers 2000: 166); and more.

all of them expose one to penalty, censure or deprivation" (emphasis added). Within contemporary feminist scholarship, oppression—across lines of gender, race, class, sexual orientation, and ability—is further understood as intersectional and mutually reinforcing (Crenshaw 1989; Dill and Zambrana 2009). Patriarchy, racism, classism, heterosexism, and ableism are envisioned as interlocking structures of power that systematically bestow privileges on members of dominant groups while putting members of subordinate groups at a structural disadvantage.

Relational autonomy theorists have identified two fundamental ways in which oppression impairs autonomy: (1) by distorting or warping an individual's preferences and desires, and (2) by denying people an adequate range of choices. First, many feminists have been concerned with the ways in which oppression molds women's desires and hampers the free formation of their authentic preferences (Oshana 1998; Stoljar 2000; Cudd 2006). Oppressive practices often produce desires within individuals that limit their horizons and thwart their abilities to engage in the world, even if they are not being directly coerced by laws or others. For example, restrictive and oppressive gender socialization might pressure women into internalizing patriarchal values and norms. Insidious feminine socialization could encourage women to defer to the authority of husbands instead of making their own decisions, for example. Internalizing oppression also offers those in subordinate positions all sorts of incentives to minimize friction and become complicit in their own subordination. Second, a person's autonomy is hampered if her options are trivial, lack variety, or come at a significant personal cost (Raz 1986; Nussbaum 1999; Stoljar 2014).[8] Possessing freedom of choice in the abstract does not guarantee that a person's life will be enriched by choosing between options if he or she has few realistic or desirable alternatives from which to choose. Making the best of a bad situation is not equivalent to making a genuinely autonomous choice. Indeed, feminist theorists like bell hooks (2015: 5) actually see a deeply constrained horizon of possibility as a telltale sign that a person experiences oppression, since, according to her definition, "being oppressed means the *absence of choices*." From this angle, relationality and interdependence in-and-of themselves are not the antonym of autonomy—oppression is.

Of course, socialization, whether it is oppressive or not, always complicates the concept of autonomy, and not just for those who are subordinated. How can one be self-governing if society shapes and deeply forms the self? Selves and their personal decisions are never free of external determinants or

---

[8] This is often referred to as the "freedom to do otherwise condition" (Stoljar 2014: 238).

pressures to conform. Decisions are not made in social vacuums divorced from all socio-material constraints, and no individual is ever "outside of power" or able to create his or her desires, preferences, and options *ex nihilo*. Additionally, social life necessarily requires that each individual square his or her own goals with those of others while negotiating interpersonal relationships and the inevitable resource limitations that render actual societies far from ideal. Nancy Hirschmann (2014: 81) eloquently describes this ever-present conundrum, writing:

> Autonomy is fundamentally about capabilities ... specifically the ability to assess one's choices, to reflect critically about them, and to make choices that allow one to exert some control over one's life. Thus, there must be a self. But if we are always and already socially constructed, then how can autonomy actually exist? What purpose does the notion of "self-rule" really serve if the "self" is always already constructed and produced through complex webs of relationships ... Indeed, how can there be a "self" necessary to the idea of "self-rule"?

As Hirschmann notes, what is "inside" the self (that is, capacities, desires, preferences) is to a certain degree produced by what is "outside" (that is, social relations, language, norms). Thus, social constructivism breaks down the duality of inner and outer in such a way that it becomes difficult to explain how individuals form certain preferences or why they make certain choices rather than others (Hirschmann 2014: 74).

Not only are our desires, preferences, and options necessarily socially constructed, but they are also inevitably limited by forces beyond our control. Even the wisest, most well-informed, thoroughly planned choices do not always turn out as intended. The best-laid plans often go awry, and human beings can control only so much. Life is messy and unpredictable, and a person's capacities and opportunities to chart his or her own path and determine his or her own fate are tempered by the human condition of finitude, or one's limits in the face of an unpredictable and contingent future shared with others.[9]

Social constructivism and the human condition of finitude certainly complicate the exercise of autonomy. However, rather than resign ourselves to the notion that these forces make the exercise of autonomy futile, we think that it is our task, to borrow a phrase from Nancy Fraser (1995: 69), to make "normative distinctions between better and worse subjectivating practices." The selves who self-govern are largely products of their environments, but the

---

[9] For a lengthier discussion of the concept of finitude, see Patchen Markell (2003).

impact that the wider social environment can have on autonomy is complicated, since it can include both enabling and limiting effects. The connection between autonomy and "the social" is multidimensional and diverse, so we need to clarify which relationships and social norms are beneficial, benign, or neutral, and distinguish them from those that are oppressive and harmful. By distinguishing between better and worse socialization practices, we can develop the normative criteria needed to decry oppressive relationships and condemn hierarchical power relationships. As Martha Nussbaum (1999: 256) reminds us, taking account of social construction does not "force us into rootless relativism; instead, it opens up a space for normative argument, political criticism, and reasoned change." By revealing the contingency and mutability of things taken to be "natural," predetermined, or fixed, social construction allows that things can be different and provides opportunities to make political claims that things should be different. Put simply, social construction opens up possibilities for deconstruction and the reconstruction of a more emancipatory future.

Value

Autonomy is highly prized within the liberal tradition, and its normative value is often attached to the notion of human dignity. Dignity is omnipresent in scholarship on law, philosophy, and political theory, but it remains a notoriously vague and elusive term. Too many proponents invoke dignity without further explanation, writing as if we can simply intuit this common-sense concept. The concept has become so overused that some have gone so far as to characterize dignity as an empty platitude devoid of any meaning or critical purchase at all (Macklin 2003; McCrudden 2008; Pinker 2008). Although we will leave the task of a comprehensive definition to others, it is nevertheless useful to spell out the relationship between autonomy and dignity for the purposes of our analysis.

At the most basic level, human dignity connotes that there is something morally special about the human person and that each human being has an inherent worth that affords him or her an equal moral status. In turn, this status generates demands that human beings be treated in ways that allow them to live a good life. Indeed, in practice, it is often those who have been subjected to undignified treatment—to degradation, oppression, and humiliation—who have most vocally asserted their dignity as an act of resistance. As Jürgen Habermas (2010: 466) observes, the appeal to human dignity "feeds off the outrage of the humiliated."

48   Prenatal Genetic Testing, Abortion, and Disability Justice

However, the fact that dignity is used to describe both the *foundation* and the *content* of just treatment has created a great deal of confusion. In order to clarify autonomy's normative value in relationship to dignity, therefore, it is useful to distinguish between what Paul Formosa and Catriona Mackenzie (2014) refer to as "status dignity" (the foundation for moral consideration) and "achievement dignity" (the content of moral treatment). According to Formosa and Mackenzie, status dignity requires one to have a "dignified or respect-worthy status." It is to be an entity worthy of respectful treatment, and this worthiness is assumed to be inalienable and permanent. The core question underpinning status dignity is, "what is the basis or ground of dignity and why do some beings have it and others do not?" To have achievement dignity, by contrast, is "to be in a dignified state." Achievement dignity is a matter of degree; one can have more or less of it, and it can come and go depending on the way in which one is treated or how one behaves. The core question underpinning achievement dignity is, "how should beings with dignity be treated by themselves and others?" Although a person can be stripped of achievement dignity by being placed in degrading circumstances, such treatment would violate but not eliminate dignity based on status (Formosa and Mackenzie 2014: 877–8).

For their part, many liberal theorists have posited a close link between autonomy and status dignity, arguing that persons are owed dignified status—and are worthy of the moral obligations that accompany this status—based on the possession of certain specific intellectual attributes or capacities for autonomy. This tradition reaches back to Immanuel Kant ([1785] 1998). Kant envisions the capacity to be autonomous as the ability to be self-governing, or to legislate moral laws and universalize maxims that are rationally self-chosen. Rational beings can go beyond simply following rules laid down by external authorities, like religious leaders, to judge for themselves whether an action is morally right or wrong. Central to Kant's theory of dignity is the claim that to be a rational person is to have a status or worth that is unlike that of any other kind of being. It is not as members of the biological species that we have status dignity, but as rational beings who are capable of moral autonomy and self-legislation. As Kant ([1785] 1998: 43) declares, "autonomy is therefore the ground of the dignity of human nature and of every rational creature."

We take issue with the historical linkage between autonomy and status dignity, and we challenge the idea that people must be capable of autonomy to have the status of a moral equal with inherent worth. After all, some members of our human community, including those with severe brain damage or cognitive impairment, will never be capable of any degree of autonomous choice or action, even if they receive accommodations and a great deal of support from others. We find it deeply troubling when philosophers give the impression that a life devoid of the capacity for autonomy is a meaningless or even subhuman life, unworthy of moral consideration and just treatment.[10] It is still possible to lead a full and good life even if one is incapable of making important life decisions and choices for oneself. Eva Kittay (2005: 110) captures this simple truth when she reflects on what living a dignified life might mean for her daughter Sesha, who has multiple cognitive and physical impairments:

> When Sesha was born ... I saw a human tragedy. But I have since learned—from her, from the disability community and from my own observations—that she is capable of having a very good life, one full of joy, of love, of laughter: a life that includes the appreciation of some of the best of human culture, great music and fine food, and the delights of nature, water, the scent of flowers, the singing of birds. No she cannot participate in political life ... read a book or engage in moral reasoning, but her life is richly human and full of dignity.

Put simply, there is more to being human than being self-governing. Ableism reigns supreme when receipt of moral consideration or political personhood is contingent upon the possession of certain specific skills or capacities presumed necessary for self-governance. Human history reveals that arguments deployed to exempt one group of people from dignified treatment have too often been taken up by those seeking to justify oppressive practices. Indeed, dehumanization is precisely the basis on which horrific atrocities have been justified. If the foundation for treating individuals with moral respect rests on their possession of intellectual attributes or capacities, then it may be considered acceptable to treat cognitively disabled human beings in repugnant ways. For example, one could attempt to justify the practice of euthanizing infants born with Down syndrome, as Helga Kuhse and Peter Singer (1985) have done. We therefore remain deeply suspicious of any idea postulating a gradation among human beings, or of any other argument that dehumanizes persons for the purpose of exempting them from the community of moral

---

[10] Political philosophers who deny the status dignity of individuals with significant cognitive disabilities often compare them to non-human animals who have similar or greater cognitive abilities (see McMahan 1996, 2009; Singer 1993, 2009). For example, Jeff McMahan (2009: 604) suggests that "differences of moral status are grounded in differences of psychological capacity." Likewise, Peter Singer (2009: 575) argues that we ought to consider abandoning "the idea of the equal value of all humans, replacing that with a more graduated view in which moral status depends on some aspects of cognitive ability."

subjects. Alternatively, a more inclusionary approach simply bases status dignity on one's species membership.[11] After all, we are all *Homo sapiens*, or, to borrow a phrase from the feminist theorist Adrienne Rich (1976), we are all "of woman born."[12]

Yet, while autonomy is not and should not be tied to status dignity, autonomy and achievement dignity are interrelated. Respecting and supporting a person's capacities and opportunities for autonomy comprise an important component of dignified treatment in a decent society. As Joseph Raz (2009: 221) explains, "respecting human dignity entails treating humans as persons capable of planning and plotting their future. Thus respecting people's dignity includes respecting their autonomy, their right to control their future." People are more likely to feel respected and dignified when they live in a society that allows them to answer questions about the meaning of their own life, and that provides them with opportunities to chart their own path. Philosopher Sarah Buss (2012: 647–8) describes the widely shared impulse to want a say over the course of one's own life path:

> We want to have a say in the conditions under which we act. We want to (be able to) "think for ourselves" in a way that is incompatible with thoughtlessly following the crowd. We want to be more than mere creatures of instinct. We want to have genuine alternatives.

Because human beings vary in many significant ways—and have different preferences, desires, and visions of what the good life entails—our individuality should be celebrated. By contrast, people often feel degraded when their path in life is completely determined, dictated, and controlled by others. Thus, autonomy enhancement constitutes a form of dignified treatment.

Our normative defense of autonomy is qualified by a recognition that it is one among many possible elements of dignified treatment that contribute to a flourishing life. It is not necessarily the most important aspiration on a list that would also include welfare, purpose, belonging, and much else.[13]

---

[11] As Doris Schroeder (2010: 121) points out, the use of dignity in international law attributes dignity to all human beings without reference to capacity. For more on the link between status dignity and species membership, see Martha Nussbaum (2006).

[12] In a similar way, Thomas Scanlon (1998: 185) affirms the full moral status of all human beings, a status that is based on "the ties of birth": "the mere fact that a being is 'of human born' provides a strong reason for according it the same status as other humans ... The tie of birth gives us good reason to want to treat them [human beings lacking rational capacities] 'as humans' despite their limited capacities." Along these lines, Eva Kittay (2009: 625) also argues that all human beings, including those with severe cognitive disabilities, should be afforded status dignity, since "we are *all* some mother's child."

[13] As Steven Wall (1998: 185) makes clear, "autonomy is not all that matters. It is one, but only one, component of a fully good life." This means that it is not an ideal that all people, no matter what their circumstances, have conclusive reason to value and pursue above all else. Similarly, Marina Oshana (2003:

Autonomy in Political Theory **51**

For example, a person cannot effectively live in a dignified state when she must constantly struggle to stay alive or meet her basic material needs. Meeting rudimentary needs for food, education, housing, and healthcare is at least as important as promoting a comparatively abstract philosophical principle.[14] It may not always be appropriate to place the attainment of autonomy at the forefront of everyone's normative values or political agenda. This does not mean that we do not have an obligation to ensure that people's lives are dignified in other ways. For example, people with severe cognitive disabilities should still not be susceptible to wrongdoing, violence, poverty, humiliation, and the like. Hence, even though we value autonomy a great deal (enough to write a book about it), we acknowledge that there is more to being human than being self-governing, and it is a mistake to suppose that we can ever reduce our essential human-ness to a single capacity or activity. Experiencing pleasure, connecting with other species and the natural environment, and receiving and bringing joy to others are just a few additional measures of a meaningful life. In sum, even though this book champions autonomy, we do not want to fetishize the concept, overstate its value, or give the impression that a person without the capacities for autonomous decision-making is unworthy of moral respect and dignified treatment.

Politics

At this point readers might wonder whether we should abandon liberal ideas of autonomy altogether. After all, liberal theory is at least partly to blame for the failure adequately to protect the autonomy of members of historically marginalized groups. However, we do not think it would be wise for either feminists or disability theorists to abandon liberalism altogether. In our view, it is possible to inherit liberalism's focus on the autonomous individual without replicating falsehoods about atomistic individualism or perpetuating masculinist and ableist assumptions about selfhood. As liberal feminists have persuasively argued, liberalism is still a tradition worth preserving. The commitment to dignified treatment of all human beings, the importance of legitimate limits on sovereign power, the respect for individuality, and the idea that legitimate government is grounded in the consent of the people are all worthwhile normative political values (Eichner 2010: 9–10).

103) instructively notes: "Not everyone will include an autonomous life among the goals that he or she regards as integral to well-being."

[14] Referring to Dostoevsky, Isaiah Berlin ([1958] 1969: 171) similarly concedes: "There are situations in which boots are superior to Pushkin; individual freedom is not everyone's primary need ... The Egyptian peasant needs clothes or medicine before, and more than, personal liberty."

52 Prenatal Genetic Testing, Abortion, and Disability Justice

Our motivation, therefore, is to rethink autonomy without giving it up. How can we value the ideal while rejecting its baggage? We argue that this can be accomplished by reconfiguring autonomy to accommodate the inescapable facts of human interdependence, sociality, and vulnerability. A conception of relational autonomy under a perfectionist liberal framework can most effectively meet these requirements.[15] Using autonomy enhancement as a guiding political principle, we propose a version of perfectionist political theory that sees the proper function of the state and society as implementing policies and practices that ensure that the capacities and opportunities of citizens for autonomy are protected and actively promoted.

The ongoing debate between political and perfectionist liberals matters for our purposes because these schools of thought differ greatly on what respect for autonomy entails in political practice. Mainstream political liberals, such as John Rawls and Ronald Dworkin, stylize respect for autonomy as governmental non-interference and neutrality. If autonomy is a natural state that exists prior to social and governmental arrangements, showing respect entails a "hands-off" approach. Moreover, it is assumed that the state should not interfere in private decisions or impose a preferred way of life, since it is not the business of the state to advance a particular conception of the good. Rather, the state should safeguard the ability of citizens to judge for themselves how they want to live their lives, so long as they do not harm others. The neutrality principle's formulation, as described by Ronald Dworkin (1995: 191), is familiar but worth reiterating:

> It is a fundamental, almost defining, tenet of liberalism that the government of a political community should be tolerant of the different and often antagonistic convictions its citizens have about the right way to live: that it should be neutral, for example, between citizens who insist that a good life is necessarily a religious one and other citizens who fear religion as the only dangerous superstition.

If autonomy is considered a relational capacity that must be actively cultivated within caring relationships, however, its exercise requires far more than keeping out of the way. It also demands a commitment to actively supporting and shaping persons into self-governing citizens. In this regard, relational autonomy offers a radical alternative to liberalism's commitment to non-interference by mandating positive action to procure the conditions (that is, care, education, economic security, non-subordination) necessary

---

[15] For more on the difference between political and perfectionist liberalism, see Martha Nussbaum (2011). For a lengthier discussion of perfectionist liberalism and its relationship to feminism, see Kimberly Yuracko (2003).

for autonomous choice. A paradigm shift follows: in addition to looking for the absence of excessive legal intervention into citizens' private lives, we must also turn our attention to creating favorable socio-political conditions that facilitate people's decision-making capacities and opportunities.

Feminist theorist Catriona Mackenzie (2014) usefully lays out the political implications. After diagnosing "how social domination, oppression, stigmatization, and injustice can thwart individual autonomy," Mackenzie (2014: 23) argues, political action should be committed to "proposing how specific social relations, practices, and institutions might be reformed in such a way as to protect and foster individuals' autonomy." Politically, this commitment requires a collective obligation to redesign social scaffolding—our political and economic institutions, education systems, kinship networks, social relations, and cultural norms—better to facilitate self-governance in various realms of people's lives. This obligation points to two goals. The first involves cultivating the capacities that individual self-governance requires through care, education, and protection from the tyranny of those who might try to manipulate, coerce, and repress others' personal preferences and desires. The second involves ensuring that individuals inhabit a social, political, and economic environment that makes a wide range of attractive options available. To lead autonomous lives, people have to have the ability to select among an adequate range of feasible and attractive options. Autonomy is not just about making personal choices; it is about having desirable options from which to choose.

One of the primary criticisms leveled at perfectionist liberalism develops from a concern that it uses the coercive power of the state to take sides on questions of justice and the good life. By permitting the state to select certain conceptions of the good for favorable treatment, critics argue that it is disrespectful to the people who do not value personal autonomy as a core component of a good life. William Galston (1995: 525–6) articulates this line criticism:

> The promotion of personal autonomy is not among the shared liberal purposes. Autonomy is one possible mode of existence in liberal societies—one among many others; its practice must be respected and safeguarded; but the devotees of autonomy must recognize the need for respectful coexistence with individuals and groups that do not give autonomy pride of place ... Any liberal argument that invokes autonomy as a general rule of public action in effect takes sides in the ongoing struggle between reason and faith, reflection and tradition.

According to Galston, perfectionist liberalism suffers from the same fault as any other comprehensive doctrine in that it disrespects ways of life that do

54 Prenatal Genetic Testing, Abortion, and Disability Justice

not involve recognizing the value upon which it is based. For example, a state that actively values and promotes autonomy is disrespectful toward citizens, such as religious conservatives, whose ways of life do not value autonomous living.

In our view, such charges of disrespect can be overstated. First, as Joseph Raz (1986) insists, the liberal state, no matter how hard it tries, cannot remain perfectly neutral. Although neutrality may be desirable in theory, it is implausible in political practice, since every culture favors certain ways of living over others, including liberal ones. Thus, Raz insists that, instead of pretending to remain neutral, the liberal state should actively promote the well-being of its citizens in accordance with overarching liberal principles. Raz's understanding (1986: 425) of well-being is intimately linked to autonomy, which on his account is an important component of human flourishing and "an essential element of the good life." Therefore, a state that wants to promote the well-being and dignity of its citizens has a duty to provide the conditions necessary for citizens to be the authors of their lives and "control, to some degree, their own destiny, fashioning it through successive decisions throughout their lives" (Raz 1986: 369).

Second, perfectionism can remain committed to pluralism and stay content-neutral about the substance of individual choices. As Raz (1986: 395) again notes, autonomy can be promoted in a liberal society "without commitment to the substance with the valuable forms of life with which it is bound up." We concede that our vision for the basic structure of society is not neutral, since it establishes a substantive standard for judging social institutions according to whether they undermine or enhance citizens' autonomy. We want our public institutions and social practices actively to develop the decision-making capacities of citizens, make a range of options available to them, and protect them from oppression, so that they are able to pursue their own life paths. Yet perfectionist theories can concern themselves with the design of an autonomy-enhancing political structure while remaining content-neutral and respectful of a broad range of individual decisions.[16]

Recall our earlier claim that negative liberty and autonomy are complementary ideals. In order to couple a theory of autonomy with a theory of negative liberty, Nancy Hirschmann (2014) recommends that we do not build in potentially stigmatizing substantive constraints. Hirschmann (2014: 75) insists that ultimately "the individual self must make her own choices" for her own reasons. We can critically interrogate and scrutinize questions about selfhood, desire, and authenticity. Collectively, we can also redesign the basic

---

[16] Natalie Stoljar (2017) also defends perfectionist liberalism against the accusation that it is incompatible with the value of respect for personal choices.

structure of society to enhance people's capacities and opportunities to affect, shape, and direct their own life. But only individuals themselves can come up with their own answers to life's big questions as they make their own choices. Nobody else, not even medical and legal experts or political philosophers, should answer personal questions about the good life for others or make intimate life decisions on their behalf.

Conclusion

As we have shown in this chapter, autonomy is a multidimensional and pliable concept that spans different schools of political thought. The concept certainly has its fair share of supporters and critics (and those, like us, who are critical supporters). As feminists and critical disability studies scholars have persuasively argued, the lived experiences and interests of able-bodied men have been overrepresented in mainstream liberal thinking on autonomous living and what it entails. This history of exclusion prompted relational autonomy theorists to reconfigure the concept adequately to account for the social and relational nature of persons and make autonomy compatible with the human condition of interdependency. Thanks to the pioneering efforts of relational autonomy theorists, we see no need for feminists and disability studies scholars to turn their backs on autonomy and its emancipatory potential. The relational tradition of autonomy can rethink the concept to resist existing hierarchies and move toward social justice.

Ultimately, autonomy does some heavy lifting in this book: it serves as both (1) an aspirational ideal for progressive reproductive justice politics, and (2) a standard against which to judge the legitimacy of governmental interventions into women's private reproductive lives. Chapter 2 extends this analysis to think more concretely about women's reproductive autonomy in the age of reprogenetics. As we show in Chapter 3, reproduction turns out to be an especially interesting and important area in which to think about how autonomy operates in practice, especially now that technological and genetic interventions are the new normal in obstetric practice.

References

Abrams, Kathryn (1999). "From Autonomy to Agency: Feminist Perspectives on Self-Direction," *William and Mary Law Review*, 40/3: 805–46.

Berlin, Isaiah ([1958] 1969). "Two Concepts of Liberty," in *Four Essays on Liberty*. Oxford: Oxford University Press, 118–72.

Bérubé, Michael (2009). "Equality, Freedom, and/or Justice for All: A Response to Martha Nussbaum," *Metaphilosophy*, 40/3–4: 352–65.

Buss, Susan (2012). "Autonomous Action: Self-Determination in the Passive Mode," *Ethics*, 122/4: 647–91.

Cavalieri, Giulia (2018). "Looking into the Shadow: The Eugenics Argument in Debates on Reproductive Technologies and Practices," *Monash Bioethics Review*, 36/1–4: 1–22.

Christman, John (1991). "Autonomy and Personal History," *Canadian Journal of Philosophy*, 21/1: 1–24.

Crenshaw, Kimberle (1989). "Demarginalizing the Intersection of Race and Sex: A Black Feminist Critique of Antidiscrimination Doctrine, Feminist Theory and Antiracist Politics," *University of Chicago Legal Forum*, 1/8: 139–67.

Cudd, Ann (2006). *Analyzing Oppression*. New York Oxford University Press.

Davy, Laura (2015). "Philosophical Inclusive Design: Intellectual Disability and the Limits of Individual Autonomy in Moral and Political Theory," *Hypatia: A Journal of Feminist Philosophy*, 30/1: 132–48.

Denbow, Jennifer (2015). *Governed through Choice: Autonomy, Technology, and the Politics of Reproduction*. New York: New York University Press.

Dill, Bonnie Thorton, and Ruth Enid Zambrana (2009). *Emerging Intersections; Race, Class, and Gender in Theory, Policy, and Practice*. New Brunswick, NJ: Rutgers University Press.

Dworkin, Gerald (1988). *The Theory and Practice of Autonomy*. Cambridge: Cambridge University Press.

Dworkin, Ronald (1995). "Foundations of Liberal Equality," in *Equal Freedom: Selected Tanner Lectures on Human Values*, ed. Stephen Darwall. Ann Arbor, MI: University of Michigan Press, 190–306.

Eichner, Maxine (2010). *The Supportive State: Families, Government, and America's Political Ideals*. Oxford: Oxford University Press.

Engster, Daniel (2021). "Care Ethics and Liberal Freedom," in Asha Bhandary and Amy Baehr (eds), *Caring for Liberalism: Dependency and Liberal Political Theory*. New York: Routledge, 97–119.

Farrar, Cynthia (1988). *The Origins of Democratic Thinking*. Cambridge: Cambridge University Press.

Feinberg, Joel (1984). *Harm to Self*. Oxford: Oxford University Press.

Formosa, Paul, and Catriona Mackenzie (2014). "Nussbaum, Kant, and the Capabilities Approach to Dignity," *Ethical Theory and Moral Practice*, 17/5: 875–92.

Fraser, Nancy (1995). "False Antitheses," in Seyla Benhabib, Judith Butler, and Drucilla Cornell (eds), *Feminist Contentions: A Philosophical Exchange*. New York: Routledge, 59–74.

Fraser, Nancy (1997). *Justice Interruptus: Critical Reflections on the "Postsocialist" Condition*. New York: Routledge.

Friedman, Marilyn (2003). *Autonomy, Gender, Politics*. Oxford: Oxford University Press.

Frye, Marilyn (1983). *The Politics of Reality: Essays in Feminist Theory*. Berkeley, CA: Crossing Press.

Galston, William (1995). "Two Concepts of Liberalism," *Ethics*, 105/3: 516–34.

Govier, Trudy (1993). "Self-Trust, Autonomy, and Self-Esteem," *Hypatia: A Journal of Feminist Philosophy*, 8/1: 99–120.

Habermas, Jürgen (2010). "The Concept of Human Dignity and the Realistic Utopia of Human Rights," *Metaphilosophy*, 41/4: 464–80.

Haworth, Lawrence (1986). *Autonomy: An Essay in Philosophical Psychology and Ethics*. New Haven, CT: Yale University Press.

Hirschmann, Nancy (2003). *The Subject of Liberty: Toward a Feminist Theory of Freedom*. Princeton: Princeton University Press.

Hirschmann, Nancy (2008). *Gender, Class, and Freedom in Modern Political Theory*. Princeton: Princeton University Press.

Hirschmann, Nancy (2014). "Autonomy? Or Freedom? A Return to Psychoanalytic Theory," in Andrea Veltman and Mark Piper (eds), *Autonomy, Oppression, and Gender*. Oxford: Oxford University Press, 61–84.

Hobbes, Thomas ([1651] 1994). *Leviathan*, ed. Edwin Curley. Indianapolis: Hackett Publishing Company.

hooks, bell (2015). *Feminist Theory: From Margin to Center*. New York: Routledge.

Kant, Immanuel ([1785] 1998). *Groundwork of the Metaphysics of Morals*, trans. and ed. Mary Gregor. Cambridge: Cambridge University Press.

Kittay, Eva Feder (1999). *Love's Labor: Essays on Women, Equality, and Dependency*. New York: Routledge.

Kittay, Eva Feder (2005). "Equality, Dignity and Disability," in Mary Ann Lyons and Fionnuala Waldron (eds), *Perspectives on Equality: The Second Seamus Heaney Lectures*. Dublin: Liffey Press, 95–122.

Kittay, Eva Feder (2009). "The Personal is Philosophical is Political: A Philosopher and Mother of a Cognitively Disabled Person Sends Notes from the Battlefield." *Metaphilosophy* 40(3-4): 606–27.

Kuhse, Helga, and Peter Singer (1985). *Should the Baby Live? The Problem of Handicapped Infants*. New York: Oxford University Press.

Locke, John ([1690] 1980). *Second Treatise of Government*, ed. C. B. MacPherson. Indianapolis: Hackett Publishing Company.

Lomasky, Loren (1987). *Persons, Rights, and the Moral Community*. Oxford: Oxford University Press.

McCrudden, Christopher (2008). "Human Dignity and Judicial Interpretation of Human Rights," *European Journal of International Law*, 19/4: 655–724.

Mackenzie, Catriona (2014). "Three Dimensions of Autonomy: A Relational Analysis," in Andrea Veltman and Mark Piper (eds), *Autonomy, Oppression, and Gender*. Oxford: Oxford University Press, 15–41.

Mackenzie, Catriona, and Natalie Stoljar (2000) (eds). *Relational Autonomy: Feminist Perspectives on Autonomy, Agency, and the Social Self*. New York: Oxford University Press.

Macklin, Ruth (2003). "Dignity is a Useless Concept," *BMJ* 327/7429: 1419–20.

McMahan, Jeff (1996). "Cognitive Disability, Misfortune, and Justice," *Philosophy and Public Affairs*, 25/1: 3–35.

McMahan, Jeff (2009). "Cognitive Disability and Cognitive Enhancement," *Metaphilosophy*, 40/3–4: 582–605.

Markell, Patchen (2003). *Bound by Recognition*. Princeton: Princeton University Press.

Meyers, Diana Tietjens (1989). *Self, Society, and Personal Choice*. New York: Columbia University Press.

Meyers, Diana Tietjens (2000). "Intersectional Identity and the Authentic Self? Opposites Attract!," in Catriona Mackenzie and Natalie Stoljar (eds), *Relational Autonomy: Feminist Perspectives on Autonomy, Agency, and the Social Self*. Oxford: Oxford University Press, 151–80.

Mill, John Stuart ([1859 2008). *On Liberty and Other Essays*, ed. John Gray. Oxford: Oxford University Press.

Nedelsky, Jennifer (1989). "Re-Conceiving Autonomy: Sources, Thoughts, and Possibilities," *Yale Journal of Law & Feminism*, 1/1: 7–36.

Nozick, Robert (1974). *Anarchy, State, and Utopia*. New York: Basic Books.

Nussbaum, Martha (1999). *Sex and Social Justice*. Oxford: Oxford University Press.

Nussbaum, Martha (2006). *Frontiers of Justice: Disability, Nationality, and Species Membership*. Cambridge, MA: Harvard University Press.

Nussbaum, Martha (2011). "Perfectionist Liberalism and Political Liberalism," *Philosophy & Public Affairs*, 39/1: 3–45.

Okin, Susan Moller (1989). "Humanist Liberalism," in Nancy Rosenblum (ed.), *Liberalism and the Moral Life*. Cambridge, MA: Harvard University Press, 39–53.

Oshana, Marina (1998). "Personal Autonomy and Society," *Journal of Social Philosophy*, 29/1: 81–102.

Oshana, Marina (2003). "How Much should we Value Autonomy?," *Social Philosophy and Policy*, 20/2: 99–126.

Pateman, Carole (1988). *The Sexual Contract*. Cambridge: Polity Press.

Pinker, Steven (2008). "The Stupidity of Dignity," *New Republic*, May 28, https://newrepublic.com/article/64674/the–stupidity–dignity.

Raz, Joseph (1986). *The Morality of Freedom*. Oxford: Oxford University Press.

Raz, Joseph (2009). *The Authority of Law: Essays on Law and Morality*, 2nd edn. Oxford: Oxford University Press.

Rich, Adrienne (1976). *Of Woman Born: Motherhood as Experience and Institution*. New York: W. W. Norton & Company.

Roberts, Dorothy (1997). *Killing the Black Body: Race, Reproduction, and the Meaning of Liberty*. New York: Pantheon Books.

Rousseau, Jean-Jacques ([1755] 2008). *The Social Contract*, trans. Christopher Betts. Oxford: Oxford University Press.

Scanlon, Thomas (1998). *What we Owe to Each Other*. Cambridge, MA: Harvard University Press.

Schroeder, Doris (2010). "Dignity: One, Two, Three, Four, Five, Still Counting," *Cambridge Quarterly of Healthcare Ethics*, 19/2: 118–25.

Showden, Carisa (2011). *Choices Women Make: Agency in Domestic Violence, Assisted Reproduction, and Sex Work*. Minneapolis, MN: University of Minnesota Press.

Simplican, Stacy Clifford (2015). *The Capacity Contract: Intellectual Disability and the Question of Citizenship*. Minneapolis, MN: University of Minnesota Press.

Singer, Peter (1993). *Practical Ethics*, Second Edition. Cambridge: Cambridge University Press.

Singer, Peter (2009). "Speciesism and Moral Status." *Metaphilosophy* 40(3–4): 567–81.

Sophocles ([441 BCE] 1991). *Antigone*, trans. David Greene. Chicago: University of Chicago Press.

Stoljar, Natalie (2000). "Autonomy and the Feminist Intuition," in Catriona Mackenzie and Natalie Stoljar (eds), *Relational Autonomy: Feminist Perspectives on Autonomy, Agency, and the Social Self*. Oxford: Oxford University Press, 94–111.

Stoljar, Natalie (2014). "Autonomy and Adaptive Preference Formation," in Andrea Veltman and Mark Piper (eds), *Autonomy, Oppression, and Gender*. Oxford: Oxford University Press, 227–52.

Stoljar, Natalie (2017). "Relational Autonomy and Perfectionism," *Moral Philosophy and Politics*, 4/1: 27–41.

Vehmas, Simo (1999). "Discriminative Assumptions of Utilitarian Bioethics Regarding Individuals with Intellectual Disabilities," *Disability & Society*, 14/1: 37–52.

Wall, Steven (1998). *Liberalism, Perfectionism, and Restraint*. Cambridge: Cambridge University Press.

Wendell, Susan (1996). *The Rejected Body: Feminist Philosophical Reflections on Disability*. New York: Routledge.

Westlund, Andrea (2009). "Rethinking Relational Autonomy," *Hypatia: A Journal of Feminist Philosophy*, 24/4: 26–49.

Young, Iris Marion (1990). *Justice and the Politics of Difference.* Princeton: Princeton University Press.

Young, Robert (1986). *Personal Autonomy: Beyond Negative and Positive Liberty.* New York: Routledge.

Yuracko, Kimberly (2003). *Perfectionism and Contemporary Feminist Values.* Bloomington, IN: Indiana University Press.

2

Reproductive Autonomy and Genomic Medicine

Reproduction involves choices—lots of difficult, deeply personal choices. Do I want to have children? Which contraceptive should I use to avoid pregnancy? Should I terminate an unplanned pregnancy? How many children do I want to have? Should I get pregnant, adopt, or hire a surrogate? Do I want to give birth in a hospital or at home? Do I want to raise a child alone, with a partner, or with extended family? These decisions are far from trivial. Reproductive choices often have serious and lasting consequences, especially for women, since they are still commonly expected to take primary responsibility for child-rearing.

In the United States, reproductive choices are often limited. Legal restrictions on the use of contraceptives, the criminalization of abortion, and state-sanctioned forced sterilization are among the many limits that have robbed women of control over their own bodies and compromised their reproductive interests. In response, feminists have advocated that women make their own reproductive choices, so that others—including male relatives, government officials, religious leaders, and physicians—cannot unduly interfere with their capacities to do so. Today there is a general feminist consensus that women must be able to choose for themselves whether, when, and how they will have and raise children in order to exercise some measure of control over their lives and freely to be able to participate in society as equals. Thus, political demands for expanded access to contraception, the legalization of abortion, and freedom from involuntary sterilization remain high on the feminist agenda.

Prenatal genetic testing technologies can further facilitate reproductive autonomy by giving pregnant women information about the genetic traits that their prospective children might have, information they can choose to have available. It can expand reproductive options by allowing prospective parents to exert some limited control over the genetic make-up of their children. Individuals who do not wish to have a child with Down syndrome,

Prenatal Genetic Testing, Abortion, and Disability Justice. Amber Knight and Joshua Miller, Oxford University Press.
© Amber Knight and Joshua Miller (2023). DOI: 10.1093/oso/9780192870957.003.0003

62 Prenatal Genetic Testing, Abortion, and Disability Justice

for example, can utilize prenatal tests to detect the extra copy of chromosome twenty-one and abort the fetus if the condition is prenatally diagnosed. In this way, the technology can enable women to make private decisions that align with their personal preferences and values.

Yet, this book illustrates how prenatal genetic screening technologies can actually thwart women's reproductive rights in practice and serve less emancipatory purposes—such as neo-eugenic, neoliberal cost-containment efforts—when deployed in a context marked by structural inequalities. The wider implication is that, while prenatal genetic screening offers the potential of greater choice, those choices remain unduly constrained by oppressive policies and norms today. As we demonstrate in the following chapters, women face tremendous medical, economic, and sociocultural pressures to accept the offer of testing and terminate pregnancies when a fetal genetic impairment is diagnosed.

Before we delve into the specific medical practices, public policies, and cultural norms that limit or expand women's options surrounding prenatal screening technologies and selective abortion, this chapter weaves together insights from Chapter 1 to evaluate the extent to which women exercise reproductive autonomy in the age of reprogenetics. Our main goal is to persuade feminist theorists who are hesitant to embrace the state as a resource in the fight for reproductive justice to change their minds. According to Sujatha Jesudason (2009: 908), many members of the reproductive rights movement "have avoided discussions about an affirmative role for government in regulation, protection, and oversight primarily because of fears that that role will extend to limiting access to abortion and other family-planning technologies." Yet, as we hope the preceding discussion about perfectionist liberalism and relational autonomy has shown, important works in political theory have advanced the idea that government can play an active role in shaping and supporting autonomous citizens to the benefit of members of socially marginalized groups. Building from this school of thought, we make the case that genuine reproductive autonomy requires both governmental restraint and active support, suggesting that restraint and action can work in tandem to enlarge women's reproductive options. From our point of view, the relevant debate is not about whether the state plays a role, but how it does so.

In the first section, we discuss what reproductive autonomy means in practice and discuss the insufficiencies of a framework that equates reproductive autonomy with the right to privacy and governmental non-interference. Embracing a relational notion of choice, as articulated by the contemporary reproductive justice movement, we think about how women's decisions to use or decline prenatal screening technologies are socially constituted and situated. Specifically, reproductive preferences are constituted by cultural expectations that "good mothers" will use biotechnologies to control reproductive outcomes and produce "normal" or even "perfect" babies. In addition, women's options are situated by various socioeconomic realities, including the restraints imposed by poverty and a lack of reliable and affordable childcare arrangements. The next section evaluates the normative significance of reproductive autonomy, envisioning it as a form of dignified treatment that respects women's bodily autonomy and political personhood. Here we distance ourselves from those who would defend prenatal genetic screening on neo-eugenic grounds. Finally, we discuss what respect for reproductive autonomy entails in political practice, making the case that the liberal state has a positive social obligation to bring about an autonomy-enhancing social structure that gives women choices really worth having as they decide whether they want to undergo prenatal testing, terminate a pregnancy following a positive result, carry the fetus to term, raise a child with a disability with dignity, or choose adoption.

Meaning

In the United States, mainstream thinking on reproductive autonomy has a strong heritage in liberal political thought, as reflected in a long line of constitutional decisions that ground women's reproductive rights in the right to privacy.[1] In *Griswold* v. *Connecticut* (1965), the Supreme Court struck down a Connecticut law that banned the use of contraceptives, ruling that a married couple has a right of privacy that cannot be infringed upon by a state law criminalizing contraceptive use.[2] The privacy rationale underpinning *Griswold* paved the way for *Roe* v. *Wade* (1973). The Supreme Court's decision in *Roe*, which struck down government restrictions on abortion, hinges on a constitutional right to privacy found in the due process clause of the Fourteenth Amendment.[3] Thus construed, reproductive autonomy is tantamount to governmental restraint.

[1] See *Griswold* v. *Connecticut* (1965), *Eisenstadt* v. *Baird* (1972), *Roe* v. *Wade* (1973), and *Planned Parenthood* v. *Casey* (1992).

[2] While the Court explained that the Constitution does not explicitly protect a right to privacy, the various guarantees within the Bill of Rights create penumbras that establish a right to privacy.

[3] Although the Court ruled that the right to privacy is broad enough to encompass a woman's decision whether or not to terminate her pregnancy, the ruling made it clear that this right was not absolute; it could be limited for a "compelling state interest"—namely, protecting the health of the mother and protecting "potential life." To balance women's privacy rights against these state interests, the Court created the trimester framework.

64   Prenatal Genetic Testing, Abortion, and Disability Justice

Early feminist theorizing and activism were deeply indebted to this liberal tradition. In order to free decision-making power from the clutches of the state and paternalistic medical establishments, mainstream "pro-choice" feminist discourse emphasized the importance of defending a woman's right to privacy and self-determination in a medical setting. As Onora O'Neill (2002: 253) observes: "Appeals to the right to choose were extended to express not only the idea that reproduction is in very many respects an area of life in which persons have a right to make their own choices, but the thought that it is a domain in which nobody else has any right to determine what they shall do in any respect." Framing abortion as a medical procedure and positioning pregnant women as patients with rights to make free and informed decisions about their own medical care, early feminists thus conceived of reproductive rights as negative rights to non-interference. In essence, they wanted to ensure that women could refuse sex, access contraception, procure abortions, and decline sterilization without being forcibly prevented from doing so. These goals are reflected in the widely adopted feminist mantra that "my body belongs to me."

More recently, feminist theorists have come to argue that, even while protecting women's decisions from government interference, a negative liberty framework is insufficient to think about how many women actually go about making authentic reproductive decisions in practice. As Dorothy Roberts (1997: 309) insists, "the traditional concept of liberty makes the false presumption that the right to choose is contained entirely within the individual and not circumscribed by the material conditions of the individual's life." This false presumption disadvantages many women. In a series of decisions, the Supreme Court has protected reproductive choices from some acts of coercive state interference, but it has absolved the state from any responsibility to ensure that citizens have access to the resources needed for the effective implementation of their reproductive choices. Consider the Court's ruling in *Harris* v. *McRae* (1980), which upheld the Hyde Amendment, a legislative provision barring the use of federal Medicaid funding to pay for abortion services, even those deemed medically necessary for the health of the mother. Justice Stewart, who delivered the majority opinion, made it clear that reproductive autonomy is a negative right and that the state's role in securing it is minimal. "Although the liberty protected by the Due Process Clause affords protection against unwarranted government interference with freedom of choice in the context of certain personal decisions," Stewart declares, "it does not confer an entitlement to such funds as may be necessary to realize all the advantages of that freedom."[4]

By allowing the material hardships that limit many reproductive decisions to go uncorrected, the liberal state does little for women living at the margins of social and economic life. So understood, the right to privacy is more empty gesture than substantive right if a woman cannot afford to pay for contraception, or if she cannot raise a wanted child without falling more deeply into poverty. Even in a post-*Roe* landscape, abortion remains inaccessible for thousands of women each year because of socioeconomic barriers, including prohibitive expenses, remote locations, a shortage of service providers, and the persistent harassment of both abortion providers and women obtaining abortions at clinics across the country.[5]

Not only are women's reproductive choices socioeconomically situated, but their reproductive preferences are often socially constituted as well. Even intimate reproductive desires that are formed within a protected sphere of legal privacy can be socially pressured, manipulated, or misinformed. For example, many women from socially dominant groups (that is, white, wealthy, heterosexual, able-bodied, cisgendered) have had their reproductive autonomy restricted by sexist social expectations that they will inevitably and "naturally" undertake and enjoy the mothering role (Thurer 1994; Douglas and Michaels 2004). Owing to pervasive gender stereotypes, motherhood has often been assumed to be an essential part of "respectable womanhood," if not a woman's highest calling or greatest achievement. Susan Brownmiller (1984: 214) explains how "womanhood" and "motherhood" are often conflated, noting,

> Love of babies, any baby and all babies, not only one's own, is a celebrated and anticipated feminine emotion, and a woman who fails to ooh and awe at the snapshot of a baby or cuddle a proffered infant in her arms is instantly suspect. Evidence of a maternal nature, of a certain innate competence when handling a baby or at least some indication of maternal longing, becomes a requirement of gender.

Ideological associations between womanhood and motherhood are so pervasive, so apparently natural, that alternatives to childrearing may appear as abhorrent deviations where they appear at all. Maternal ideology amounts to

---

[4] See also *Webster* v. *Reproductive Health Services* (1989), wherein the Court held that the due process clause did not require states to enter into the business of abortion, nor did it create an affirmative right to governmental aid in the pursuit of constitutional rights.

[5] A study for the Guttmacher Institute found that three-fourths of abortion patients in 2014 were low income—49% lived at or below the federal poverty level, and 26% lived slightly over the federal poverty line (Jerman, Jones, and Onda 2016).

invidious socialization and is thus especially harmful for women who cannot imagine their future selves without their own biological children.

Just as restrictive gender norms have pressured women from socially dominant groups into having children, many women continue to experience the social expectation that they should be primarily responsible for childcare once children are born. Indeed, until relatively recently, women were incentivized to privilege motherhood over other life pursuits by discriminatory policies and workplace practices that barred or discouraged their participation in public life and the pursuit of educational opportunities and careers. Even now, American women are legally permitted to pursue careers, but unsupportive policies and unrealistic workplace norms—including unguaranteed and unpaid family-leave policies, unsubsidized childcare costs, inflexible work hours, and so on—make it so difficult to balance work and parenting obligations that many mothers "opt out" of the paid workforce to stay at home with their kids (Gornick and Meyers 2008; Williams 2010; Engster 2015).

Women from socially marginalized groups (that is, racial minorities, poor, queer, disabled, trans, and/or non-binary), by contrast, have faced a different set of social pressures and constraints. Many have had their reproductive desires shaped by oppressive socialization patterns that actively dissuade them from bearing and raising children (Roberts 1997). For example, many disabled women who are making decisions about family planning are bombarded with ableist messages that they are unfit for motherhood, incapable of parenting (regardless of their actual or potential capacities), and/or potential breeders of defective offspring who should avoid reproduction altogether (Knight 2017). Moreover, socioeconomic obstacles too frequently create financial hurdles to accessing contraceptives, using abortion services, and bearing and raising children in a safe, healthy, and financially secure environment.

In sum, a negative liberty theoretical framework for reproductive autonomy, while politically important, is ill equipped to analyze the wider socioeconomic and political forces that steer women's reproductive choices toward socially prescribed outcomes and/or make certain options practically unavailable. The right to privacy thus falls short of providing women with reproductive options really worth having. The limitations of the privacy framework underscore the need to embrace a relational conception of autonomy that can establish a contextual relationship between individual choice and persistent social inequalities *without* abandoning the commitment to government non-intervention in protecting women's reproductive decisions.

Let us now consider these lessons in light of decisions surrounding prenatal genetic screening and selective abortion. Women who live in states without prenatal non-discrimination laws currently enjoy a large degree of negative liberty: prenatal screening technologies are (*de jure*) voluntary, and selective abortion is (*de jure*) legal. Yet, even in these states, private decisions are not immune from material constraints and social pressures. Consider a pregnant woman's choice of whether or not to consent to the genetic screening procedure in the first place. If a pregnant woman who lives below the poverty line feels that the procedure is necessary to protect her family from the additional financial hardships that often accompany the experience of raising a child with a genetic impairment, can we really say that the decision to undergo screening is voluntary in a practical sense? We suggest that a decision to use prenatal screening made out of financial fear—in a society without adequate social safety nets for those living with disabled family members—falls short of being as autonomous as it should be in a liberal society. By the same token, if the procedure becomes a routine part of prenatal care, and doctors discuss prenatal genetic screening as a "no-brainer" that it would be irresponsible to decline, can we say that the availability of prenatal genetic screening enhances women's reproductive choices? The absence of overt coercion does not make a choice fully autonomous, even if doctors or the state do not directly interfere with the decision.

In recent years, women of color have been at the forefront of struggles to shift the concept of reproductive autonomy from a negative liberty paradigm to a more encompassing theoretical framework that connects reproductive choice to a wider social justice agenda (Roberts 1997; Smith 2005; Price 2010, 2011; Ross and Solinger 2017). In collaboration with grassroots organizations spearheaded by women of color—including Generations Ahead, Asian Communities for Reproductive Justice, and SisterSong—scholars have critically analyzed how women's capacities and opportunities to make meaningful choices about their reproductive lives are shaped by intersecting systemic oppressions such as racism, sexism, classism, heterosexism, transphobia, and ableism. By emphasizing how reproductive decisions cannot be understood separately from an analysis of the social context in which they occur, reproductive justice scholars reconceptualize reproductive autonomy by insisting that women should have decisional control over their bodies as well as access to the resources they need to prevent pregnancy and also to conceive, bear, and raise children with dignity. In doing so, advocates of reproductive justice open the possibility that the state can play a vital role in securing the external conditions necessary for reproductive choices to be effectively realized, even

68 Prenatal Genetic Testing, Abortion, and Disability Justice

if many are hesitant to enlist the state in the pursuit for reproductive justice. We explore the possibility of an affirmative state duty further in the sections below.

Value

Prenatal genetic screening and selective abortion are controversial, since matters related to conception, pregnancy, birth, and childrearing touch upon people's core moral values. As a result, ethical questions about the development and use of prenatal genetic screening and selective abortion continue to be fiercely debated in moral philosophy and bioethics. In this book, we defend the normative value of prenatal screening technologies and selective abortion on the grounds that these technologies have the potential to enhance women's reproductive options and secure women's political equality. In doing so, we disavow eugenic justifications for their usage. Like Rayna Rapp (1999: 50), we aim to "contest the eugenic and stigmatizing definition of disabilities which seems to underlie prenatal diagnosis, while still upholding the rights of individual women to determine what kind of medical care, and what sorts of pregnancy decisions, are in their own best interests."

The fact of the matter is that prenatal genetic testing and selective abortion cannot be adequately understood apart from the history of eugenics.[6] The eugenics movement—which gained prominence in the United States at the turn of the twentieth century—sought to "better" society by controlling reproduction. A foundational premise of twentieth-century eugenics was the idea that heredity was linked to social problems such as poverty and crime.[7] Attempts to improve the gene pool by preventing those deemed "undesirable" from reproducing led to repressive practices, including forced sterilization programs across the majority of American states.[8] Many American politicians and policymakers eventually retreated from explicit eugenic policies and practices after the rise of Hitler and the ensuing unease with Nazi-like racial supremacy, but subtle forms of eugenic logic are still deeply entrenched

---

[6] For a more developed discussion of the threads tying the eugenics movement to current reproductive genetic technologies, see Christopher Gyngell and Michael Selgelid (2017) and Gabrielle Goodrow (2019).

[7] The word "eugenics" stems from the Greek word *eugenes*, which means "good in stock."

[8] In the notorious case of *Buck* v. *Bell* (1925), the Supreme Court upheld Virginia's state compulsory sterilization statute after a cognitively disabled woman named Carrie Buck was sterilized against her will owing to her "incompetence." In the majority opinion, Justice Oliver Wendell Holmes infamously declared: "It is better for all the world, if instead of waiting to execute degenerate offspring for crime, or to let them starve for their imbecility, society can prevent those who are manifestly unfit from continuing their kind. The principle that sustains compulsory vaccination is broad enough to cover cutting the fallopian tubes. Three generations of imbeciles are enough." While state-level involuntary sterilization statutes have been struck down since *Buck*, the case still has not been explicitly overruled almost a century later.

Reproductive Autonomy and Genomic Medicine **69**

in much American political thinking.[9] To be clear, prenatal genetic screening and selective termination are *de jure* voluntary, so their resemblance to practices as nefarious as government-mandated forced sterilization should not be overstated.[10] Nonetheless, forms of neo-eugenic thinking have survived into the modern era and continue to permeate contemporary debates about the permissibility and desirability of prenatal screening technologies and selective termination.

For example, some proponents value prenatal genetic screening procedures and selective abortion as cost-cutting devices that can eliminate genetic disorders that would otherwise impose costly financial burdens on society. From this line of thought, it costs less to fund prenatal screening programs and subsidize termination than it does to retrofit inaccessible buildings, finance long-term care services, fund special education programs, and so on.[11] Dan Brock (2005: 391), for example, makes the case that the avoidance of "societal harm ... could in some cases outweigh individuals' reproductive and childrearing rights and interests." He is particularly concerned with economic harms that might result from the choice to bring children into the world who will have "extremely expensive health care needs," and he defends the relevance of savings considerations in thinking about whether prenatal genetic testing should be publicly subsidized in healthcare systems. In his view, "the other members of the health service do at least have a legitimate interest in limiting the health care costs that will be externalized upon them" (Brock 2005: 391). Brock is hardly alone in this line of thinking. Most recently, Elizabeth Beck (2020) has argued that prenatal non-discrimination acts—which ban selective abortions—are objectionable because they will pose a financial burden on society (not because they violate women's reproductive autonomy). Forcing women to carry fetuses with Down syndrome to term will probably mean that many children with disabilities will end

---

[9] Some disability studies scholars would have misgivings about our use of the word "subtle," arguing that these technologies are inherently eugenic because they built on the principle of "selection and eradication" (see Hubbard 1986; Saxton 2013; Garland-Thomson 2020). These technologies were developed and made available—partly at public expense—to allow prospective parents to identify genes for traits they prefer that their fetuses do not have. For such critics, prenatal genetic screening illustrates the defining intent of eugenics: to limit the births of individuals (or groups of individuals) who are deemed unfit or undesirable.

[10] Tom Shakespeare (1998) usefully makes a distinction between what he calls "strong" and "weak" eugenics. According to Shakespeare (1998: 669), "strong eugenics" is defined as "population-level improvement by control of reproduction via state intervention," while "weak eugenics" is defined as "promoting technologies of reproductive selection via non-coercive individual choices." Prenatal genetic screening and selective abortion fall under the "weak" categorization.

[11] In the early the 1970s, Zena Stein, Mervyn Susser, and Andrea Guterman (1973: 307) praised the fact that "almost total prevention of Down syndrome could be achieved by screening all pregnant women using amniocentesis and selective abortion." In an attempt to convince the broader community to embrace these developments, they also argued that "the cost of screening mothers over 30 years of age is certainly less than that of caring for cases of Down syndrome" (Stein, Susser, and Guterman 1973: 308).

up in foster care, which will create "an astronomical financial burden on an already belabored child welfare system" (Beck 2020: 725). Simply put, Beck defends the legality of selective abortion in order to contain costs in the foster-care system.

If we work from Dorothy Roberts's characterization (2009: 796) of eugenics as "the belief that reproductive strategies can improve society," it is easy to see how eugenic logic often undergirds the endorsement of prenatal genetic screening and selective abortion for financial gain. The celebration of prenatal genetic testing and abortion as a way to end disability and reduce its corollary expenses is problematic, because it feeds into the eugenic premise that social goals, like a balanced budget, can best be achieved by controlling reproduction and prenatally determining who shall and shall not inherit the earth based on the net economic value they add to society. Such a position overlooks the fact that legitimate state interests—such as improving the population, reducing suffering, and containing costs in a context of scarce resources—can be met far more effectively through strategies that have nothing to do with controlling women's reproductive lives. Concerned with improving the population? Make an effort to invest in education, human development, medical infrastructure, and care work. Motivated to reduce human suffering? Start by eliminating malnutrition, homelessness, and gun violence. Want to save scarce resources? Tax the rich their fair share and reallocate resources away from the military industrial complex. Most social goals should not be pursued at the expense of women's reproductive rights.

As far as we are concerned, the only good reason to defend the value of prenatal genetic screening and selective abortion is on the grounds that they allow women to have more control over their pregnancies and empower them to decide whether or not to bring a fetus to term according to their own values and conceptions of the good life. Why is reproductive autonomy a normative value worth championing? For their part, many liberal theorists have valued women's capacities to make autonomous choices about their bodies and reproductive futures as an important component of dignified treatment in a decent society. The Supreme Court has relied upon the concept of dignity to reject limitations upon the woman's right to choose an abortion prior to viability. Writing for the majority in *Planned Parenthood of Southeastern Pennsylvania* v. *Casey* (1992), Justice O'Connor made the case, writing:

These matters, involving the most intimate and personal choices a person may make in a lifetime, choices central to personal dignity and autonomy, are central to the liberty protected by the Fourteenth Amendment. At the heart of liberty is the right to define one's own concept of existence, of meaning, of the universe,

Reproductive Autonomy and Genomic Medicine   **71**

and of the mystery of human life. Beliefs about these matters could not define the attributes of personhood were they formed under compulsion of the State.[12]

From this perspective, respect for reproductive autonomy entails the obligation to allow people independently to form their own preferences, develop their own interests, and make their own medical decisions about their own bodies and pregnancies free from excessive government interference.

Many feminists have also valued reproductive autonomy as a component of dignified treatment. Betty Friedan, a co-founder of the National Organization for Women, made such an argument in a speech to an abortion-rights conference in Chicago in February 1969. Friedan asserted: "there is no freedom, no equality, no full human dignity and personhood possible for women until we assert and demand the control over our own bodies, over our own reproductive process" (quoted in Greenhouse and Siegel 2019: 56). Laws criminalizing abortion deny women the authority to shape their own lives, Friedan argued. Many other feminists have followed this line of thinking, portraying the ability legally and safely to obtain an abortion as an ingredient of women's human dignity. According to Drucilla Cornell (1995), the experiences of pregnancy and motherhood bear significantly on how one's life will be lived, so a woman's ability to decide the outcome of her pregnancy is crucial to her sense of self. To deny a woman authorial control infringes on her bodily integrity and identifies her with a function rather than "as a self who projects and continuously re-imagines herself and the meaning of her embodiment" (Cornell 1995: 58). Thus, denying women reproductive autonomy denies them dignity, because it objectifies them as instruments of reproduction and reduces them to a "walking uterus" or "fetal incubator." This type of degrading treatment positions a woman as less than a fully human adult responsible for her own choices.

If treating women in a dignified manner means respecting their reproductive choices, it follows that pregnant women should be able to choose whether to use prenatal genetic screening and to decide how they want to move forward with their pregnancy based on the information they learn from the results. In a diverse society characterized by a variety of lived values, we expect that people in similar situations will inevitably make different choices. The genetic characteristics and health status of one's prospective children might matter a great deal to some people, while they may play little part in the reproductive decisions of others. As a matter of dignified treatment, we should respect reproductive choices to employ these technologies, and

---

[12] *Planned Parenthood of Southeastern Pennsylvania et al. v. Casey* 505 U.S. 833 (1992), 851.

72 Prenatal Genetic Testing, Abortion, and Disability Justice

we should respect those to forgo them as well. Respect means that prenatal screening technologies should be available to all who want to access them, but their use should be truly voluntary instead of routinized to the point that they seem compulsory.

The same goes for selective abortion. On the one hand, pregnant women should never have to endure the indignity of forcibly carrying an unwanted pregnancy to term. Nor should they have to experience the indignity and danger of seeking an illegal abortion or inducing miscarriage through non-medical means. The fact of the matter is that bearing and raising a child with a genetic impairment may not fit into everyone's life plan, and some prospective parents may wish to avoid the birth of a fetus for a range of reasons.[13] Hence, so-called prenatal non-discrimination acts, which prohibit abortion in cases of fetal genetic impairment, violate women's autonomy and constitute a form of degrading (rather than dignifying) treatment. On the other hand, some people may want to bring a fetus with a prenatally diagnosed genetic impairment into the world and welcome the child into their families after she is born. This means that oppressive social pressures that effectively steer women towards terminating genetically impaired fetuses—including ableist medical counseling, the realistic threat of poverty following the birth of a child with expensive "special needs," and the privatization and feminization of child-rearing labor and care for disabled dependants—are also degrading.

Consistent with the principle of negative liberty, we think that even individual decisions made out of pernicious social conditioning are worthy of respect and should not be forcibly overridden by the government. We believe that it is never acceptable paternalistically to coerce women into certain choices in the name of autonomy, or to leverage the power of the state to force women into making certain reproductive decisions "for their own good." What individual women decide to do with these technologies, and how they go about making these decisions, is ultimately up to them.[14] The point is to allow women to decide for themselves, while taking collective responsibility for creating a fair and just context within which decisions are made. As we argued in Chapter 1, we hope to avoid paternalistic governance and retain a

---

[13] Although at times individual women's reproductive decisions may be colored by ableist or eugenic ideals, we agree with Tom Shakespeare's contention (1998: 672) that "the decisions underlying selective termination may often be about the social implications of bringing up a disabled child, not a eugenic unwillingness to bring disabled people into the world."

[14] For example, if a woman chooses to defer to a religious leader in deciding what to do after receiving positive test results from prenatal genetic testing, that is her prerogative. We are satisfied so long as her decision to act non-autonomously is made in a context where she has the opportunity to live her life autonomously. After all, part of what autonomy involves is allowing people some amount of room to reject autonomous living.

commitment to the right to privacy by tethering our theory of autonomy to a political commitment to negative liberty.

While we are adamant about respecting women as the final arbiters of their own life choices, we also think about respect in a more capacious manner than many mainstream liberals. Respect for personal autonomy is not just as a passive orientation or form of toleration; it also involves active cultivation and promotion. If our current social and political arrangements are so constraining on individual choice that they rise to the level of oppression, respect cannot be achieved by staying out of the way. Respect also requires that the political community take affirmative steps actively to cultivate and nourish opportunities for personal autonomy so that members of "dispossessed and disempowered groups share the means to be self-determining" (Roberts 1997: 312). These affirmative steps imply institutional reforms—including comprehensive sex education in state schools, overhauls to health insurance and long-term care systems, and changing cultural norms about "good mothers" and "perfect babies"—that dismantle oppressive social and political forces so that women of all backgrounds have a range of viable options to choose among as they make reproductive choices and engage with prenatal genetic screening technologies.

Finally, it is also worth noting that our normative defence of reproductive autonomy can coincide with Eva Kittay's call for humility. Kittay (2019: 68) takes up a firmly pro-choice position vis-à-vis prenatal genetic screening and selective abortion by maintaining that "enlarging choices for those who have lacked much choice, such as women and sexual minorities, should be viewed as a positive thing". Yet she warns that new reproductive technologies might offer "the false assurance that, as a result of choice, everything will be as we wish it (or think we wish it)" (Kittay 2019: 76). Reproduction has become increasingly technologized following medical and scientific advances, and this technologization makes it seem as though reproduction is a phenomenon that is under the complete control of human beings and their instruments. Kittay (2019: 75) is not critical of these developments, per se, but she offers up the occasion to question the limits of choice, recognize the unpredictability of fortune, and acknowledge how human ability to control reproductive outcomes is at best partial and incomplete. For instance, bodies may not cooperate with reproductive choices owing to factors like infertility, and the genetic make-up of children will at least partly be determined by the vagaries of the genetic lottery. Prenatal genetic screening cannot detect or eliminate all cases of physical and mental impairment, nor can it guarantee that a child will have a natural aptitude for any particular skill, such as maths or sports. Kittay (2019: 96) champions choice, but also urges her

74 Prenatal Genetic Testing, Abortion, and Disability Justice

reader humbly to "make each choice aware, if only dimly, that we may not get what we signed up for". Parenthood is always a plunge into the unknown and uncontrollable. This point is also important to consider, as most impairments are acquired over the life cycle. Comparatively fewer impairments are congenital.[15] In the end, it is perfectly consistent to promote reproductive autonomy as a form of dignified treatment owed to women in a decent society without perpetuating the myth that our reproductive fates are completely up to us.

Politics

Volumes have been written about the political struggle to carve out a sphere of privacy that places women's reproductive decisions out of the reach of government, including the decisions to prevent pregnancy through contraception and terminate a pregnancy up until viability (Solinger 2013; Sanger 2017). This struggle has been deeply contested and tiresomely repetitive. The fight for women's reproductive rights is relentless. Victories are hard fought, frequently repealed, and in constant danger of being overturned. Access to legalized abortion is in jeopardy in state legislatures across the country as ever more restrictions are envisioned and passed.

Even though the battle to protect women's reproductive rights is ongoing, fighting against intrusive state power is not enough. Rosalind Pollack Petchesky (1990) explains why.[16] According to Petchesky, positive social rights get pushed to the side when the right to privacy is regarded as the chief end of reproductive politics.[17] She describes the shortcomings with a negative liberty privacy-centered strategy, writing:

> Until privacy or autonomy is redefined in reference to the social justice provisions
> that give it substance for the poorest women, it will remain not only a class-biased

---

[15] Reliable data about rates of congenital disability are hard to come by. However, Jeffrey Brosco (2010) found that the incidence of intellectual and developmental disability has stayed constant over time. Even though fewer people with genetic congenital impairments are being born following the advent of prenatal screening and selective abortion, scientific developments and medical advances have also improved survival rates of those who would previously not have survived, including those born preterm and individuals who have acquired cognitive impairment from traumatic brain injuries or dementia in old age.

[16] See also Catherine MacKinnon's critique of the right to privacy and its negative impact on women's lives. MacKinnon (1989: 193) argues that political appeals to privacy have usually functioned to shore up existing hierarchies in the private realm. In her words, "the existing distribution of power and resources within the private sphere are precisely what the law of privacy exists to protect."

[17] Social rights can generally be understood as rights that afford every citizen the social and economic conditions necessary to fulfill their basic human needs, such as the rights to healthcare, an adequate standard of living, and education. For more on the distinction between civil and social rights, see T. H. Marshall's famous work *Citizenship and Social Class* (1950).

Reproductive Autonomy and Genomic Medicine   75

and racist concept but an antifeminist one, insofar as it is premised on a denial of social responsibility to improve the conditions of women as a whole. (Petchesky 1990: pp. xxv–xxvi)

This means that "leaving people alone" in a libertarian sense may actually impede reproductive autonomy in a context of structural inequality. In the absence of positive rights to economic resources and social goods, which would provide access to healthcare, a living wage, education, and so on, women at the social margins—especially poor women, women with disabilities, and/or women of color—will lack the wherewithal to exercise their reproductive choices in practice.[18]

Feminist legal scholars have expanded their criticisms on the insufficiencies of a negative liberty framework for a progressive reproductive justice agenda in recent years. Robin West (2009) persuasively argues that negative constitutional rights may be necessary to "keep the state off our backs and out of our lives." Yet, on their own, negative rights also "run the risk of legitimating the injustices we sustain in the insulated privacy so created" (West 2009: 1398). That is, the inordinate focus on negative liberty does not just divert attention from social justice matters or eclipse the concern with social rights. Rather, according to West, the attainment of negative legal rights actually *legitimates* the lack of social rights and undermines claims for public support for ensuring reproductive autonomy in a more robust way. *Roe* may have constitutionalized the "right to choose" within a legal zone of privacy, but, according to West (2009: 1411), this ruling also legitimized "the lack of public support given parents in fulfilling their caregiving obligations" at the same time. West (2009: 1411) explains how the privacy strategy backfired, writing:

By giving pregnant women the choice to opt *out* of parenting by purchasing an abortion, we render parenting a market commodity, and thereby systematically legitimate the various baselines to which she agrees when she opts *in*: an almost entirely privatized system of childcare, a mixed private and public but prohibitively expensive healthcare system, and a publicly provided education system that delivers a product, the quality of which is spotty at best and disastrously inadequate at worst. Narrowly, by giving her the choice, her consent legitimates the parental burden to which *she* has consented.

---

[18] For example, the Hyde Amendment, originally enacted in 1977, is a legislative provision that bans the use of federal funds for abortion services in all but the most extreme circumstances—including cases of rape, incest, or life endangerment. This provision abdicates any positive responsibility to ensure that poor women have the resources to exercise their choice to receive abortion services.

76   Prenatal Genetic Testing, Abortion, and Disability Justice

Put differently, the rhetoric of private choice following *Roe* has undercut arguments in favor of the development of what West (2001) refers to elsewhere as positive "caregiver rights," or the positive rights of parents and other caregivers to public assistance for their caregiving work. The struggles of parenthood are considered private battles, because women presumably volunteered for the financial and social hardships when they freely chose to have children. As a constitutionally protected private choice, every individual is considered free to choose or reject parenthood, but parents have no special claim on public assistance, since state support for childcare would be unfair to non-parents who made a different choice.[19] In sum, the privacy argument that clinched *Roe*'s victory also limited its prospects by severing reproductive autonomy from issues of economic and social justice.

The political costs of the privacy strategy have become especially apparent within discussions about parenting children with disabilities following the routinization of prenatal genetic screening. For example, some responsibility-sensitive egalitarians have suggested that parents should bear the costs of raising and caring for disabled children that they deliberately and avoidably chose to have when they could have chosen to have non-disabled children instead (Steiner 2002; Clayton 2006). If children with disabilities are expected to cost more than they benefit economically, they cannot be regarded as public or "socialized" goods that would then entitle parents to state subsidies designed to offset child-rearing costs. In this way, the choice to carry and raise a disabled child is equated with an expensive lifestyle choice. The view is that parents who knowingly and deliberately choose to have genetically impaired children that will need additional resources to flourish should be personally liable for the increased costs associated with their private preferences and choices. By undermining political claims to public assistance, the negative right of privacy created in *Roe* actually undermines the reproductive autonomy of prospective mothers who want to raise a child with Down syndrome in an ableist society.

What lessons can be learned from these criticisms? In an ironic twist, the lack of public support for the choice to birth and raise a child with an impairment is in fact legitimized by the "pro-choice" rhetoric that lent itself to a libertarian framework around freedom from government intrusion. When the decision knowingly to parent a child with a disability is equated with an expensive lifestyle choice or consumer preference, the related assumption is that any hardships related to raising disabled children in an ableist society fall within the domain of personal responsibility for private preferences

---

[19] Anne Alstott (2004: 60) refers to this as the "private project objection" to the collective responsibility for childcare.

rather than the domain of collective support for shared vulnerability and human development. The wider implication is that the mainstream reproductive rights movement has elevated the rights of affluent women at the expense of poor women, who are disproportionately women of color, working-class women, and women with disabilities. Wealthy families who want to birth and raise a child with a genetic impairment may be able to do so successfully and make ends meet with their own resources but the privatization of childcare that follows reinforces the disadvantages of attempting to raise children at or near poverty.

Where do we go from here? To begin, if the narrow focus on the legal right to privacy—and the attendant issues of contraception and abortion—does not serve all women well, the agenda needs to be broadened. Many affluent, white, able-bodied women may be content with the privacy rights that have been secured under *Griswold* v. *Connecticut* (1965) and *Roe* v. *Wade* (1973), but many women of color, poor women, and women with disabilities have not enjoyed these gains to the same degree. Contraceptives, abortion services, as well as prenatal healthcare services can be out of reach and prohibitively expensive in a privatized healthcare system. Relatedly, the myopic focus on the right to privacy obscures forms of reproductive injustice that are more likely to affect women at the social margins. The privacy framework does not capture the concerns of poor women of color who face pressures to accept contraception or sterilization in exchange for welfare benefits, for example, or the challenges that women from low-income families face if they want to birth and raise a child with an impairment but cannot afford to risk additional financial ruin. Thus, if the reproductive justice movement is to be effective, it must broaden its agenda to champion a range of issues outside abortion or risk alienating poor women, women of color, and women with disabilities.

Another takeaway is that cross-movement mobilization and coalition politics are required in the face of formidable political opposition. The biotechnology industry, medical associations, the Catholic Church, and other "pro-life" factions of the conservative Right are well-funded and well-organized stakeholders in policy debates about the development and application of prenatal screening technologies and selective abortion practices. This means that any long-standing tensions between the disability rights movement and the reproductive rights movement are counterproductive for progressive politics.[20] In recent years, scholars and activists committed to an intersectional framework have refused to accept the bifurcation of these social movements

---

[20] The long-standing tensions between the disability rights movement and the reproductive rights movement on the issue of prenatal genetic screening have been well documented. See Keith Sharp and Sarah Earle (2002) and Martha Saxton (2013).

78 Prenatal Genetic Testing, Abortion, and Disability Justice

by working under the assumption that reproductive rights include attention to disability rights, and vice versa.[21] Cross-movement dialogue is central to their visions of a progressive form of coalition politics. In order to forge alliances between reproductive justice, racial justice, women's rights, and disability rights organizations, regular convenings—including conferences, meetings, roundtables, and so on—are productive. These types of collaborations should be as diverse as possible and include a cross-section of women from various racial, religious, and class backgrounds who have different sexual orientations and abilities. Participants need not expect consensus or agreement on all issues or values, but they need to provide a space where each group can share its unique perspective on reprogenetics, discuss its members' key challenges and struggles, and make clear what each organization wants other people to understand and respect about their experiences (Jesudason 2009: 911). The basic working premise is that grappling with differences in earnest can build solidarity. As Dorothy Roberts and Sujatha Jesudason (2013: 316) argue, "the radical potential for intersectionality lies in moving beyond its recognition of difference to build political coalitions based on the recognition of connections among systems of oppression as well as on a shared vision of social justice."[22]

The last lesson is that an active state is not always an impediment to free choice. To the extent that reproductive rights activists have been willing to the engage the state, they have turned to the judicial branch. The Courts have generally curtailed excessive state intrusion into people's lives, but, according to some feminist legal scholars, one reason that the mainstream reproductive rights framework has fallen short of achieving the goals of the reproductive justice movement is because it has relied too heavily on the court system and rights-focused litigation (West 2009; London 2011). According to these critics, litigation is disempowering, because it elevates the role that elites play

---

[21] See Roberts 2005, 2009; Jesudason 2009; Kafer 2013; Piepmeier 2013; Saxton 2013; Jarman 2015

[22] Dorothy Roberts and Sujatha Jesudason (2013) provide a concrete historical example of a successful coalition-building process through a case study of the non-profit organization Generations Ahead. Founded in 2008, Generations Ahead was a social justice organization based in Oakland, California. Its stated mission was to bring diverse communities together to expand the public debate around genetic technologies and promote policies that protect human rights. Generations Ahead's *modus operandi* was collaborative. It worked with a network of reproductive rights, racial justice, disability rights, and queer rights groups—including Planned Parenthood Federation of America, the American Civil Liberties Union, the LGBT Center of New York, and the Disability Rights Education Defense Funds, among many others—to increase diverse participation in public debates and policymaking on reprogenetic technologies. Unfortunately, Sujatha Jesudason decided to close Generations Ahead in 2012 owing to lack of funding and budgetary constraints. Yet, this organization is worthy of emulation, since it adopted an intersectional framework at the movement-building level to identify genuine common ground, create authentic alliances, and more effectively advocate for shared policy priorities.

Reproductive Autonomy and Genomic Medicine **79**

in making change by relying on judges and lawyers. This reliance is problematic, because clients generally have minimal opportunities to participate in the process or to shape the outcome when lawyers advocate on their behalf. Also, owing to their elite social status, lawyers in strategic decision-making positions tend to downplay class issues in social movements, since they are not directly affected by the sting of poverty themselves.

In addition, constitutional law has a limited use, since courts lack the tools to implement remedies for systemic social or structural problems (London 2011; Alstott 2015). The Constitution grants individuals a significant degree of latitude to assert negative liberty and live freely from excessive state intervention in private life, but individuals have no constitutional right to claim any social rights or economic resources needed to take control of their reproductive lives. Court rulings have refused to make the leap from protecting negative rights to ensuring social rights by absolving the state from any affirmative obligation to ensure that its citizens have the means to execute their choices. From the Court's perspective, a woman's reproductive autonomy remains sufficiently protected, even if her choice is made more difficult based on financial constraints. In sum, the court system is not designed to alter the balance of power, since courts do not make decisions that shift resources or affect the delivery of health services.

In order to reallocate wealth and social resources, legislation—not litigation—is instrumental for social transformation. Indeed, many significant battles over reproductive politics have been waged in the legislative arena since the 1970s. Having lost before the Supreme Court, abortion opponents shifted the fight to Congress and state legislatures effectively to dilute the impact of the *Roe* ruling. Pro-life federal and state legislators have chipped away at women's access to abortion services by various means, including: ending Medicaid funding for abortions; limiting insurance coverage and requiring pre-abortion counseling (which often requires physicians to read a state-mandated script with misleading and unsubstantiated health information); requiring invasive ultrasound imaging; insisting on mandatory waiting periods; and demanding parental consent requirements for minors (Guttmacher Institute 2021).

Rather than count on the Court to provide answers, or shy away from any engagement with the state and operate exclusively as a social movement within civil society, a reproductive justice approach needs to direct more attention and resources to thinking about how state and federal legislation can play an active role in guarding and even enhancing autonomy. Public policies can be leveraged to protect against structures of social inequality that diminish women's opportunities to form and execute reproductive choices.

80 Prenatal Genetic Testing, Abortion, and Disability Justice

What is needed, therefore, is a formative and active liberal state committed to cultivating its citizens' capacities and opportunities for self-government. Affirmative steps may need to be taken to make sure that the choice is well informed (that is, the passage of the Kennedy–Brownback Act) and free from undue financial burdens (that is, repeal the Hyde Amendment and pass legislation to fund long-term care services for families who choose to continue pregnancies following a positive diagnosis).

To be clear, the turn toward a more active legislative agenda for reproductive justice need not abandon respect for privacy or compromise on the issue of abortion. It would be foolish to turn our backs on privacy, since abortion is on the chopping block in state legislatures across the United States The point that we are trying to make, following the lead of relational autonomy theorists, is that restraint and action are complementary dimensions of how the state can protect and promote its citizens' capacities for self-determination (McClain 2006: 42). Governmental non-interference is necessary but insufficient. It is necessary, because excessive governmental intrusion poses a significant threat to autonomy. Criminalizing abortion, for example, limits women's abilities to govern their own bodies and determine their own life paths, and the courts need to protect the right to privacy. Yet restraint is also insufficient, because the government must often take proactive measures to create the social conditions that foster citizens' opportunities to make autonomous reproductive decisions. For instance, state legislatures need to fund sexual education programs in state schools that facilitate informed reproductive choice. Reproductive justice also advocates the need to rally for legislation to reduce disparities in reproductive healthcare so that all women can access affordable quality prenatal and postnatal care.

Finally, we also recognize that politics takes place outside the halls of government. Litigation and legislation are not the only tools of social transformation. Legal change is by itself inadequate to enact broader transformations, since legislation is difficult to pass if progressive movements cannot marshal popular support for changes. Civil society is a space where public opinion on reproductive politics is shaped, so consciousness-raising groups, street protests, and other forms of contentious politics that move the needle in favor of reproductive justice are valuable forms of democratic struggle as well. In addition, as many relational autonomy theorists maintain, barriers to reproductive choice can be internal, owing to pernicious social conditioning, ignorance, and manipulation. Reproductive preferences are often formed by social norms, but norms cannot simply be "fixed" through policy change.

Gender roles, stereotypes about "fit" and "unfit" parents, and cultural norms about normalcy need to be contested and challenged in the cultural realm.

When we think about these political implications of a reproductive justice framework for the purpose of expanding women's reproductive autonomy in the context of prenatal screening and selective abortion, it is clear that active government support and progressive social transformation will call for many legislative and cultural changes. The remaining chapters of this book are devoted to the task of spelling out which changes should be made and how.

Conclusion

Can we really have it both ways? Can we place the social factors that sway women towards termination at center stage, and then turn around and make normative claims that the state should nevertheless respect a woman's choice to abort following a positive fetal diagnosis (that is, "my body, my choice")? Emily Jackson (2000) is skeptical that we can have our cake and eat it too.[23] She is concerned that incorporating an analysis of social construction into a discussion of reproductive autonomy risks disrespecting and discrediting the legitimacy of an individual woman's reproductive choices. If all our choices are inevitably affected by the situation in which we find ourselves, dwelling on the social factors that shape and circumscribe a woman's decision to get an abortion takes us down a dangerous path. "To suggest that a woman's desire for an abortion is only worthy of respect if it is unmediated by external influences is unrealistic," Jackson (2000: 480) writes, "and would in practice invalidate most individuals' decisions about their medical treatment."

As we hope to have shown, there is nothing untoward about taking into account the influence of various forms of oppression over reproductive decision-making. By making a commitment to negative liberty part and parcel of our theory of autonomy, we maintain that the pregnant woman is the sole person authorized to make her own reproductive choices about prenatal screening and selective abortion. This means that a woman's desire to use prenatal screening technologies and procure an abortion following a positive diagnosis is worthy of respect, even if it is affected by external influences, including oppressive ones. Nevertheless, an appreciation for the ways in which women's reproductive choices have been shaped by medical institutions, the economic mode of production, the legal system, and

---

[23] See also Samuel Bagenstos (2006), who is also hesitant to use government regulation to counteract social pressures that impede free reproductive choice.

82 Prenatal Genetic Testing, Abortion, and Disability Justice

the social structure in which we live enriches our notion of what counts as a choice worthy of the name and allows us to think about how to enlarge women's options in the pursuit of a more just future.

References

Alstott, Anne (2004). *No Exit: What Parents Owe their Children and What Society Owes Parents*. Oxford: Oxford University Press.

Alstott, Anne (2015). "Neoliberalism in US Family Law: Negative Liberty and Laissez-Faire Markets in the Minimal State," *Law and Contemporary Problems*, 77/2: 25–42.

Bagenstos, Samuel (2006). "Disability, Life, Death, and Choice," *Harvard Journal of Law and Gender*, 29/2: 425–63.

Beck, Elizabeth (2020). "The Hollow Shell of Ohio H.B. 214: A Critical Examination of the Consequences of Down Syndrome Discrimination Laws," *University of Pittsburgh Law Review*, 81/3: 697–734.

Brock, Daniel (2005). "Shaping Future Children: Parental Rights and Societal Interests," *Journal of Political Philosophy*, 13/4: 377–98.

Brosco, Jeffrey (2010). "The Limits of the Medical Model: Historical Epidemiology of Intellectual Disability in the United States," in Eva Feder Kittay and Licia Carlson (eds), *Cognitive Disability and its Challenge to Moral Philosophy*. Malden, MA: Wiley–Blackwell, 27–54.

Brownmiller, Susan (1984). *Femininity*. New York: Linden Press.

Clayton, Matthew (2006.) *Justice and Legitimacy in Upbringing*. Oxford: Oxford University Press.

Cornell, Drucilla (1995). *The Imaginary Domain: Abortion, Pornography and Sexual Harassment*. New York: Routledge.

Douglas, Susan, and Meredith Michaels (2004). *The Mommy Myth: The Idealization of Motherhood and how it has Undermined Women*. New York: Free Press.

Engster, Daniel (2015). *Justice, Care, and the Welfare State*. Oxford: Oxford University Press.

Garland-Thomson, Rosemarie (2020). "How We Got to CRISPR: The Dilemma of Being Human," *Perspectives in Biology and Medicine*, 63/1: 28–43.

Goodrow, Gabrielle (2019). "Biopower, Disability and Capitalism: Neoliberal Eugenics and the Future of ART Regulation," *Duke Journal of Gender, Law, and Policy*, 26/2: 137–55.

Gornick, Janet, and Marcia Meyers (2008). "Creating Gender Egalitarian Societies: An Agenda for Reform," *Politics and Society*, 36/3: 313–49.

Greenhouse, Linda, and Reva Siegel (2019). "The Unfinished Story of *Roe v. Wade*," in Melissa Murray, Kate Shaw and Reva Siegel (eds), *Reproductive Rights and Justice Stories*. St Paul, MN: Foundation Press, 53–75.

Guttmacher Institute (2021). *Banning Abortions in Cases of Race or Sex Selection or Fetal Anomaly*. New York: Guttmacher Institute, https://www.guttmacher.org/evidence-you-can-use/banning-abortions-cases-race-or-sex-selection-or-fetal-anomaly.

Gyngell, Christopher, and Michael Selgelid (2017). "Twenty-First-Century Eugenics," in Leslie Francis (ed.), *The Oxford Handbook of Reproductive Ethics*. Oxford: Oxford University Press, 141–58.

Hubbard, Ruth (1986). "Eugenics and Prenatal Testing," *International Journal of Health Services*, 16/2: 227–42.

Jackson, Emily (2000). "Abortion, Autonomy, and Prenatal Diagnosis," *Social & Legal Studies*, 9/4: 467–94.

Jarman, Michelle (2015). "Relations of Abortion: Crip Approaches to Reproductive Justice," *Feminist Formations*, 27/1: 46–66.

Jerman, Jenna, Rachel Jones, and Tsuyoshi Onda (2016). *Characteristics of US Abortion Patients in 2014 and Changes since 2008*. New York: Guttmacher Institute, https://www.guttmacher.org/report/characteristics-us-abortion-patients-2014.

Jesudason, Sujatha (2009). "In the Hot Tub: The Praxis of Building New Alliances for Reprogenetics," *Signs: Journal of Women in Culture and Society*, 34/4: 901–24.

Kafer, Alison (2013). *Feminist, Queer, Crip*. Indianapolis: Indiana University Press.

Kittay, Eva Feder (2019). *Learning from my Daughter: The Value and Care of Disabled Minds*. Oxford: Oxford University Press.

Knight, Amber (2017). "Disability and the Meaning of Reproductive Liberty," *Politics, Groups, and Identities*, 5/1: 67–83.

London, Sarah (2011). "Reproductive Justice: Developing a Lawyering Model," *Berkeley Journal of African-American Law and Policy*, 13/1: 71–102.

MacKinnon, Catharine (1989). *Toward a Feminist Theory of the State*. Cambridge, MA: Harvard University Press.

McClain, Linda (2006). *The Place of Families: Fostering Capacity, Equality, and Responsibility*. Cambridge, MA: Harvard University Press.

Marshall, Thomas Humphrey (1950). *Citizenship and Social Class and Other Essays*. New York: Cambridge University Press.

O'Neill, Onora (2002). *Autonomy and Trust in Bioethics*. Cambridge: Cambridge University Press.

Petchesky, Rosalind Pollack (1990). *Abortion and Woman's Choice: The State, Sexuality, and Reproductive Freedom*. Rev. edn. Boston: Northeastern University Press.

Piepmeier, Alison (2013). "The Inadequacy of 'Choice': Disability and What's Wrong with Feminist Framings of Reproduction," *Feminist Studies*, 39/1: 159–86.

Price, Kimala (2010). "What is Reproductive Justice? How Women of Color Activists are Redefining the Pro-Choice Paradigm," *Meridians*, 10/2: 42–65.

Price, Kimala (2011). "It's not just about Abortion: Incorporating Intersectionality in Research about Women of Color and Reproduction," *Women's Health Issues*, 21/3S: S55–S57.

Rapp, Rayna (1999). *Testing Women, Testing the Fetus: The Social Impact of Amniocentesis in America*. New York: Routledge.

Roberts, Dorothy (1997). *Killing the Black Body: Race, Reproduction, and the Meaning of Liberty*. New York: Pantheon Books.

Roberts, Dorothy (2005). "Privatization and Punishment in the New Age of Reprogenetics," *Emory Law Journal*, 54/3: 1343–60.

Roberts, Dorothy (2009). "Race, Gender, and Genetic Technologies: A New Reproductive Dystopia?," *Signs: Journal of Women in Culture and Society*, 34/4: 783–804.

Roberts, Dorothy, and Sujatha Jesudason (2013). "Movement Intersectionality: The Case of Race, Gender, Disability, and Genetic Technologies," *Du Bois Review: Social Science Research on Race*, 10/2: 313–38.

Ross, Loretta, and Rickie Solinger (2017). *Reproductive Justice: An Introduction*. Oakland, CA: University of California Press.

Sanger, Carol (2017). *About Abortion: Terminating Pregnancy in Twenty-First-Century America*. Cambridge, MA: Harvard University Press.

Saxton, Marsha (2013). "Disability Rights and Selective Abortion," in Lennard Davis (ed.), *The Disability Studies Reader*, 4th edn. New York: Routledge, 7–99.

Shakespeare, Tom (1998). "Choices and Rights: Eugenics, Genetics and Disability Equality," *Disability and Society*, 13/5: 665–81.

Sharp, Keith, and Sarah Earle (2002). "Feminism, Abortion and Disability: Irreconcilable Differences?," *Disability and Society*, 17/2: 137–45.

Smith, Andrea (2005). "Beyond Pro-Choice Versus Pro-Life: Women of Color and Reproductive Justice," *NWSA Journal*, 17/1: 119–40.

Solinger, Rickie (2013). *Reproductive Politics: What Everyone Needs to Know*. Oxford: Oxford University Press.

Stein, Zena, Mervyn Susser, and Andrea Guterman (1973). "Screening Programme for Prevention of Down's Syndrome," *Lancet*, 1/7798: 305–10.

Steiner, Hillel (2002). "Silver Spoons and Golden Genes: Talent Differentials and Distributive Justice," in by David Archard and Colin Macleod (eds), *The Moral and Political Status of Children*. Oxford: Oxford University Press, 183–94.

Thurer, Shari (1994). *The Myths of Motherhood: How Culture Reinvents the Good Mother*. Boston: Houghton Mifflin.

West, Robin (2001). "Rights, Capabilities, and the Good Society," *Fordham Law Review*, 69/5: 1901–32.

West, Robin (2009). "From Choice to Reproductive Justice: De-Constitutionalizing Abortion Rights," *Yale Law Journal*, 118/7: 1394–1432.

Williams, Joan (2010). *Reshaping the Work–Family Debate: Why Men and Class Matter*. Cambridge, MA: Harvard University Press.

PART II
APPLICATIONS

3

The Healthcare System

Marguerite Reardon was 39 years old and had been married for less than six months when she discovered that she was pregnant for the first time. Given her age, her initial concerns were primarily with getting pregnant in the first place. "But we were lucky," she wrote in a 2016 newspaper column, "I got pregnant with relative ease. So I assumed we had passed over the biggest hurdle associated with my 'advanced maternal' age." When offered what was in 2014 a novel non-invasive prenatal screening test, her questions were mainly about the baby's sex. In this she was not alone. A common reason that many women submit to such testing is that it can detect fetal sex at twelve weeks of pregnancy, eight weeks earlier than can an ultrasound. Reardon never considered that her prospective child might have a chromosomal atypicality, nor did she know any recent mothers her own age who had babies with Down syndrome. "And then I got the call. My daydreams shattered, and my husband and I were devastated by the news." Though she was certain that she would carry her pregnancy to term, she did consider termination: "I knew I could quietly end the pregnancy, tell friends and family I had miscarried and start again. We could put the whole thing behind us and pretend it never happened. I could get a do-over" (Reardon 2016).

Reardon, who lived in New York at the time, chose to continue her pregnancy. But she had a choice. Had she received the same diagnosis today in Kentucky, Louisiana, North Dakota, Ohio, South Dakota, or Tennessee, the decision would not have been hers to make. As of 2021, each of these states has enacted legislation barring termination in cases where selecting against genetic impairment may be a motivating cause for doing so. Several other states have introduced similar bills.[1] These changes to the political landscape cut against one of the healthcare industry's main claims in favor of NIPT—namely, that it reduces anxiety among prospective mothers (Allyse et al. 2017). Put simply, if a woman submits to screening with a mind

---

Chapter adapted with permission from: Amber Knight and Joshua Miller, "Prenatal Genetic Screening, Epistemic Justice and Reproductive Autonomy," *Hypatia*, 36 (2021), 1–21.

[1] As of 2021, Arizona, Arkansas, Kentucky, and Louisiana have actually passed prenatal non-discrimination acts, but courts have ordered temporary injunctions on the legislation, pending litigation.

Prenatal Genetic Testing, Abortion, and Disability Justice. Amber Knight and Joshua Miller, Oxford University Press.
© Amber Knight and Joshua Miller (2023). DOI: 10.1093/oso/9780192870957.003.0004

90   Prenatal Genetic Testing, Abortion, and Disability Justice

to planning a gender reveal party, or as a routine choice in "a 'well, might as well' situation," only to receive a life-changing diagnosis that restricts her reproductive options, it is difficult to see how that information has benefited her (Crabbe, Stone and Filoche 2019: 892). Especially when coupled with paltry or inaccurate information about how test results should be interpreted or what courses of action may lie ahead, such information can indeed harm prospective mothers.

In the United States, fetal diagnoses of Down syndrome lead to termination in the majority of cases (Natoli et al. 2012). Many prospective mothers choose termination after considered reflection, but many are unable to do so, because such diagnoses are not often accompanied by balanced and accurate information about Down syndrome and its impact on quality of life. In some cases, genetic counselors and other medical professionals deliver diagnoses without offering any further information, while in other cases the information is incomplete or misleading. Moreover, many medical professionals discuss the prospect of raising a child with a genetic impairment as a tragedy for the child or a burden for the family that inevitably results in suffering, stress, and diminished quality of life. In addition, wrongful birth lawsuits—which make physicians susceptible to financial liability if they fail to inform prospective parents of the availability of prenatal genetic screening procedures and the risks of having a child with a genetic impairment—further incentivize medical professionals to routinize screening and stress the benefits of termination. Ultimately, ableist attitudes and perverse legal incentives exert pressures on prospective mothers that unjustly color the decision-making process.

In response, several states have passed legislation referred to as "information acts," which are designed to enhance women's reproductive autonomy by providing a fuller range of information related to Down syndrome and related conditions. Information acts grew out of the pro-information movement of the disability rights campaign over a decade ago. The pro-information movement developed in response to the fact that medical professionals—the very people on whom many pregnant women rely as their primary source of information and counseling as they make reproductive decisions—often exhibit ableist attitudes and provide misinformation to patients. To counterbalance this skewed perspective, members of the pro-information movement want prospective parents to be given more balanced, up-to-date information and literature about the lived experience of conditions like Down syndrome, so that pregnant women have a fuller and more nuanced idea of what it might mean to give birth to and raise a child with a genetic impairment.

At the federal level, the Prenatally and Postnatally Diagnosed Conditions Awareness Act (2008), co-sponsored by Senators Edward Kennedy (D-MA) and Sam Brownback (R-KS), was passed to strengthen patient support networks, increase referrals to support services for women who receive a positive diagnosis of Down syndrome and similar conditions, and guarantee that patients have access to up-to-date and accurate information about test results and the range of outcomes associated with the diagnosed conditions. While the Act authorizes federal public health agencies to award grants and contracts related to the collection and distribution of information, no specific funds were appropriated for the law. It also lacks any enforcement provision. As disability rights organizations realized that the federal statute would have little (if any) impact, they directed most of their efforts toward the state level.

Although information acts can, in principle, enhance women's reproductive autonomy, pro-life organizations have managed to highjack information acts to advance their anti-abortion agendas.[2] For example, Louisiana's information act prohibits the state from recognizing materials that "explicitly or implicitly present termination as a neutral or acceptable choice," and Indiana and Texas's laws also prohibit medical professionals from recognizing termination as an option following a positive test result. Moreover, "conscience clauses" in Virginia and Nebraska now allow genetic counselors to refuse to share any information that conflicts with their moral or religious beliefs, even allowing them to withhold results for fear that termination will result in turn. As we will argue, these clauses threaten to undermine practices of informed consent that buttress even the thinnest conceptions of patient autonomy and undoubtedly impinge upon women's reproductive autonomy more broadly.

These ongoing political battles about prenatal testing and state regulation raise a host of timely theoretical questions pertinent to feminist theorists, as well as for those interested in the politicization of information more broadly. Especially in a "post-truth" informational landscape littered with "alternative facts" and "fake news," partisanship and other sources of political belief play increasingly prominent roles in shaping how we regard institutions as arbiters of trustworthiness. As historian Sophia Rosenfeld (2019: 20) explains: "Post-truth is, at heart, a struggle over *people* as holders of epistemic authority and over their different *methods* of inquiry and proof in an intensely partisan era." In this chapter, we are concerned with the epistemic dimensions of these political struggles and grapple with the following questions: What types of information should be included in discussions about prenatal testing

---

[2] The shift from pro-information to anti-abortion legislation has occurred largely owing to the fact that disability rights organizations have less funding and political power than pro-life groups.

92 Prenatal Genetic Testing, Abortion, and Disability Justice

and diagnosis, and how does that information enhance or diminish women's reproductive autonomy? What counts as a legitimate knowledge claim within these contexts? Who has epistemic authority in these discussions, and whose views are discredited? And, as a matter of social justice, which normative political obligations need to be fulfilled so that information about prenatal testing and diagnosis can simultaneously promote women's reproductive autonomy and also value people with disabilities and their family members?

Our primary goal is to reveal the power relations at play in knowledge claims about prenatal screening and diagnosis to argue that reproductive autonomy is restricted by what Miranda Fricker (2007) and others have described as epistemic injustice. According to Fricker (2007: 1), epistemic injustice is "a wrong done to somebody specifically in their capacity as a knower." We argue that medical professionals perpetuate epistemic injustice when they offer their patients distorted information (that is, information that is out of date or prejudicial) or limited information (that is, information that fails to convey all of a patient's options following a positive diagnosis, including information about termination, adoption, and what it might be like to raise a child with Down syndrome). This epistemic injustice constitutes a twofold harm: (1) people with Down syndrome and their family members who claim that parenting a child with Down syndrome may be a rewarding and joyous experience are harmed, when they are systematically silenced, disbelieved, and/or denied epistemic credibility, and (2) pregnant women are harmed, since they might make poorly informed choices without access to all relevant information. One of the wider implications of our argument is the idea that epistemic justice is a precondition of women's reproductive autonomy. Pregnant women cannot make truly voluntary and autonomous reproductive decisions if they are not getting "the whole story" or if the information they are receiving is distorted by ableist ideology or pro-life propaganda.

We begin this chapter with a brief overview of informed consent and non-directiveness as necessary but insufficient conditions of supporting women's reproductive autonomy, arguing that an adequate theory of patient autonomy must attend to the ways in which wider social forces—like ableism—influence medical decision-making. The second section more concretely examines the challenge of prenatal screening in Down syndrome cases, arguing that current medical screening and informational practices fall short of even the baseline requirements of informed consent and non-directiveness. We demonstrate how medical professionals can intentionally and unintentionally promote ableist assumptions about quality of life that implicitly, and

The Healthcare System **93**

sometimes explicitly, dissuade women from carrying pregnancies to term. This section also demonstrates how the fear of wrongful birth litigation has impacted on how healthcare providers offer prenatal screening services and counsel patients. The third section applies Miranda Fricker's theory of epistemic injustice to the patient–physician relationship. Here we observe that women who receive prenatal diagnoses of Down syndrome are rarely exposed to accounts from the lived experiences of individuals with the condition, or from those of their family members. Their stories are important, because they not only constitute a counter-narrative to the ableist assumptions prevalent in the health services community, but they also enrich prospective parents' expectations about raising a child with Down syndrome. We argue that marginalizing these narratives constitutes a testimonial injustice against the parents of children with Down syndrome while simultaneously abridging the reproductive autonomy of pregnant women. We conclude by making the case that this widescale and entrenched epistemic injustice ultimately warrants federal regulation over the type of information that physicians must make accessible to their patients in prenatal screening and diagnosis sessions.

Informed Consent and Physician Authority

Contemporary bioethics is deeply indebted to the liberal tradition, and patient autonomy has become a cornerstone of the discipline. It is now widely accepted that patients have a right to make decisions about their medical care and determine their own treatment preferences free from coercion and controlling influences. Though a sacrosanct principle of medical ethics today, this conception of patient autonomy emerged only recently. Until the middle of the twentieth century, medical paternalism, and the idea that "doctor knows best," was the prevailing norm throughout North America and Western Europe. After a series of abuses—including Nazi medical war crimes in Germany and the Tuskegee Syphilis Study in the United States—public outcry led to radical reformulations of the patient–physician relationship.[3] Codified in documents such as the *Nuremberg Code* (1949) and the *Belmont Report* (1979), these alternative norms adopted a politically liberal orientation, envisioning patient rights in distinctly negative terms.

---

[3] A full account of bioethics emerging as a response to such crises lies beyond the scope of this chapter. For detailed overviews, see David Rothman (2003).

94 Prenatal Genetic Testing, Abortion, and Disability Justice

Owing to these social and legal changes, it is no longer acceptable for physicians paternalistically to prescribe treatment for their patients without their patients' input and authorization. Instead, medical professionals are expected to guide and counsel patients as they make medical decisions for themselves. The principal means by which physicians and other healthcare providers respect patient autonomy is by obtaining informed consent after presenting relevant information and options in a non-directive manner. The *Nuremberg Code* first established an explicit connection between informed consent and autonomy as an international standard of medical research practice, affirming that "the voluntary consent of the human subject" is "absolutely essential" to medical experimentation using human subjects:

> [The] person involved should have legal capacity to give consent; should be so situated as to be able to exercise free power of choice, without the intervention of any element of force, fraud, deceit, duress, over-reaching, or other ulterior form of constraint or coercion; and should have sufficient knowledge and comprehension of the elements of the subject matter involved, as to enable him to make an understanding and enlightened decision.[4]

The Code's emphasis on a subject's categorical right to free, informed, non-coerced decision-making generates a duty whereupon researchers and physicians must facilitate autonomy through the non-directive disclosure of information relevant to the patient's health and well-being. By this standard, withholding or manipulating information pertinent to making an informed choice constitutes negligence and causes a harm to the patient.[5]

We find a similar view of patient autonomy described in American jurisprudence, where the foundational case for informed consent, *Canterbury v. Spence* (1972), also accounts for the practical difficulty of meeting the *Nuremberg Code*'s standards.[6] As Judge Spottswood Robinson writes in the Court's decision: "True consent to what happens to one's self is the informed exercise of choice, and that entails an opportunity to evaluate

---

[4] The *Belmont Report* also explicates the harm entailed in violating autonomy: "To show lack of respect for an autonomous agent is to repudiate that person's considered judgments, to deny an individual freedom to act on those considered judgments, or to withhold information necessary to make a considered judgment, when there are no compelling reasons to do so" (National Commission for the Protection of Human Subjects of Biomedical and Behavioral Research 1979).

[5] The Supreme Court has repeatedly stated the value and constitutionality of state action to ensure that medical decisions concerning reproduction and abortion are fully informed. In *Planned Parenthood of Central Missouri v. Danforth* (1976) the Court ruled: "The decision to abort ... is an important, and often a stressful one, and it is desirable and imperative that it be made with full knowledge of its nature and consequences. The woman is the one primarily concerned, and her awareness of the decision and its significance may be assured, constitutionally, by the State."

[6] *Canterbury v. Spence* 464 F2d 784 (DC Circ., 1972).

knowledgeably the options available and the risks attendant upon each" (*Canterbury* v. *Spence*: 780). A patient's capacity to exercise autonomous medical choice is, therefore, subject to informational, cognitive, and—we shall argue—epistemic conditions:

> The average patient has little or no understanding of the medical arts, and ordinarily has only his physician to whom he can look for enlightenment with which to reach an intelligent decision. From these almost axiomatic considerations springs the need, and in turn the requirement, of a reasonable divulgence by physician to patient to make such a decision possible ... It may oblige the physician to advise the patient of the need for or desirability of any alternative treatment promising greater benefit than that being pursued. (*Canterbury* v. *Spence*: 780)

The Court's connection between information and decision-making alerts us to concerns about how informational disparities translate into power dynamics between patients and their healthcare providers, and how the inherent power imbalance of the patient–physician relationship makes the exercise of patient autonomy challenging in practice.

Indeed, even in the current age of Internet research and WebMD, patients often trust the goodwill and expertise of medical professionals over all other sources, relying on them as primary providers of authoritative and reliable medical information.[7] After all, medical professionals have extensive medical training and requisite credentials that most patients do not, creating an asymmetry of knowledge and skill between patient and medical provider. This means that physicians often serve as gatekeepers of medical knowledge, and thus have the power to determine what information is deemed relevant to patient decision-making. This status grants them the opportunity to empower patients with information to enhance free decision-making, but it also affords them the capacity to silence and manipulate. In their influential *Principles of Biomedical Ethics* (2013), Tom Beauchamp and James Childress draw our attention to the ways in which manipulation and framing effects may filter or distort information and, by extension, abridge patient autonomy. Often, physicians and other healthcare professionals are biased with respect to what qualifies as *fact* or legitimate knowledge, so they may omit

---

[7] While several studies conducted in the United States have indicated that public trust in physicians has declined from 73% in 1966 to 34% in 2012, Americans still trust the medical system more than other institutions such as Congress, religious institutions, and the police (Blendon, Benson and Hero 2014). Observing that rates of public trust have remained higher in many West European countries, some researchers have blamed this decline on the commodification of healthcare in the United States (Huang et al. 2018). When patients do consult other sources of information, such as those found on the Internet, they are motivated by a desire to play a more active role in their treatment rather than by a distrust of their physicians (Hu et al. 2012).

some sources of information from consideration. Importantly, Beauchamp and Childress (2013: 139) stress that this dynamic is often unintentional:

> In health care, the most likely form of manipulation is informal manipulation, a deliberate act of managing information that alters a person's understanding of a situation and motivates him or her to do what the agent of influence intends. Many forms of informational manipulation are incompatible with autonomous decision-making. For example, lying, withholding information, and misleading by exaggeration with the intent to lead persons to believe what is false all compromise autonomous choice. The manner in which a health care professional presents information ... can also manipulate a patient's perception and response.

Even well-intentioned physicians cannot know all facets of how their patients will make decisions about their health, decisions that are, as Beauchamp and Childress (2013: 126) acknowledge, only partially medical to begin with.

In addition to physicians being positioned as gatekeepers of information, the information that medical professionals choose to disclose often carries significant clout. Patients who lack medical training, or who even lack access to higher education, may be inclined to weigh the information presented by healthcare providers so heavily that they defer to them without question. As Rayna Rapp (1988: 133) explains: "Science speaks the language of universal authority," so physicians' biomedical knowledge—which is presumed to be well tested, objective, and trustworthy—is difficult to challenge or refute. Moreover, physicians are experts with a privileged status in modern social life beyond the strict boundaries of the medical field. Being a doctor is socially respectable, and physicians are generally held in high esteem. Despite efforts to shift professional norms away from paternalism and toward a more cooperative engagement between physicians and their patients, medicine maintains a hallowed social position that resists change.

In sum, scholars generally agree that obtaining informed consent through non-directive counseling is a tangible way to promote patient autonomy and deconstruct the power imbalance inherent in the patient–physician relationship. While informed consent and non-directiveness may be desirable ideals to guide clinical conduct, many physicians fail to live up to them in practice. The following section examines how ableist socialization and legal incentives impact on the content and delivery of information about prenatal screening in current medical practice. Often using language laden with tragic pathology, physicians and genetic counselors sometimes presuppose termination when delivering fetal diagnoses of Down syndrome to prospective mothers.

In other cases, conscience clauses empower healthcare professionals who personally oppose abortion to limit what information about fetal health they choose to share. Whether healthcare professionals regard termination as a given or off the table, their attitudes can color the information they provide, restricting women's reproductive autonomy in the process.

(Mis)Informed Choice from Biased and Limited Information

In the previous section, we argued that medical professionals have considerable epistemic power. This power translates into an attendant responsibility to provide patients with accurate and comprehensive medical information—in a clear and non-directive manner—so that patients themselves can make autonomous decisions about their medical care. In the case of prenatal genetic screening, many physicians attempt to live up to this responsibility. However, several studies have demonstrated that a substantial portion of them do not. Some medical professionals draw prominently upon their own values when discussing patients' options, which is especially problematic, given that several studies have shown that physicians and genetic counselors often harbor ableist biases (Kothari 2004; Klein 2011; Reynolds 2017, 2018). Medical professionals are disproportionately able-bodied and socialized within a wider ableist culture, so it should come as little surprise that many are likely to misunderstand, misjudge, and mischaracterize the lived experience of Down syndrome. Not only do many physicians lack first-hand experience with cognitive disability in their personal lives, but studies suggest that few obstetricians and genetic counselors have access to disability-sensitive course curricula or direct contact with individuals with intellectual impairments during their medical training (Sanborn and Patterson 2014).

What is important to consider is how wider ableist biases and beliefs subsequently enter into patient–physician exchanges in ways that threaten to diminish women's reproductive autonomy. In practice, some medical professionals have tried explicitly to alter prospective parents' decisions by offering biased counseling. Others, however well intentioned, have less perceptibly (and perhaps even subconsciously) exerted undue influence over reproductive decisions by framing and presenting information in such a way that certain options are not considered viable, reasonable, or worth pursuing.[8]

---

[8] In a survey of nearly 500 primary-care physicians who have prenatally diagnosed Down syndrome, 13% admitted that they emphasized the negative aspects of the condition so that parents would favor a termination, and 10% actively urged parents to terminate (Skotko 2005).

98 Prenatal Genetic Testing, Abortion, and Disability Justice

To begin, there is often a default expectation on the part of physicians that pregnant women will all want to undergo prenatal testing in the first place. Prenatal screening is often presented as a "no-brainer," as a routine part of prenatal care, and some women may not feel that they actually have a choice to opt in or out. It is just what pregnant women do this day and age.[9] The subtle expectation that responsible parents automatically undertake prenatal screening hinders reproductive autonomy by reinforcing an environment in which women come to believe that it is the only course of action to take. Some parents have even reported feeling pressured and badgered into testing when they have deliberately opted not to.

Consider the experience of Valle Dwight. When Valle and her husband discussed their options and decided that they would not want to terminate their pregnancy even if an amniocentesis came back with a positive result for Down syndrome, they shared their decision to forgo testing with their physician. The following excerpt from Valle's conversation with her doctor demonstrates how her physician second-guessed her decision:

> "Even if the baby has Down syndrome," I told the doctor, "I won't terminate the pregnancy, so what difference does it [the test] make?"
>
> "Well, that's what everyone says," she told me. "But they change their minds when they get the test results." (quoted in Soper 2007: 5)

In these types of interactions, physicians who dismiss their patients' preferences or express disbelief and disapproval when their patients choose a course of action that they would not have chosen for themselves violate their commitment to non-directive counseling.[10]

Scholars have also documented how diagnostic discussions often draw on negative stereotypes and unsubstantiated assumptions about what it is like to live with Down syndrome or raise a child with the condition (Lalvani 2011). Some medical professionals underestimate what people with Down syndrome can do by offering empirically inaccurate and gloomy predictions, telling prospective parents that their future child may never walk, talk, or read, and/or that he or she will remain dependent for the entirety of his or her life with no potential for success or fulfillment. Yet the medical conditions, traits, and abilities of people with Down syndrome vary widely and

---

[9] Studies have shown that some women who have undergone prenatal genetic screening and diagnostic testing did not understand what they were signing up for. They had a limited understanding of the procedure and the potential impact of the results (Parham, Michie, and Allyse 2017).

[10] Gareth Thomas (2017) describes similar dynamics in his ethnographic study of two clinics in the United Kingdom, recording instances when providers immediately booked amniocentesis after a positive screen, or a termination immediately after diagnosis, even before the patient herself requested these steps.

cannot be predicted before distinct individuals are born. Screening simply cannot predict the severity of symptoms in cases of Down syndrome, let alone estimate the degree or longevity of care that the child may need. Even the language used to convey a diagnosis is overwhelmingly and presumptively negative. Studies have shown that physicians often rely on the discourse of "tragedy," "burden," "grief," and "loss" when delivering positive diagnoses (Rapp 1999). When physicians use negative language to describe a parent's potential quality of life raising a child with Down syndrome, they foreclose the possibility that it might be a gratifying or rewarding experience.

Some prospective parents have even reported that physicians have openly promoted the termination of the pregnancy (Rapp 1993; Lalor et al. 2007; Dixon 2008). In 2016, Courtney Baker posted an open letter to her physician on the Internet after he tried to convince her to abort following a positive diagnosis. She explains the harm that he caused her, writing,

> I came to you during the most difficult time in my life. I was terrified, anxious and in complete despair ... But instead of support and encouragement, you suggested we terminate our child. I told you her name, and you asked us again if we understood how low our quality of life would be with a child with Down syndrome. You suggested we reconsider our decision to continue the pregnancy. From that first visit, we dreaded our appointments. (quoted in Brown 2016)

Rather than allowing pregnant women to arrive at their own fully informed decisions, some doctors overtly counsel from their own point of view to pressure patients into termination. Doing so harms women by violating principles of non-directiveness that betray the trust underpinning the patient–physician relationship. Like Martha Swartz (2006), we argue that physicians *qua* physicians have overriding fiduciary commitments to treating patients in ways that honor patients' interests, not their own. As she writes: "The patient's autonomous expression of her interests should set the course for medical decision-making, guided by the health care professional's advice" (Swartz 2006: 278). While the physician's advice should derive from both clinical evidence and professional ethics, personal and unsubstantiated beliefs about the quality of life with a child with Down syndrome should play no part in that counsel.

Ableist socialization is not the only force at play in shaping physicians' interactions with patients in clinical settings. The legal landscape also plays a vital role. In particular, wrongful birth lawsuits, which are governed by traditional medical malpractice and negligence principles, loom large in many

100 Prenatal Genetic Testing, Abortion, and Disability Justice

physicians' minds (Pergament and Ilijic 2014; Brown 2016). In wrongful birth lawsuits, parents who give birth to a child with a genetic impairment can file a cause of action alleging that their doctor deprived them of the opportunity to make an informed decision about whether to terminate the pregnancy.[11] This deprivation can occur if physicians fail fully or accurately to communicate information (in a timely manner) about the availability of screening and diagnostic tests, their relative levels of invasiveness and risk for each type of procedure, the percentage of false negatives and positives offered by the test chosen, the results, and/or the implications of the results. If physicians are held liable, parents can recover costs associated with past and future medical expenses for the child, parents' lost income, and emotional distress.[12] Relatively few wrongful birth lawsuits are filed each year in the United States, and an even smaller handful actually make it to trial, but physicians are now on high alert after a spate of relatively high-profile cases that ended in multimillion-dollar verdicts. Deborah Pergament and Katie Ilijic (2014) explain the implications, arguing that physicians have started routinely to order tests and counsel patients with affected pregnancies about the benefits of termination to shield themselves from liability and the threat of financial ruin. This may be especially true in private medical practices in jurisdictions that allow for recovery of damages in excess of malpractice insurance policy limits (Pergament and Ilijic (2014: 1441–2).

Even when patient–physician exchanges are not directly tainted by bias or driven by fears of litigation, the information that medical professionals provide is often partial and incomplete. Physicians, by the very nature of their work, primarily focus on the medical complications and health risks associated with Down syndrome (Skotko 2005; Skotko, Capone, and Kishnani 2009; Sheets et al. 2011a). Down syndrome is a genetic condition that is caused by an extra copy of the twenty-first chromosome. People with Down syndrome generally have mild to moderate cognitive delays, low muscle tone, and higher chances for a variety of other health issues over their lifespan. Roughly half of those with Down syndrome are born with cardiovascular problems that often require surgery in early infancy. Individuals with Down syndrome are also at an increased risk of leukemia and thyroid problems,

---

[11] In the United States, the majority of states recognize wrongful birth claims as a cause of action either by statute or by common law, but a handful of states have enacted statutes to outlaw wrongful birth claims. For a deeper discussion of prohibitory statutes and state-level variation, see Dov Fox (2019).

[12] In wrongful birth cases, courts across states are divided on the question of what damages are recoverable and the measure of such damages. For more on wrongful birth and the recovery of damages, see Haley Hermanson (2019).

The Healthcare System **101**

as well as some minor illnesses and disorders, such as: sleep apnea, gastrointestinal blockages, hearing loss, seizures, poor vision, and skeletal problems.[13] Medical prognoses are undeniably important sources of information for reproductive decision-making. However, a long list of potential health problems is not enough to go on when a pregnant woman is considering all of her reproductive options; it is just one piece of the information puzzle.

Genetic information, on its own, offers potentially important yet insufficient information to make an informed choice. It can tell us (with varying levels of accuracy) the likelihood of whether or not a fetus has or does not have a particular genetic marker, but that is all. Rosemarie Garland-Thomson (2020) is concerned that the people administering these genetic technologies exaggerate what they can discover from the results, since "genetic information actually tells us much less than it appears to predict." As she further explains:

> Such a preemptive diagnosis doesn't give us meaningful information about that person's capabilities, relationships, or actual lived life. Such genetic knowledge, like the knowledge that someone has the gene for maleness, really predicts little about how a particular lived life actually unfolds: genetic knowledge tells us something, but not very much. (Garland-Thomson 2020: 35)

In the absence of a fuller picture of how a prospective child's life might unfold—information that no prospective parent can ever really access—prenatal screening can therefore promote what Adrienne Asch and David Wasserman (2005) have called "synechdocal thinking," which involves taking a single trait to represent the whole. Prenatal screening and diagnosis for a condition such as Down syndrome, for example, encourage a view of a fetus that focuses only on a single trait—the additional copy of chromosome twenty-one—and ignores any other relevant aspects of who that fetus could become in the future. According to Asch and Wasserman (2005: 174–5), it is problematic to let the part stand in for the whole. How could one piece of genetic information possibly predict whether the experience of raising that child will meet parental expectations?

Thus, expectant parents also need access to information on what day-to-day life is like for people living with or raising a child with Down syndrome in order to make a fully informed decision in accordance with their own values and life plans. Yet, studies show that physicians rarely mention how prospective parents can access information about the lived experience of Down

---

[13] For a comprehensive list of medical conditions with a higher prevalence in individuals with Down syndrome, see David Wright (2011).

102 Prenatal Genetic Testing, Abortion, and Disability Justice

syndrome, nor do they sufficiently discuss public services that are available to support families who choose to continue their pregnancies (Sheets el al. 2011a). Reflecting on his experience raising his son Jamie, who has Down syndrome, Michael Bérubé explains how testimonies are sources of information that should be more frequently used to supplement clinical information. As he explains:

> Alongside the information about possible health risks, I'd offer prospective parents the testimony of various families—parents and siblings—of people with Down syndrome, as well as the testimonies of people with Down's themselves. The message: if you choose to have this child, your life may become richer and more wonderful than you can imagine, and the child will grow to be a loving, self-aware, irreplaceable member of the human family. *And* if you choose to have this child, your life may become more arduous and complicated than you can imagine ... The reason you need a variety of family testimonies, for those prospective parents who are uncertain about abortion and curious about whether they can cope with a "disabled" child, is simply that people with Down syndrome are individuals ... (Bérubé 1996: 82–3)

Bérubé concedes that testimonial information can only go so far. The experience of one person or family cannot stand in for all members of the Down syndrome community, and there is no way to predict what one's own experience will be based on other peoples' experiences.[14] Nevertheless, he makes a convincing case that personal testimonies are important sources of information for prospective parents considering their reproductive options, because they have the potential to dispel the widespread belief that Down syndrome necessarily entails relentless agony, suffering, stress, and low quality of life for the child and family, and in doing so offer a fuller and more nuanced sense of the potential challenges and rewards of raising a child with Down syndrome. The wider implication is that facilitating informed decision-making requires balance in the information provided.

In sum, the information provided by healthcare professionals leaves much to be desired.[15] It is often biased or incomplete to the detriment of women's reproductive autonomy, since pregnant women cannot freely make decisions about their reproductive futures and personal well-being—without excessive influence or manipulation—when information is misleading or omitted

---

[14] Similarly, Skotko et al. (2015: 11) remind us that, even though individuals with Down syndrome share a common diagnosis, "the same extra chromosome does not script a common playbook for family relationships," since each individual and family experience is unique.

[15] As Adrienne Asch (2003: 334) observes, "it is clear that many [medical] professionals do not practice in a way that legitimates the choice to maintain a pregnancy of a fetus affected by a disabling trait."

from discussion. The paradox is obvious: even though prenatal screening is touted as a means of enhancing choice in theory, in practice it can actually undermine autonomy. To be clear, we understand that medical expertise and clinical information about Down syndrome are essential ingredients of informed choice. Moreover, it is often the case that patients are unable to interpret the results of genetic screenings, so they must put their trust in physicians and genetic counselors, who have undergone extensive medical training. Physicians' exercise of epistemic authority is not always or necessarily a bad thing. Our main concern is with instances wherein incomplete or misleading information is tainted by ableist bias or provided in a non-directive manner.

In the following section, we further examine the ways in which physicians' knowledge and epistemic power can trump, discredit, and invalidate the legitimacy of testimonial knowledge provided by people with Down syndrome and their family members. We show how medical professionals' tendency to dismiss and overlook testimony on the lived experience of Down syndrome constitutes an epistemic injustice, one that violates the dignity of people with disabilities and also translates into diminished reproductive autonomy for prospective parents.

Testimonial Injustice and Its Harm

In recent years, social scientists have identified and analyzed what has been dubbed the "disability paradox," which refers to the persistent finding that people with disabilities report having a good or excellent quality of life in contrast to the widespread ableist expectation that disabled lives are inevitably agonizing, tragic, and even so bad that they might not be worth living at all (Albrecht and Devlieger 1999 Wasserman, Bickenbach, and Wachbroit 2005). For example, in a survey of 284 people with Down syndrome who were asked to rate their quality of life, the vast majority of respondents reported being happy and fulfilled (Skotko, Levine, and Goldstein 2011). Specifically, 99 percent reported that they were happy with their lives, 96 percent liked how they looked, and 97 percent liked who they were. Only a very small percentage (roughly 4 percent) expressed sadness or strong dissatisfaction with their quality of life.[16] Relatedly, in a survey of roughly 2,500 family members,

---

[16] According to the authors of the study, the cause of their sadness appeared to be the byproduct of unfavorable social circumstances, including living in a group-home setting that was socially isolating, rather than stemming from sadness owing to their functional skills or lack thereof (Skotko, Levine, and Goldstein 2011: 2366).

parents and siblings of individuals with Down syndrome also reported being happy and satisfied with their lives, despite acknowledging the challenges that sometimes accompany living with and/or caring for someone with the genetic condition. Nearly all parents reported loving and being proud of their child with Down syndrome, and about 79 per cent said their outlook on life was actually *more* positive because of their son or daughter. Brothers and sisters also reported a favorable perspective (Skotko et al. 2015). Beyond surveys, qualitative analyses (Green 2007; Lalvani 2008, 2011; Piepmeier 2013, 2015) and memoirs or autobiographical accounts from parents (Bérubé 1996; Soper 2017; Adams 2013; Kaposy 2018; Piepmeier 2021) discuss how raising a child with Down syndrome can be an enriching, joyful, and desirable experience (although parenting any child inevitably has its tough and undesirable moments too).

In contrast, medical professionals tend to have more negative quality-of-life assessments of Down syndrome than individuals whose lives are directly affected by the condition (Ormond et al. 2003; Saxton 2013). Most healthcare professionals focus on the medical or functional aspects of impairment when assessing quality of life, viewing disability as intrinsically negative and equated with suffering. Healthcare professionals tend to focus inordinately on the negative aspects of an individual's impairment instead of viewing impairment as simply one factor in the context of multiple elements that influence the quality of a person's life. This medicalized assessment is clearly at odds with the broader notion of quality of life embraced by disability studies scholars and many people with disabilities themselves, which encapsulates biomedical and social variables, such as control over one's life choices and social acceptance and support.

The problem is not simply that there are conflicting criteria for and assessments of quality of life. There is also evidence that medical professionals often disregard the experiential knowledge created by individuals with Down syndrome and their family members when personal testimony conflicts with their pre-existing assumptions and expectations.[17] Skeptics of positive parental testimony dismiss it as unreliable for various reasons: the parents are clearly in denial and find it easier unrealistically to "sugar-coat" the situation and delude themselves than come to terms with their "tragic" circumstances;

---

[17] Cooley et al. (1990) evaluated genetic counselor and parent responses to a video describing parents' experiences in raising a child with Down syndrome. They found that the two groups' responses to the film differed significantly: 14% of twenty-nine genetic counselors versus 89% of thirty-six parents felt the film accurately portrayed parental experiences. The majority of the genetic counselors who viewed the film rated it as being "too positive," refusing to believe that the benefits of parenting a child with Down syndrome could outweigh the challenges.

parents are afraid to admit that they are disappointed and would have preferred an able-bodied child, because they might be viewed as bad parents if they do not appear to love their child unconditionally; they are expressing an adaptive preference because they have never raised a "normal" child, so they do not know what they are missing out on; and/or their emotional investment in their child with Down syndrome distorts their rational and "objective" judgment. In sum, medical professionals offer various rationales to justify their incredulous reception of positive parental testimony. Of course, personal testimony (like other types of information) is always fallible and open to critique. However, discounting testimony after careful consideration is a very different thing from saying it is simply obvious or common sense that disability is a "Bad Thing" and that people with Down syndrome and their family members who have a positive outlook on their lives are kidding themselves or trying to disguise their despair.

We argue that this type of dismissal constitutes what has come to be referred to as epistemic injustice, specifically a form of testimonial injustice. According to Miranda Fricker (2007: 1), epistemic injustice is "a wrong done to someone specifically in their capacity as a knower." Fricker further distinguishes two types of epistemic injustice: testimonial injustice and hermeneutical injustice. Testimonial injustice occurs when prejudice causes a hearer to give a deflated level of credibility to a speaker's word, such as when a police officer does not believe someone just because he is a person of color. Hermeneutical injustice occurs when collective interpretative resources put someone at an unfair disadvantage when it comes to making sense of their social experience, such as when a woman cannot portray her experience of sexual harassment because she lives in a cultural context that lacks the concept (Fricker 2007: 1). Overall, Fricker argues that the social practice of giving information to others and interpreting our experiences is integral to a person's identity, agency, and dignity, so epistemic injustice should be considered a deep source of harm that affects a person's life as a whole.

Extending this idea to the case at hand, we argue that the disability paradox is indicative of structural testimonial injustice.[18] Ableist assumptions interfere with the ability of able-bodied people to hear, understand, or believe the knowledge claims of people with disabilities and their family members. Rather than take the testimony of people with disabilities seriously, non-disabled people tend to project their own fears and fantasies. Medical

---

[18] For more on how the people with disabilities experience rampant testimonial justice, see Elizabeth Barnes (2016), Shelley Tremain (2017), and Jackie Leach Scully (2018).

professionals may confidently think that they can accurately intuit what it is like to have Down syndrome or to raise a child with the condition, but it seems that they tend both to overestimate the negative effects of impairment on a person's quality of life and also to fail to recognize many of the socially induced barriers to well-being.

Of course, medical practitioners are hardly alone in jumping to conclusions about what life must be like with Down syndrome. "Among people with little exposure to disabled people," writes Marsha Saxton (2013: 123), "it is common to think that this [positive testimony] is a romanticization or rationalization of someone stuck with the burden of raising a damaged child." We are singling out medical professionals because they are in a unique position to cause considerable harm to free reproductive choice. On the one hand, medical professionals often possess what Miranda Fricker calls "credibility excess," where knowers, based on their identity or social position, are granted more credibility than they might merit in some cases. On the other hand, people with Down syndrome and the family members often experience what Fricker (2007: 17) refers to as "credibility deficits," wherein a prejudice deflates the credibility afforded the speaker. Because of this power imbalance, the information offered by physicians can easily eclipse or drown out other types of information. Michael Bérubé (1996: 47) spells out the implications, writing: "If we had no way of knowing how loving, clever, and 'normal' a child like Jamie can be, we would simply have to rely on the advice of 'experts'. And if those experts told us there was no way to raise such a child, we would probably believe them."

In the following section, we consider how the state—specifically, the federal government—has an obligation to ensure that the social scaffolding necessary for pregnant women to exercise informed, non-directed decision-making is available. Honoring that obligation will require the state to refrain from banning disability-selective abortions, but it will also introduce a commitment for it to take a more active role in regulating and standardizing information.

"Pro-Choice" Defense of Government Regulation

By now it should now be clear that far too many medical professionals fall short of the ideals of non-directiveness and informed consent that underpin even the thinnest standards of patient autonomy. So how do we fix this problem? Scholars in the humanities and social sciences, disability rights activists, and members of the medical and scientific community have furnished answers to this question by developing various recommendations to improve physician–patient relations and facilitate informed decision-making. In this section, we survey these recommendations and call for several policy reforms: (1) state-funded medical schools should include disability training as part of their standard curricula; (2) lawmakers should reassess or repeal conscience clauses; (3) public and private health insurance companies should cover genetic counseling services so that wrongful birth litigation is effectively unnecessary; and (4) Congress should adequately fund the Kennedy–Brownback Act.

To begin, the current education system is not producing physicians with the requisite disability cultural competencies, so structural reform in the medical education system is warranted. According to survey data, medical professionals have reported feeling unprepared to treat patients with disabilities or patients pregnant with disabled fetuses in a manner informed by the lived experience of disability and its cultural components (Santoro et al. 2017). Studies have also shown that nearly a third of genetic counselors have been dissatisfied with the disability training they obtained in their graduate programs (Sanborn and Patterson 2014). In order to remedy the fact that medical professionals often do not recognize the social dimensions of disability, nor receive sufficient training on how to do so in their course curricula, Anita Ho (2011) advises medical professionals to adopt a posture of epistemic humility when discussing prognoses and available treatment options with patients. In her words:

> Epistemic humility is a disposition as well as a commitment. It arises out of professionals' acknowledgment of the boundary of their expert domain as well as their fallibility. It means a commitment to make realistic assessment of what one knows and does not know, and to restrict one's confidence and claims to knowledge only to what one actually knows about his/her specialized domain. In particular, it is a recognition that knowledge creation is an interdependent and collaborative activity. (Ho 2011: 117)

As she describes it, epistemic humility requires physicians to be open to multiple forms of inquiry and knowledge, including subjective testimonies, in a collaborative project of knowledge production. An ethos of humility can curb the all-too-common tendency among clinicians to undermine the epistemic authority of people with disabilities and their family members.

State-funded medical schools can facilitate a culture of epistemic humility by including disability training in their standard curricula. The Association of American Medical Colleges (AAMC) has recommended that medical schools

108 Prenatal Genetic Testing, Abortion, and Disability Justice

create specially designed curricula to teach disability cultural competency. However, it is ultimately up to faculty and administrators to decide whether or how to do so, since these measures are encouraged, but not required, for accreditation and licensure. The result is that medical schools vary greatly in the content and delivery of their disability curricula and training (Crossley 2015; Santoro et al. 2017). Disability cultural competency is completely overlooked at some medical schools, though a notable few have begun formally implementing disability training in their programs. The approach developed at the Jacobs School of Medicine and Biomedical Sciences at the University of Buffalo is especially promising. Integrated over four years of medical training and consisting of formal lectures, interviews, and clinical rotations, the program culminates in a four-week elective course in which students meet patients with disabilities and their families as well as patient advocacy groups and community organizations (Symons, McGuigan, and Akl 2009). By inviting people with disabilities and their families to share their own narratives, such programs recover the epistemic value of testimony while inculcating an ethos of humility among early-career physicians. As one student wrote in a reflective piece following an encounter with disabled patients and their families: "This was the first step in opening our eyes to the necessity of being able to fully understand what it means to care for those that may have an impaired ability to care for oneself" (Symons, McGuigan, and Akl 2009: 78). While this specific approach may not work for all medical schools, we nevertheless argue that state-funded medical schools should be incentivized or even required formally to integrate a requirement for curriculum on disabilities into its accreditation standards.[19]

Second, we encourage lawmakers to reassess and/or repeal conscience clauses, especially those that permit physicians to restrict patients' access to the balanced information necessary for decisional autonomy. Having rapidly expanded in the wake of *Roe*, most existing conscience clauses are vaguely written and deeply problematic for patients attempting to make autonomous decisions about their reproductive health. Troublingly, many women may not even realize that their healthcare provider or institution has policies against certain procedures related to reproductive care—including abortion—until it is too late for them to choose another provider (Swartz 2006: 289). At a minimum, physicians have a duty to inform patients of any personal convictions that may inform their approach to care, thereby allowing patients to decide as early as possible whether to continue the relationship. As Holly

---

[19] Although the specific enforcement mechanisms that could be used remain up for debate, it might be worthwhile to use Title IX legislation as a template for thinking about how to develop training programmes or even craft financial penalties for non-compliance.

Lynch (2008: 217–18) suggests: "Revelation of a potential mismatch will allow the patient to seek an alternative provider before investing a substantial amount of time and energy in developing a relationship with the refuser, and before a time-sensitive situation arises that could inhibit the search for an alternative physician." Insofar as the patient–physician relationship should promote mutual respect, safeguard trust, and focus on patient care, such disclosures are a necessary practice in respecting patient autonomy. Vaguely written and devoid of standards explicating acceptable reasons for refusal and timelines for disclosure, existing conscience clauses undermine patient autonomy. Repealing conscience clauses would not prevent some physicians from masking cryptonormative recommendations as value-neutral clinical advice, but doing so would remove the cover of law from those who would impose their own beliefs upon their patients. The bottom line is that prospective parents cannot exercise their right to make an informed decision when material information is withheld.

Third, if wrongful birth lawsuits encourage physicians to order tests for patients and emphasize the benefits of termination for affected pregnancies, reform is necessary. However, instead of encouraging statutory prohibitions on wrongful birth claims, we suggest a different route forward. In wrongful birth cases, the purported injury at stake is the lost choice to make an informed decision. Gross negligence (that is, a botched test or a misinterpreted result) can lead to the injury, so wrongful birth litigation, like other forms of medical malpractice tort law, is needed to uphold high standards of medical care and hold doctors accountable for poor-quality work. One way to keep these lawsuits in place while preventing healthcare providers from feeling compelled to peddle the procedure would be to cap the damages that plaintiffs can collect. Another strategy involves thinking about wrongful birth claims in relationship to patients' access to genetic counseling services. Genetic counseling is a time-consuming activity, and some physicians may not have the requisite training or time to provide quality pre- and post-test counseling.[20] Despite the benefits of genetic counseling, reimbursement remains limited, so few clinics or private practices hire counselors. Sometimes genetic counselors are hired directly by the testing company, so genetic counseling is reimbursed as a hidden cost of the procedure and covered by private insurance providers (Wolff and Wolff 2018). However, while nearly all state Medicaid plans cover some of the costs of screening and diagnostic

---

[20] Bryan Gammon et al. (2016) interviewed prenatal healthcare providers in the United States, and many interviewees reported that there was not enough time for them adequately to counsel and educate patients on their options about the NIPT procedure and the results, further noting that limited reimbursement disincentivizes them from spending any additional time with patients.

110 Prenatal Genetic Testing, Abortion, and Disability Justice

procedures, fewer states cover the costs of genetic counseling services to help patients make sense of their results (Gadsboll et al. 2020). Indeed, genetic counseling remains unrecognized by the Centers for Medicare and Medicaid Services (CMS) as a profession that can independently bill, or that state Medicaid agencies will independently cover as "medically necessary" (Romano et al. 2019). This needs to change. The more legislative support that pregnant women receive to access genetic counseling services and make genuinely free and informed choices, the less likely it is they will ever need to turn to the court system to file wrongful birth claims after a child with a genetic impairment is born. Hence, from our perspective, wrongful birth litigation is "too little, too late." Public and private health insurance providers should cover the costs of genetic counseling services, so that patients can access reliable and affordable pre- and post-test genetic counseling services. In turn, as wrongful birth claims become effectively obsolete, the legal pressure that physicians feel may dissipate.

Finally, we recommend that the federal government adequately fund the Kennedy–Brownback Act. To take a step back, medical practitioners and professional organizations have set their own standards for best practices to deliver information and counsel patients, but not all clinicians have chosen to follow these recommendations. In 2011, the National Society of Genetic Counselors (NSGC) developed and published guidelines on how to communicate a positive diagnosis of Down syndrome following screening to "ensure that families are consistently given up-to-date and balanced information about the condition." These guidelines specifically recommend that medical professionals "balance the negative aspects of Down syndrome, such as birth defects, medical complications, and developmental delay, with positive aspects like available treatments, therapies, and the ability for people with Down syndrome and their families to enjoy a high quality of life" (Sheets et al. 2011b: 435). Additional recommendations include providing patients with referrals to necessary specialists, as well as contact information for local support services, including reference lists available from the National Down Syndrome Society (www.ndss.org) and the National Down Syndrome Congress (www.ndsccenter.org).

Non-profits have crafted useful resources as well. The Lettercase National Center for Prenatal and Postnatal Resources, which is part of the University of Kentucky's Human Development Institute, prepared a booklet titled "Understanding a Down Syndrome Diagnosis." This booklet is available in print and online for expectant parents who have received a prenatal diagnosis of Down syndrome but have not yet made decisions regarding their pregnancy options. Developed in collaboration with Down syndrome advocates and professional medical organizations, the booklet discusses medical issues and developmental delays that children with Down syndrome typically face, as well as contact information for medical specialists, Down syndrome advocacy groups, and support organizations. Importantly, the publication also addresses pregnancy termination and adoption as options.

These initiatives are commendable, and the proposed tactics offer a powerful corrective to the narrowly clinical and generally pessimistic counsel that pregnant women whose fetuses are diagnosed with Down syndrome typically receive from doctors. That said, these proposals are entirely voluntary, since they are designed to persuade medical professionals to change their practice and rhetoric. Physicians do not have any incentive or obligation to adhere to these guidelines. Given the deeply entrenched ableist biases that pervade Western medicine, we are not optimistic that adequate solutions can be achieved by these voluntary individual-level measures. Reproductive autonomy is a matter of justice, and women should be guaranteed access to comprehensive, balanced, and up-to-date information—they should not have to depend on the goodwill of individual physicians, nor should they need to rely on good fortune to live in a state with an exemplary disability information act.

In order to standardize medical practice across states and uphold the integrity of information related to prenatal testing for the sake of women's autonomy, we recommend that the federal government adequately fund the Kennedy–Brownback Act. This funding will allow the Department of Health to collect and disseminate accurate, up-to-date, comprehensive information about test results and the range of outcomes associated the diagnosed condition. Additional information should include patient support networks, including information about how expectant parents of fetuses diagnosed with Down syndrome can connect with other parents who have had the same experience through First Call programs.[21] In turn, medical providers should then be required to make this information accessible to patients via written materials.[22]

---

[21] First Call programs are comprised of volunteer parent mentors who listen, share, answer questions, and provide valuable information about the challenges and rewards of raising a child with Down syndrome.

[22] It would be a mistake to allow the government to intrude into the communication between patients and providers, since physicians need room to use their professional discretion. For example, physicians should not be forced to recite a congressionally scripted statement or perform a medically unnecessary and invasive procedure on patients against their will. We are merely suggesting that physicians be required to provide information-rich, well-vetted, federally approved written information to women who receive positive prenatal test results for Down syndrome to supplement the clinical counseling they will receive.

112 Prenatal Genetic Testing, Abortion, and Disability Justice

At this point, feminist readers may be wondering to what extent our call for governmental regulation in the name of women's autonomy differs from pronatalist abortion-related informed consent statutes, often labelled "Woman's Right to Know" Acts. Although the exact content of each statute varies from state to state, these pieces of legislation typically require physicians to share specific details with patients, including information about the risks of the termination procedure, graphic material about fetal development and termination, and information regarding assistance to women deciding whether to continue their pregnancies. The professed aim of these statutes is to promote women's autonomy (or a woman's "right to know"), suggesting that women confronting the choice to have an abortion need special safeguards to protect them from misunderstanding the nature and consequences of their decision and from the regret that might come from having an abortion without understanding important facts about the procedure beforehand. In *Planned Parenthood of Southeastern Pennsylvania v. Casey* (1992), the Supreme Court upheld the constitutionality of Pennsylvania's law, affirming the permissibility of states to require physicians to supply pregnant women with material designed to discourage abortion as a means of ensuring that women's choices are "mature and informed."[23]

We distinguish our call for federal funding for the Kennedy–Brownback Act from state-level "Woman's Right to Know" Acts along three dimensions. First, our proposal is addressing a substantiated problem (that is, the premise that misinformation about Down syndrome colors prenatal screening and selective abortion has been well documented), while state-level "Woman's Right to Know" Acts do not. The *Casey* decision cites the potential for psychological harm and regret as justifications for making supplementary information about non-selective abortion available to women:

> In attempting to ensure that a woman apprehend the full consequences of her decision, the State furthers the legitimate purpose of reducing the risk that a woman may elect an abortion, only to discover later, with devastating psychological consequences, that her decision was not fully informed. (882)

That is, "Woman's Right to Know" Acts aim to reduce the risk of psychological harm without showing that a significant portion of women have actually been put at risk. At best, these risks seem to be hypothetical possibilities rather than common occurrences. There is no proof that women are not already sufficiently informed of the risks and benefits of abortion, and the potential

---

[23] The *Casey* decision upheld a number of regulations regarding abortion, including an informed consent requirement, a twenty-four-hour waiting period, and a parental notification requirement.

link between abortion and psychological harm or regret remains unsubstantiated. In his majority opinion, Justice Kennedy admitted that there are "no reliable data" that women having abortions experience greater regret than do women continuing unwanted pregnancies. Hence, like protections for voter fraud, "Woman's Right to Know" Acts are "solutions in search of a problem," so to speak. The state is pre-emptively protecting patients from the unproven risks of psychological harm that may follow from a lack of information and understanding, although we have no compelling reason to suspect that women seeking non-selective abortions are in fact making their decisions without adequate information in the first place. In contrast, a federal disability information act would protect women's reproductive decision-making capacities from a substantiated threat: widespread ableist bias in the medical community.

Second, while the Kennedy–Brownback Act mandates that *supplemental* material be made available to patients, "Woman's Right to Know" Acts allow the government to *supplant* the information that physicians provide, sometimes even going so far as to make doctors recite a state-approved medical script. Even though *Casey* held that states may adopt regulations that are "calculated to inform the woman's free choice" by supplying "truthful, nonmisleading information," recent studies have demonstrated that state-developed materials do not always measure up to this standard. In fact, many statutes enacted since *Casey* miserably fail the "truthful and nonmisleading" test by making bogus and misleading claims about a link between abortion and breast cancer, the psychological impact of abortion, and fetal pain.[24]

Finally, on a related note, we endorse governmental regulations designed to inform, not influence, choice. By contrast, the *Casey* decision allows states to influence, not inform, choice. According to legal scholar Sonia Suter (2013: 22):

> [*Casey*] rejected the view of *Akron* and *Thornburgh* that disclosures attempting to discourage abortions were unconstitutional. Instead, it permitted the "State to further its legitimate goal of protecting the life of the unborn by enacting legislation aimed at ensuring a decision that is *mature and informed*, even when in so doing the State expresses a preference for childbirth over abortion."

---

[24] Cynthia Daniels et al. (2016) analyzed state-authored information packets. After extracting all statements regarding embryological and fetal development from the state-developed brochures given to patients before the abortion procedure (a total of 896 statements about fetal development across 23 states), they recruited a team of 7 specialists in embryological and fetal anatomy through the American Academy of Anatomists to evaluate the medical accuracy of the materials. The study finds that nearly one-third of the informed consent information is medically inaccurate (Daniels et al. 2016: 191). Moreover, their findings indicate that medically unsubstantiated information is concentrated primarily in the earlier weeks of pregnancy, when women are most likely to seek an abortion (Daniels et al. 2016: 194).

114   Prenatal Genetic Testing, Abortion, and Disability Justice

Thus, even if mandated disclosure of information relating to fetal development and pregnancy assistance "might cause the woman to choose childbirth over abortion," the Court allowed states to influence a woman's choice toward childbirth. This type of influence is manipulative, rather than autonomy enhancing.

Hence, it seems that "Woman's Right to Know" Acts are less about protecting the integrity of genuine informed choice and more about discouraging abortion by making it a more cumbersome and shame-filled process.[25] In our view, pregnant women who choose to undergo prenatal screening cannot be self-determining if the information they are given is biased toward one outcome. When left to their own devices, medical professionals err on the side of providing and framing information in a manner that is biased toward termination. Yet, following the *Casey* decision, state governments can provide information that encourages women to choose childbirth over abortion. In order to remove constraints to individual choice that result from undue influence in medical settings and state legislatures, governmental regulation at the federal level can potentially ensure that prenatal screening actually works for the sake of women's autonomy by better informing—not influencing or manipulating—women's reproductive decisions.

Conclusion

Ultimately, we recognize the potential risks of legitimizing government regulation in the terrain of reproductive rights, and we certainly hope that our pro-autonomy rationale for regulating the delivery of information about prenatal screening will not fuel the call for more stringent restrictions on abortion in general. To prevent the anti-abortion movement from co-opting the rhetoric of women's rights, we want to be perfectly clear about our position: we argue that the federal government has an obligation affirmatively to allocate the funds to ensure that up-to-date, comprehensive, and balanced information is made accessible to pregnant women who choose to undergo prenatal screening in order to promote informed choice, but it is up to the pregnant patients ultimately to decide what they want to do with the information.

---

[25] Brittany Leach (2020: 321–2) also identifies an obvious disjuncture between the pro-life movement's professed "pro-woman messaging" and the actual intent of this type of legislation. Even though pro-life activists package themselves as "the true advocates for women" who protect women from a "corrupt and profit-driven abortion industry," the ultimate aim of statutes like "Women's Right to Know" Acts is to compel women to "choose life," not to protect women's reproductive autonomy or promote gender equality.

References

Adams, Rachel (2013). *Raising Henry: A Memoir of Motherhood, Disability, and Discovery*. New Haven, CT: Yale University Press.

Albrecht, Gary, and Patrick Devlieger (1999). "The Disability Paradox: High Quality of Life Against All Odds," *Social Science and Medicine*, 48/8: 977–88.

Allyse, Megan, et al. (2017). "Offering Prenatal Screening in the Age of Genomic Medicine: A Practical Guide," *Journal of Women's Health*, 26/7: 755–61.

Asch, Adrienne (2003). "Disability Equality and Prenatal Testing: Contradictory or Compatible?," *Florida State University Law Review*, 30/2: 315–41.

Asch, Adrienne and David Wasserman (2005). "Where is the Sin in Synecdoche? Prenatal Testing and the Parent-Child Relationship," In Quality of Life and Human Difference: Genetic Testing, Health Care, and Disability, edited by Wasserman, David, Jerome Bickenbach, and Robert Wachbroit, pp 172–216. Cambridge: Cambridge University Press.

Barnes, Elizabeth (2016). *The Minority Body: A Theory of Disability*. Oxford: Oxford University Press.

Beauchamp, Tom, and James Childress (2013). *Principles of Biomedical Ethics*. 7th edn. New York: Oxford University Press.

Bérubé, Michael (1996). *Life as we Know it: A Father, a Family, and an Exceptional Child*. New York: Vintage Books.

Blendon, Robert, John Benson, and Joachim Hero (2014). "Public Trust in Physicians: US Medicine in International Perspective," *New England Journal of Medicine*, 371/17: 1570–2.

Brown, Genevieve Shaw (2016). "Mom and Baby with Down Syndrome Mail Letter to Doctor who Suggested Abortion," *ABC News*, 7 June, https://abcnews.go.com/Lifestyle/mom–baby–syndrom email–letter–doctor–suggested–abortion/story?id=39666410.

Cooley, Carl, et al. (1990). "Reactions of Mothers and Medical Professionals to a Film about Down Syndrome," *American Journal of Diseases in Children*, 144/10: 1112–16.

Crabbe, Rebecca, Peter Stone, and Sara Filoche (2019). "What are Women Saying about Noninvasive Prenatal Testing? An Analysis on Online Discussion Forums," *Prenatal Diagnosis*, 39/10: 890–5.

Crossley, Mary (2015). "Disability Cultural Competence in the Medical Profession," *Saint Louis University Journal of Health Law and Policy*, 9/1: 89–110.

Daniels, Cynthia, et al. (2016). "Informed or Misinformed Consent? Abortion Policy in the United States," *Journal of Health Politics, Policy and Law*, 41/2: 181–209.

Dixon, Darrin (2008). "Informed Consent or Institutionalized Eugenics? How the Medical Profession Encourages Abortion of Fetuses with Down Syndrome," *Issues in Law and Medicine*, 24/1: 3–59.

Fox, Dov (2019). *Birth Rights and Wrongs: How Medicine and Technology are Remaking Reproduction and the Law*. Oxford: Oxford University Press.

Fricker, Miranda (2007). *Epistemic Injustice: Power and the Ethics of Knowing*. Oxford: Oxford University Press.

Gadsboll, Kasper, et al. (2020). "Current Use of Noninvasive Prenatal Testing in Europe, Australia, and the USA: A Graphical Presentation," *Acta Obstetricia et Gynecologica Scandinavica*, 99/6: 722–30.

Gammon, Bryan Leigh, et al. (2016). "'I Think we've Got Too Many Tests!' Prenatal Providers' Reflections on Ethical and Clinical Challenges in the Practice and Integration of Cell-Free DNA Screening," *Ethics, Medicine, and Public Health*, 2/3: 334–41.

Garland-Thomson, Rosemarie (2020). "How We Got to CRISPR: The Dilemma of Being Human," *Perspectives in Biology and Medicine*, 63/1: 28–43.

Germany (Territory under Allied Occupation, 1945–1955: US Zone) (1949). *Trials of War Criminals before the Nuremberg Military Tribunals under Control Council Law no. 10*. Washington: US Government Printing Office.

Green, Sara Eleanor (2007). "'We're Tired, not Sad': Benefits and Burdens of Mothering a Child with a Disability," *Social Science and Medicine*, 64/1: 150–63.

Hermanson, Haley (2019). "The Right Recovery for Wrongful Birth," *Drake Law Review*, 67/2: 513–59.

Ho, Anita (2011). "Trusting Experts and Epistemic Humility in Disability," *International Journal of Feminist Approaches to Bioethics*, 4/2: 102–23.

Hu, Xinyi, et al. (2012). "The Prepared Patient: Information Seeking of Online Support Group Members Before Their Medical Appointments. Journal of Health Communication 17 (8): 960–78.

Huang, Ellery Chih-Han, et al. (2018). "Public Trust in Physicians: Health Care Commodification as a Possible Deteriorating Factor: Cross-Sectional Analysis of 23 Countries," *Inquiry: The Journal of Health Care Organization, Provision, and Financing*, 55: 1–11.

Kaposy, Chris (2018). *Choosing Down Syndrome: Ethics and New Prenatal Testing Technologies*. Cambridge, MA: MIT Press.

Klein, David Alan (2011). "Medical Disparagement of the Disability Experience: Empirical Evidence for the 'Expressivist Objection'," *AJOB Primary Research*, 2/2: 8–20.

Knight, Amber and Joshua Miller (2021), "Prenatal Genetic Screening, Epistemic Justice and Reproductive Autonomy," *Hypatia*, 36: 1–21

The Healthcare System **117**

Kothari, Sunil (2004). "Clinical (Mis)judgements of Quality of Life after Disability," *Journal of Clinical Ethics*, 15/4: 300–7.

Lalor, Joan, et al. (2007). "Unexpected Diagnosis of Fetal Abnormality: Women's Encounters with Caregivers," *Birth*, 34/1: 80–8.

Lalvani, Priya (2008). "Mothers of Children with Down Syndrome: Constructing the Sociocultural Disability," *Intellectual and Developmental Disabilities*, 46/6: 436–45.

Lalvani, Priya (2011). "Constructing the (M)other: Dominant and Contested Narratives on Mothering a Child with Down Syndrome," *Narrative Inquiry*, 21/2: 276–93.

Leach, Brittany (2020). "Whose Backlash, against whom? Feminism and the American Pro-Life Movement's 'Mother–Child' Strategy," *Signs: Journal of Women, Culture, and Society*, 45/2: 319–28.

Lynch, Holly Fernandez (2008). *Conflicts of Conscience in Healthcare: An Institutional Compromise*. Cambridge, MA: MIT Press.

National Commission for the Protection of Human Subjects of Biomedical and Behavioral Research (1979). *The Belmont Report: Ethical Principles and Guidelines for the Protection of Human Subjects of Research*. Washington: United States Government Printing Office.

Natoli, Jaime, et al. (2012). "Prenatal Diagnosis of Down Syndrome: A Systemic Review of Termination Rates (1995–2011)," *Prenatal Diagnosis*, 32/2: 142–53.

Ormond, Kelly, et al. (2003). "Attitudes of Health Care Trainees about Genetics and Disability: Issues of Access, Health Care Communication, and Decision Making," *Journal of Genetic Counseling*, 12/4: 333–49.

Parham, Lindsay, Marsha Michie, and Megan Allyse (2017). "Expanding Use of cfDNA Screening in Pregnancy: Current and Emerging Ethical, Legal, and Social Issues," *Current Genetic Medicine Reports*, 5/1: 44–53.

Pergament, Deborah, and Katie Ilijic (2014). "The Legal Past, Present and Future of Prenatal Genetic Testing: Professional Liability and Other Legal Challenges Affecting Patient Access to Services," *Journal of Clinical Medicine*, 3/4: 1437–65.

Piepmeier, Alison (2013). "The Inadequacy of 'Choice': Disability and what's Wrong with Feminist Framings of Reproduction," *Feminist Studies*, 39/1: 159–86.

Piepmeier, Alison (2015). "Would It Be Better for Her Not to be Born? Down syndrome, Prenatal Testing, and Reproductive Decision-Making." Feminist Formations 27 (1): 1–24.

Piepmeier, Alison (2021). *Unexpected: Parenting, Prenatal Testing, and Down Syndrome*, ed. Rachel Adams and George Estreich. New York: New York University Press.

Rapp, Rayna (1988). "Moral Pioneers: Women, Men, and Fetuses on a Frontier of Reproductive Technology," *Women and Health*, 12/1–2: 101–16.

Rapp, Rayna (1993). "Amniocentesis in Sociocultural Perspective," *Journal of Genetic Counseling*, 2/3: 183–96.

Rapp, Rayna (1999). *Testing Women, Testing the Fetus: The Social Impact of Amniocentesis in America*. New York: Routledge.

Reardon, Marguerite (2016). "'I didn't Know I would be Able to Love her the Way I Do': A Mother's Story of Down Syndrome," *CBS News*, 22 March, https://www.cbsnews.com/news/down–syndrome–mothers–story/.

Reynolds, Joel (2017). "'I'd Rather be Dead than Disabled': The Ableist Conflation and the Meanings of Disability," *Review of Communication*, 17/3: 149–63.

Reynolds, Joel (2018). "Three Things Clinicians should Know about Disability," *American Medical Association Journal of Ethics*, 20/12: 1181–7.

Romano, Neil, et al. (2019) (chairman). *Genetic Testing and the Rush to Perfection: Part of the Bioethics and Disability Series*. Washington: National Council on Disability, https://ncd.gov/sites/default/files/NCD_Genetic_Testing_Report_508.pdf.

Rosenfeld, Sophia (2019). *Democracy and Truth: A Short History*. Philadelphia, PA: University of Pennsylvania Press.

Rothman, David J. (2003). *Strangers at the Bedside: A History of how Law and Bioethics Transformed Medical Decision-Making*. Hawthorne, NY: Aldine de Gruyter.

Sanborn, Erica, and Annette Patterson (2014). "Disability Training in the Genetic Counseling Curricula: Bridging the Gap between Genetic Counselors and the Disability Community," *American Journal of Medical Ethics Part A*, 164A: 1909–15.

Santoro, Jonathan, et al. (2017). "Disability in US Medical Education: Disparities, Programmes and Future Directions," *Health Education Journal*, 76/6: 753–9.

Saxton, Marsha (2013). "Disability Rights and Selective Abortion," in Lennard Davis (ed.), *The Disability Studies Reader*. 4th edn. New York: Routledge, 87–99.

Scully, Jackie Leach (2018). "From 'She would Say that, wouldn't she?' to 'Does she Take Sugar?': Epistemic Injustice and Disability," *IJFAB: International Journal of Feminist Approaches to Bioethics*, 11/1: 106–24.

Sheets, Kathryn, et al. (2011a). "Balanced Information about Down Syndrome: What is Essential?," *American Journal of Medical Genetics Part A*, 155: 1246–57.

Sheets, Kathryn, et al. (2011b). "Practice Guidelines for Communicating a Prenatal or Postnatal Diagnosis of Down Syndrome: Recommendations of the National Society of Genetic Counselors," *Journal of Genetic Counseling*, 20/5: 432–41.

Skotko, Brian (2005). "Prenatally Diagnosed Down Syndrome: Mothers who Continued their Pregnancies Evaluate their Healthcare Providers," *American Journal of Obstetrics and Gynecology*, 192/3: 670–7.

Skotko, Brian, et al. (2015). "Family Perspectives about Down Syndrome," *American Journal of Medical Genetics Part A*, 9999A: 1–12.

Skotko, Brian, George Capone, and Priya Kishnani (2009). "Postnatal Diagnosis of Down Syndrome: Synthesis of the Evidence on How Best to Deliver the News," *Pediatrics*, 124/4: 751–8.

Skotko, Brian, Susan Levine, and Richard Goldstein (2011). "Self-Perceptions from People with Down Syndrome," *American Journal of Medical Genetics Part A*, 155: 2360–9.

Soper, Kathryn Lynard (2007) (ed.). *Gifts: Mothers Reflect on how Children with Down Syndrome Enrich their Lives*. Bethesda, MD: Woodbine Press.

Suter, Sonia (2013). "The Politics of Information: Informed Consent in Abortion and End-of-Life Decision Making," *American Journal of Law & Medicine*, 39/1: 7–61.

Swartz, Marth (2006). "Conscience Clauses or Unconscionable Clauses: Personal Beliefs versus Professional Responsibilities," *Yale Journal of Health Policy, Law, and Ethics*, 6/6: 269–350.

Symons, Andrew, Denise McGuigan, and Elie Akl (2009). "A Curriculum to Teach Medical Students to Care for People with Disabilities: Development and Initial Implementation," *BMC Medical Education*, 9–78.

Thomas, Gareth (2017). *Down's Syndrome Screening and Reproductive Politics: Care, Choice, and Disability in the Prenatal Clinic*. London: Routledge.

Tremain, Shelley (2017). "Knowing Disability, Differently," in Ian James Kidd, José Medina, and Gaile Pohlhaus, Jr (eds), *The Routledge Handbook of Epistemic Injustice*. New York: Routledge, 175–83.

Wasserman, David (2005). "The Nonidentity Problem, Disability, and the Role Morality of Prospective Parents," *Ethics*, 116/1: 132–52.

Wasserman, David, Jerome Bickenbach, and Robert Wachbriot (2005) (eds). *Quality of Life and Human Difference: Genetic Testing, Healthcare, and Disability*. New York: Cambridge University Press.

Wolff, Nicholas, and Jon Wolff (2018). "A Commentary on Commercial Genetic Testing and the Future of the Genetic Counseling Profession," *Journal of Genetic Counseling*, 27/): 521–7.

Wright, David (2011). *Downs: The History of a Disability*. Oxford: Oxford University Press.

4

The Neoliberal Welfare State

In 2013, Ariel and Deborah Levy were awarded $2.9 million in damages after they sued Oregon's Legacy Health System in a wrongful birth lawsuit. As we explained in Chapter 3, wrongful birth litigation is a unique subset of medical malpractice claims arising from a physician's alleged negligence in failing to inform potential parents about their offspring's risk of having a birth defect or congenital impairment. According to court documents, Deborah was given a chorionic villus sampling (CVS) during her first trimester. The results came back negative for Down syndrome. A few weeks later, two ultra-sounds revealed abnormalities that sometimes indicate Down syndrome, but the Levys testified that their healthcare providers did not advise them to get an amniocentesis. Despite their physician's reassurance, their daughter was diagnosed with Down syndrome a few days after she was born (Green 2012).

Deborah claimed that Legacy's Center for Maternal–Fetal Medicine and a Legacy Lab botched the test, subsequently robbing her of informed choice and depriving her of the opportunity to terminate the pregnancy. She claimed that she would have aborted had she known that her daughter had the chromosomal marker for trisomy 21. Legacy Health System denied any negligence, responding that the test results revealed a normal genetic profile because the fetus had mosiac Down syndrome and a significant number of her cells did not contain an extra twenty-first chromosome. Ultimately, jurors found Legacy Health negligent on five counts, concluding that employees—including the doctor who took the sample and lab workers who analyzed it—failed to communicate with each other, leading to the erroneous result.

At various points throughout the trial, questions about the Levys' perceived lack of parental love and acceptance prompted their attorney, David Miller, to defend them from condemnation in the court of public opinion. He told reporters that his clients deeply loved their daughter but filed the lawsuit out of concern over how they were going to afford all the long-term care and services that she would need over the course of her lifetime. As Miller explained to Portland's *Daily Mail* (2012): "It's been difficult for them … These are parents who love this little girl very, very much … Their mission since the

Prenatal Genetic Testing, Abortion, and Disability Justice. Amber Knight and Joshua Miller, Oxford University Press.
© Amber Knight and Joshua Miller (2023). DOI: 10.1093/oso/9780192870957.003.0005

122 Prenatal Genetic Testing, Abortion, and Disability Justice

beginning was to provide for her and that's what this is all about." Miller characterized wrongful birth litigation as an ignoble means to a noble end. Even though the Levys had to state in legal documents that they would have terminated their daughter if given the chance, they actually launched the wrongful birth lawsuit with the sole purpose of guaranteeing her care and ensuring their entire family's financial security.

Wrongful birth litigation is controversial, and it has seen its fair share of critics in recent years. As we showed in Chapter 3, some scholars worry that these lawsuits have created a perverse incentive for doctors to routinize prenatal genetic screening and testing for liability purposes, pushing the procedures on patients to shield themselves from an onslaught of medical malpractice claims (Pergament and Ilijic 2014; Murdoch et al. 2017). Other scholars have taken wrongful birth litigation to task for stigmatizing disability and operating under the ableist assumption that a pregnant woman would by default opt to terminate the pregnancy if she had successfully discovered that the fetus had a high likelihood of impairment (Stein 2010; Brown 2018). Finally, another camp of critics suggests that wrongful birth litigation highlights a flawed parental attitude that misinforms other prospective parents about the experience of raising a child with a disability (Hensel 2005; Stein 2010).

We argue that wrongful birth litigation is symptomatic of a larger problem: the shortcomings of neoliberal public policy. Public services for people with disabilities and their families are limited, highly fragmented, and poorly funded in neoliberal regimes committed to small government. Parents desperately file wrongful birth lawsuits as a last-ditch effort to procure financial assistance when other venues of government support are closed to them. Put another way, parents may feel as though they have little choice but to turn to the court system in the absence of a robust commitment from state and federal legislatures to fund healthcare, long-term supports and services, and family support services. In our view, a society reliant on the privatization of public goods—the hallmark of a neoliberal state—is the underlying problem at hand.[1]

Even though wrongful birth lawsuits are still relatively rare, the financial motivations behind them are not.[2] According to Darpana Sheth (2006), many

---

[1] Long-term supports and services typically include assistance with basic activities of daily living (ADLs) such as bathing, dressing, using the toilet, or other personal care and help with instrumental activities of daily living (IADLs) such as household chores, financial management, medication management, and transportation. These services are distinguished from medical care.

[2] Rayna Rapp and Faye Ginsburg (2001: 542) found that many of their interviewees who decided to use amniocentesis were motivated by the financial fears they had about raising potentially expensive disabled children in an already "tight domestic economy."

The Neoliberal Welfare State   **123**

parents see wrongful birth litigation as a type of supplemental insurance that can help cover extraordinary costs related to disability. This financial assistance, however, comes with a cruel caveat, since it is provided only to those willing openly to claim injury from the lost opportunity to choose not to bring their child into existence, whether they genuinely feel that way or not.[3] Thus, we see wrongful birth lawsuits as a testament to the failure of public policy as well as an indication of the lengths to which some parents are willing to go to secure vital services for their children when other types of assistance have run dry.

This chapter is particularly concerned with the way in which neoliberal budget reductions and cost-containment efforts might impact on the decision-making of pregnant women who are deciding whether or not to screen for genetic impairments and what to do following a positive Down syndrome diagnosis. Pregnant women facing these choices have a lot to take into consideration, and economic concerns about raising a child with Down syndrome often enter into the equation. Although we cannot quantify precisely how many women choose to terminate out of financial fear of the costs of raising a child with heightened care needs, we strongly suspect that financial considerations come into play for many women, especially those from socially marginalized groups—including working-class women, women of color, and/or women with disabilities—who disproportionately live at or near the poverty line.[4] We are concerned about financial motivations because, as Victoria Seavilleklein (2009: 77) persuasively argues, "it is hard to make a free choice about pursuing prenatal screening options when there are not adequate socially-supported alternatives ... that would make the decision to raise a child with disabilities easier."

Hence, prospective parents weighing their options may need to take stock of the type and amount of financial assistance they can reasonably expect to receive if they decide to give birth to and raise a child with Down syndrome.

---

[3] Financial motivations certainly underpin many wrongful birth lawsuits, but they are by no means the only reason for them. As Sofia Yakren (2018) makes clear, some plaintiff-mothers file these lawsuits because they believe that negligent medical providers should be held accountable for their misconduct. Still others are resentful of the fact that they were denied valuable information that could have guided a decision to abort, especially in cases where children have a terminal impairment like Tay-Sachs.

[4] Some recent studies indicate that economic considerations play a crucial role for women seeking abortions in general. According to the Guttmacher Institute, roughly three-fourths of abortion patients came from low-income households in 2014—almost half (49%) lived under the federal poverty level, and an additional 26% lived at incomes within 200% of the poverty line (Jerman, Jones, and Onda 2016). Anecdotal evidence also indicates that the same dynamic is at play with selective abortions. Professor Elizabeth Gettig, who was a genetic counselor in the 1980s, stated that nearly all the women she treated who chose to terminate a fetus with Down syndrome did so at least partly owing to a lack of economic resources (quoted in Dixon 2008: 6). Moreover, when Rayna Rapp (1999) interviewed women who were choosing to use amniocentesis, many interviewees identified a fear of economic vulnerability as a motive for undergoing the procedure.

Twenty-five years ago, Susan Wendell (1996: 82) warned: "If they [prospective parents] are afraid of the burden of raising a child with a disability in a society where accessibility and help are far from adequate, they have reason to be afraid." As we show in the following sections, the situation has not changed since Wendell wrote those words. Bereft of adequate public long-term supports and services, many prospective parents may feel unduly pressured to use prenatal screening technologies or terminate impaired fetuses. The wider implication is that the absence of manifest coercion is not the only precondition for autonomous decision-making. Even if not coercively compelled to use prenatal screening technologies or selectively abort an impaired fetus, prospective parents can be unjustly forced by poverty (or the looming prospect of poverty) to make these decisions. Put simply, using screening technologies and aborting an impaired fetus because one cannot afford a disabled child in a society that privatizes care is not a genuine expression of reproductive freedom.

This chapter therefore places issues of political economy at center stage in discussions about prenatal genetic screening and reproductive autonomy to examine the following questions. What types of financial burdens do parents of children with disabilities face in the neoliberal economic and political landscape? Which policies are in place to offset the financial costs of care, and are they effectively designed and administered? And, as a matter of social justice, what types of policy reforms need to be fulfilled so that prospective parents who want to move forward with their pregnancies following a positive fetal diagnosis of Down syndrome can do so free from the threat of poverty or excessive financial hardship?

The first section begins with a brief sketch of the current neoliberal policy landscape. This section argues that neoliberal policies compromise the security and well-being of many families, especially families raising children with disabilities. The next section discusses the theoretical underpinnings of our current privatized model of prenatal healthcare. The goal here is to demonstrate how public services for people with disabilities have been shrinking as prenatal genetic technologies have been expanding, and how these trends are not coincidental or independent of one another. That is, we seek to show how the reduction in public services and increased funding for prenatal genetic screening both serve purposes of neoliberal policy. The third section draws on Maxine Eichner's theory of "the supportive state" to envision an alternative to neoliberal governance. Eichner offers an attractive alternative to neoliberalism by offering a normative justification for publicly sharing the costs of care grounded in a commitment to personal autonomy and human dignity. The final section envisions the specific policy reforms

The Neoliberal Welfare State **125**

that would follow from the version of liberalism that Eichner offers. We ultimately propose changing our current long-term care system for home- and community-based services from a means-tested public assistance program to a universal social insurance program.

Neoliberal Policy and Disability

Feminist legal theorists have said a great deal about how neoliberal principles and values have shaped law and policy outcomes in an American context since the end of the twentieth century (McCluskey 2003; Alstott 2015; Cooper 2017; Eichner 2017; Harbach 2019). The term "neoliberalism" is a multifaceted concept, and there is no consistent usage across disciplines.[5] For our purposes, neoliberalism refers to a mode of governmentality that extends classical economic market principles to the arrangement of political and social affairs. In a neoliberal regime, the so-called free market is the preferred organizing principle for state and social relations, which means that market efficiency rather than formative social policy is considered to be the best means to secure social welfare. From this it follows that the state's primary role is to ensure the proper conditions for economic activity and individual prosperity so that individuals can access markets freely to pursue their own interests, with the state having no affirmative obligation to provide these goods itself. The neoliberal emphasis on limited government makes low taxes more important than social welfare programs, and neoliberal government officials often strive to eliminate social services in order to reduce social spending.

Beginning at least with the Reagan administration, state–family relations in the United States have been infused with a neoliberal ethos. From that time, as Anne Alstott (2015) persuasively argues, three interrelated core neoliberal ideals—negative liberty, laissez-faire market distributions, and the minimal state—have permeated US family law and guided the development of social policy. Thus Alstott argues that goods such as caretaking and human development are assumed to be best distributed by the "invisible hand of the market," while the state's primary responsibility is to "keep its hand off" and stay out of the way as families decide how to care for their members in their own way and on their own dime. Subsequently, the *raison d'être* of family law is to fend off

---

[5] For a deeper analysis of neoliberalism as a political doctrine and a historical development, see David Harvey (2007).

126 Prenatal Genetic Testing, Abortion, and Disability Justice

excessive state intrusion into the private sphere.[6] Under the circumstances, a constricted neoliberal concern with protecting negative liberty precludes other commitments, like ensuring that families have the minimal resources needed to care for dependants and to conduct family life.

The logic of neoliberalism legitimizes minimal welfare-state provisions, since families are presumed to be able to go it alone and shoulder their own financial weight.[7] As Ahoo Tabatabai (2020: 155) succinctly argues: "Neoliberalism, with its logic of efficiency, turns to parents to provide both income and care while absolving the state of any responsibilities." The result is that most US welfare programs are designed to provide only minimal resources for family life in extraordinary circumstances, stepping in only as a last resort when families "fail" to provide for themselves (Eichner 2010; Alstott 2015). Put differently, the state provides residual rather than universal support. Governmental assistance is regarded not as a right but as an exception. The result is that many American families do not have constitutionally protected rights to goods such as housing, healthcare, cash assistance, and other social goods and services.

Neoliberalism therefore undermines the state's capacity to design social policies that promote work–family balance and shield families from financial risk. The impact on US welfare policy is undeniable, as it consistently lags behind other advantaged industrialized societies in implementing social safety nets. American citizens do not have any federal legislation to guarantee paid parental leave, parity of wages, benefits for workers who work part time in order to accommodate caretaking, or paid vacation. In fact, the US is the only member of the Organization for Economic Cooperation and Development (OECD), an intergovernmental economic organization comprised of thirty-seven democracies with market-based economies, not to offer statutory paid parental leave on a national basis.[8] Likewise, the US devotes significantly less public spending to childcare and early education than other advanced industrialized societies.[9] As a result, roughly one in seven children in America lived in poverty in 2019, making them the poorest

---

[6] Following a long line of legal precedents, the Supreme Court has determined that parental autonomy cannot be compromised by excessive governmental regulation. See *Meyer* v. *Nebraska* (1923), *Prince* v. *Commonwealth of Massachusetts* (1944), *Wisconsin* v. *Yoder* (1972), *Reno* v. *Flores* (1993), and *Troxel* v. *Granville* (2000).

[7] For a discussion of the privatization of childcare in classical liberal thought and neoliberal policy, see Daniel Engster (2010, 2015).

[8] Generally, OECD members are regarded as developed nations with high-income economies and a high Human Development Index (HDI).

[9] According to OECD (2021) data, the US's total public expenditures on early childhood education and care, as a percentage of GDP, ranked among the lowest in the Global North.

age group in the country (US Census Bureau 2020). When it comes to public support for families, or lack thereof, the US stands out among peer nations.[10]

The situation is particularly dire when disability is added into the equation. Everyone knows that it is expensive to raise a child under the best of circumstances. It is never cheap to pay for food, shelter, educational expenses, clothing, transportation, and other essential goods and services necessary to bring up children. However, parenting a child with Down syndrome usually involves sizeable financial costs beyond those incurred by parents of non-disabled children. For children with intellectual and developmental disabilities—many of whom may also have chronic medical conditions and/or need long-term supports and services to conduct activities of daily living—the added expenses can be overwhelming. Expenditures on healthcare, medication, different types of therapeutic services, special education resources, accessible transportation, assistive technologies, respite care, and so on can add up fast.[11] Some of these expenses are covered by private insurance, but many are not.[12] Although estimates vary considerably, it is widely acknowledged that it is generally more expensive to raise a child with a disability than a non-disabled child (Stabile and Allin 2012; Mitra et al. 2017). According to one study, raising a disabled child to age 18 costs more than *three* times as much as raising a non-disabled child (Wasserman 2017: 469). Costs not offset by private insurance coverage, such as rehabilitation therapy and in-home nursing care, can quickly use up every spare dollar from even a middle-class family's income.

Not only do these added out-of-pocket expenses put a strain on a family's budget, but paid employment is often difficult for many parents to sustain. In particular, many mothers of children with Down syndrome cut back on work hours or quit their jobs altogether to care for their child's heightened care needs (Parish 2006; Scott 2010). According to the Family and Individual Needs for Disability Supports (FINDS) Survey (2017), which is a national survey of family caregivers to people with intellectual and developmental disabilities, 55 percent of respondents reported having to cut back on work hours to accommodate caregiving responsibilities, and 32 percent reported giving up work entirely (Anderson et al. 2018: 7). The time required to provide

---

[10] OECD (2022b) data have consistently found that the US has one of the worst child poverty rates of any advanced industrialized society.

[11] One study estimates that medical costs for children 0–4 years old with Down syndrome are roughly twelve times higher than for those without the condition, and even higher when the diagnosis includes congenital cardiac conditions (Boulet et al. 2008).

[12] Even when families have private insurance that covers a needed healthcare service, high out-of-pocket maximum expenditures and high deductibles result in families having to shoulder a large portion of the costs of medical treatments out of pocket.

128 Prenatal Genetic Testing, Abortion, and Disability Justice

quality care, combined with a lack of accessible childcare arrangements, often compromises a parent's ability to remain in the workforce. Moreover, children with Down syndrome often have quickly changing and elevated healthcare needs that require frequent and spontaneous visits to doctor's offices and hospitals, which translate into missed workdays. Without flexible employment schedules or government-mandated paid parental leave, paid employment is hard to manage. And, owing to the sexual division of labor and the gender wage gap, it often "makes sense" for mothers to drop out of the workforce to provide unpaid care, since they tend to make less money than their male partners. These lost earnings can be difficult for many families to absorb.

In sum, the financial consequences of raising a child with a disability can be immense. Studies have found that parents of children with developmental disabilities had significantly lower savings and income at midlife compared to other parents (Parish et al. 2010). This means that families once considered middle class often find themselves surfing the edge of financial ruin with no "rainy-day" fund to weather any additional setbacks. In other cases, exorbitant out-of-pocket expenses and reduced earnings put families caring for children with disabilities at increased risk of poverty. And this risk is far too real. American families of children with disabilities are significantly more likely to live in poverty, experience food insecurity, and declare bankruptcy to extract themselves from medical debt than the general population (Sonik et al. 2016; Himmelstein et al. 2019). In fact, the US has the highest poverty rates in the developed world for households with a disabled family member. In 2009, approximately 30 percent of American households with a disabled family member were classified as poor (compared with 19 percent of "typical" American households).[13]

What kinds of social welfare policies are currently available to support families with children with disabilities who experience financial hardship? As David Mitchell and Sharon Snyder (2015: 16) have observed, neoliberalism has created a "willy-nilly approach" to service provision for people with disabilities and their family members. There is no centralized comprehensive national program to which parents can reliably turn for social services such as respite care, skilled childcare, family counseling, architectural adaptation of the home, the purchase of specialized medical equipment, and in-home nursing or long-term care. Government-funded long-term supports and services

---

[13] The US has the highest poverty rates for households with a disabled family member out of the thirty-seven member countries of the OECD (2022a). By contrast, poverty rates for families with a family member with a disability were either at a similar level or even somewhat smaller than the general population in Sweden, Norway, Iceland, Ireland, and the United Kingdom.

for individuals with disabilities vary considerably based on the state in which the child lives, the nature of the child's condition, and the family's income. All in all, the current patchwork of social policies is highly fragmented and difficult to access, lacking coordination across agencies and providers. In fact, the current hodgepodge is so bewildering that it has sparked a new industry of consultants, called "support planners," who are paid to help parents of children with disabilities navigate the bureaucratic labyrinth (Serres and Howatt 2019).

The only national program of income support is Supplemental Security Income (SSI), which pays small monthly cash benefits to incredibly poor families with the most severely impaired children. SSI is a federal mean-tested cash assistance program. Eligibility is determined by medical criteria and income and asset tests. Regarding medical criteria, a child's impairment must match or equal a list of disabilities compiled by the Social Security Administration.[14] In addition, the child's family must also have very low income and assets. In 2017, the family's countable income had to be under $735 per month, or less than $9,000 per year (Romig 2017). Moreover, an eligible recipient's countable assets could not exceed $2,000 if the child lived with one parent, or $3,000 if the child lived with two parents. Owing to the strict eligibility criteria, only a fraction of the nation's families with disabled children qualified. In 2017, roughly 1.2 million children under the age of 18 received childhood SSI benefits (Social Security Administration 2018).

While SSI reduces some material hardship by reducing the effects of deep poverty, the benefits are modest. In 2020, the maximum monthly federal payment was $783 a month. Most SSI recipients remain poor precisely because the program creates work disincentives and places strict limitations on resource accumulation. Kristin Bumiller (2013: 159) explains the implications, arguing that "the Social Security system, in effect, sets up poverty as the norm for the disabled population." Moreover, Bumiller (2013: 160) notes that, despite the inadequacies of SSI, proponents of neoliberal welfare reform have continuously attacked the program as a prime example of wasteful government spending that is in need of additional "market-reform" further to divest the state of its obligations.

Beyond income support, many families receive much-needed financial assistance through the Medicaid program.[15] Medicaid is structured as a federal–state partnership, jointly funded and administered. Federal Medicaid

---

[14] Notably, Down syndrome is included among the qualifying conditions.
[15] Medicaid and the Children's Health Insurance (CHIP) Program covered about half of American children with special healthcare needs in 2017 (roughly six million children) (Musumeci and Chidambaram 2019).

130 Prenatal Genetic Testing, Abortion, and Disability Justice

law sets broad rules but gives states considerable discretion over benefit and coverage design, so Medicaid programs vary considerably across states. Despite significant variation, Medicaid is generally provided to those with poverty-level incomes, SSI beneficiaries, and children in the foster-care system. Medicaid is vital for poor families who would otherwise not have access to health-insurance coverage, especially those where children such as those with Down syndrome require more medical care and expensive medical services than their peers (Kageleiry et al. 2017).

In addition, nearly all states have chosen to extend eligibility to middle-class families raising children with disabilities through "waiver" programs.[16] Why do middle-class families with private health insurance also need Medicaid coverage as well? Unlike private health insurance, Medicaid covers acute medical care *and* long-term supports and services. Long-term supports and services assist individuals in carrying out activities of daily living, including everyday activities (such as walking, toileting, bathing, dressing, and eating) as well as instrumental tasks (such as managing medications, meal preparation, handling finances, and household chores). Thus, Medicaid covers or shares the costs of home health aides, specialized therapies, respite care, home and/or vehicle modifications, and many other services that private insurance plans do not cover and that many families cannot afford out of pocket. Many people with Down syndrome often require assistance with activities of daily living throughout their lives. Though parents and other unpaid family members can provide this type of assistance informally, paid services often become necessary or desirable. However, the out-of-pocket costs of personal-care attendants and/or long-term therapeutic services exceed most families' earnings and savings, so Medicaid can provide coverage to defray some of these costs. Unlike state plans, Medicaid waivers allow the executive branch to circumvent federal Medicaid law and "waive" one or more Medicaid rules—for instance, family income can be disregarded as a qualification for Medicaid eligibility—in order to extend eligibility and pilot new services. Waivers have given states the flexibility to cover services that most private insurers generally do not cover, such as personal-attendant services in a home setting, and that may not be explicitly medical in nature, like installing wheelchair ramps in a home.

---

[16] Medicaid waivers "waive" one or more Medicaid rules in order to extend eligibility and services to children. The most common rule to be waived is the way income is calculated, wherein the waiver is based on the child's income instead of the parent's income. As Frank Thompson (2012) explains, there are two basic types of waivers for home- and community-based services: demonstrations (which derive from section 1115 of the Social Security Act) and more targeted initiatives focused on long-term supports and services (which derive from section 1915c of the Social Security Act).

The Neoliberal Welfare State **131**

For many families, obtaining a Medicaid waiver is a path to economic sta-bility, especially for parents providing care in a home setting.[17] Yet waiver programs have not matched demand, as evidenced by the fact that hundreds of thousands of families remain on waiting lists. Under regular Medicaid rules, states cannot limit participation, but waiver enrollment can be capped. As of 2017, more than 707,000 people with disabilities were on waiting lists for waivers, and they spent more than two years on average on those lists (Musumeci, Chidambaram, and Watts 2019). Lengthy waiting lists give an indication of how public assistance for long-term supports and services is highly coveted, yet many people's needs remain unmet.

Unlike means-tested programs, the Individuals with Disabilities Education Act (IDEA), passed in 1990, protects the rights of all qualifying children with disabilities, regardless of income, to receive a "free, appropriate, public edu-cation" in the "least restrictive environment." Children with disabilities are now often able to attend school and learn alongside their non-disabled peers. As part of a free and appropriate public education, eligible children are also entitled to an Individualized Education Program (IEP). Moreover, Part C of the IDEA program was designed to provide infants and toddlers who have disabilities and their families with early intervention services, such as speech therapy, occupational therapy, and family counseling.

Finally, the US tax system has also provided financial relief to families of children with disabilities through what Joshua McCabe (2018) refers to as the "fiscalization of social policy," wherein tax exemptions, deductions, credits, and allowances lower an individual's tax burden. Not surprisingly, the expan-sion of tax credits arose in the era of neoliberal austerity—when govern-ment was cutting back on traditional social assistance programs—precisely because tax credits (unlike traditional social programs) are classified as "rev-enue not collected" and do not show up as spending in budgets (McCabe 2018: 3). However, as Aerie Rimmerman (2015: 80–90) has observed, current tax law favors middle-class and wealthy families of children with disabilities who can benefit from dependency exemptions, capital expenditure deduc-tions (primarily excessive medical bills), and the Earned Income Tax Credit. Poor families do not have enough reported income to claim deductions, and instead must rely on means-tested programs for assistance.[18]

---

[17] Traditionally, Medicaid has had an "institutional bias." The 1965 law that created Medicaid and Medicare stipulates that states have an obligation to provide care in an institutional setting—such as a hospital, nursing home, or medical daycare—but coverage for home- and community-based services is still optional. Medicaid home- and community-based services waivers have been instrumental in getting around institutional bias.

[18] Means-tested social programs by definition set limits on beneficiaries' capacity to accumulate wealth. Through the years, various tax strategies have been developed to enable recipients of SSI and Medicaid to

132 Prenatal Genetic Testing, Abortion, and Disability Justice

Even though tax relief and more traditional social policies such as SSI, Medicaid, and IDEA have undoubtedly improved the lives of millions of people with disabilities and their family members, families of children with disabilities still report that many of their needs remain unmet. Some services— like respite care—are still incredibly difficult to come by. Almost half of the respondents in the 2017 FINDS survey said that government-funded services in their communities were decreasing, and one in five families have been waiting for services like Medicaid waivers for roughly ten years (Anderson et al. 2018: 9). Approximately nine out of ten families reported still having many out-of-pocket expenses related to caring for a family member with a disability, despite receiving some government-funded services, with roughly one-third (36 per cent) reporting expenses totaling $5,000 or more per year (Anderson et al. 2018: 9).

Long-term supports and services grow increasingly scarce as people with Down syndrome become adults and "fall off the cliff" when they become too old for the school system (Bagenstos 2015). Educational and therapeutic services provided under the IDEA—which can include transportation, subsidized housing, and vocational and life-skills training—are the only entitlements on which parents of children with Down syndrome can reliably depend. Most other forms of governmental assistance are means-tested or provisional. Once children leave the education system and lose their federal entitlements (between the ages of 18 and 22, depending on the state of residency), they face an underfunded, fragmented system in which few services are guaranteed as a matter of right.[19] The result is that many young adults with disabilities and their parents must figure out their eligibility and try to cobble together scarce services across scattered providers. Many vital supports and services fall through the cracks during the journey from adolescence to adulthood, and insufficient funding for long-term supports and services can be devastating for the millions of people with disabilities and their caregivers

save money without becoming ineligible for benefits. In addition to conventional special needs trusts (SNTs), ABLE accounts are an increasingly popular option. Passed in 2014, the Achieving Better Life Experience (ABLE) Act allows states to create tax-advantaged savings programs for eligible people with disabilities to cover qualified disability expenses. The money in an ABLE account (also known as 529 A savings accounts) or any interest it earns is not taxed. Account-holders can withdraw the money at any time tax free to pay for qualified disability expenses such as education, housing, transportation, employment training and support, assistive technology, personal support services, and healthcare expenses. In addition, contributions to an ABLE account do not impact on income and asset calculations for SSI or Medicaid. ABLE Acts can therefore help people with disabilities accumulate savings and maintain eligibility for means-tested public benefits. However, creating special needs trusts and/or ABLE accounts is confusing, time consuming, and costly, because setting them up requires the paid services of professional assistants (i.e. financial planners and lawyers), and there are often maintenance fees associated with the accounts. For more, see Nancy Susan Germany (2018) and Madeline Laser (2018).

[19] Transition teams are required by the federal government to prepare students who are receiving special education services for life after graduation by developing a transition plan.

who lack the means of obtaining the financial assistance they need. Across the US, estimates are that only 25 per cent of all adults with intellectual and developmental disabilities receive state-run services for community living, whereas 75 per cent receive little to none (Hewitt 2014).

For the purposes of our analysis, what we find especially concerning is how the lack of reliable financial assistance can also put economic and social pressure on women to use prenatal genetic screening technologies and terminate pregnancy following a positive result. Chris Kaposy (2018: 19) gets to the crux of the matter when he observes that "neoliberal economic policies and the dismantling of the welfare state have forced families into economic situations in which having a child with a disability seems like an overwhelming challenge." And this challenge is far from inevitable—the problem is not affordability but priority. How government spends money, and who benefits from that spending, reflect national priorities. The US government can fund programs to meet the needs of individuals with disabilities and their caregivers, but the neoliberal state chooses to pay for tax cuts for the wealthiest Americans or to fund subsidies for large corporations instead. The bottom line is that "the devaluation of the disabled life is expressed over and over again in the failure of our society to provide adequately for the disabled and their families" (Kittay 2000: 181).

Pregnant Women as Neoliberal Biocitizens

The causal story is not unidirectional, however. Neoliberalism and the routinization of prenatal genetic screening technologies go hand in hand. Neoliberal social policies indirectly put social pressure on women to use prenatal genetic screening technologies and to terminate their pregnancies following a positive result. And, once women have been socially expected to self-police as genetic screeners, the state can further justify its decision to limit care services for people with disabilities by making them financially responsible for deliberately choosing children with so-called special needs. Public policies can expand or reduce women's options and influence their private reproductive decisions; in turn, women's private reproductive choices have public consequences.

Dorothy Roberts's research on genetic technologies and biocitizenship is helpful in thinking about how neoliberal policy goals and the routinization of prenatal genetic screening are mutually reinforcing. Some scholars have celebrated the emergence of biocitizenship—a term that recognizes how genomic knowledge and data have changed the way that citizenship is imagined—for

134 Prenatal Genetic Testing, Abortion, and Disability Justice

enhancing individual autonomy and giving individuals unprecedented control over their own health and well-being at the genetic level. As Nicholas Rose (2007: 40) explains: "Our very biological life itself has entered the domain of decision and choice." Moreover, Rose views this development as an empowering one, in part, because "biology is no longer blind destiny ... it is knowable, mutable, improvable, eminently manipulable" (Rose and Novas 2005: 442). For her part, Dorothy Roberts is hesitant to uncritically embrace the idea that an increased capacity to use biotechnologies is empowering, especially when taking issues surrounding race and disability into account. Situating biocitizenship within a neoliberal context, Roberts (2010: 270–1) writes:

> In this neoliberal context, genetic testing serves as a form of privatization that some interpret as empowering individuals to manage their own health but that also makes the individual the site of governance through the self-regulation of genetic risk ... The new responsibilities imposed on individuals constitute a re-regulation that supports capital investment in market-based approaches to health care and other social needs, while state investment in public resources shrinks. The view of biocitizenship as all choice and freedom ignores how state policies and corporate power make individuals responsible for managing their own health because of a lack of public support.

In other words, biocitizenship may give individuals access to more information and an increased level of control over their own health and well-being, but biocitizenship simultaneously offloads responsibility for health onto individuals, who are expected to self-manage and regulate risk.

Looking specifically at reprogenetic technologies, Roberts acknowledges that most women are not directly coerced or forced to use prenatal genetic screening technologies. Nevertheless, indirect economic and social pressures wrought by neoliberalism have nevertheless tasked them with the biocivic responsibility of ensuring the genetic and economic fitness of future citizens. As a result, women are increasingly expected to self-regulate genetic risk and produce socially desirable, economically self-reliant offspring as part of their duty to act as good biocitizens who make "the 'right' genetic decisions."[20] In a neoliberal landscape, women who make reproductive choices that cause extra resources to be needed are likely to be seen as having made the "wrong" choice (Roberts 2011: 217).

---

[20] Similarly, Silja Samerski (2009: 738) argues that modern prenatal care treats pregnant women not as expectant mothers but as "managers of fetal risk profiles."

Roberts (2011: 221) is concerned that making the wrong genetic choice then "disqualifies biocitizens from claiming public support," thereby allowing the neoliberal state to "escape public responsibility for disability-related needs." She explains the implications, noting that, "in the future, the government may rely on the expectation that all pregnant women will undergo genetic testing to justify not only its refusal to support the care of disabled children, but also its denial of broader claims for the public provision of healthcare" (Roberts 2011: 221). Roberts also predicts that, by essentially privatizing the social responsibility of addressing systemic inequalities, the use of these reprogenetic technologies will exacerbate already existing injustices. "Like the punishment of minority women's childbearing," she writes, "reprogenetics is linked to the elimination of the welfare state and support for private remedies for illness and disease" (Roberts 2005: 1355). The broader takeaway is that biocitizenship reinforces neoliberal policy goals by making structural inequalities related to racism and ableism—including the social determinants of adverse health outcomes—seem like predominantly genetic issues that should be managed at the individual, molecular level instead of under the collective purview of the state. Relatedly, if biocitizens see it as their primary aim to purchase and use pharmaceuticals, reproductive technologies, and genetic tests privately to manage genetic risk and health outcomes, they may be less inclined to make demands for structural social and political changes.

On the face of it, then, prenatal genetic screening technologies seem to expand pregnant women's options, but the story is not so simple. The expansion of choice has come hand in hand with the privatized financial responsibility for the consequences of those choices. Before prenatal screening, having a child with a condition like Down syndrome was seen as a matter of chance or a roll of the genetic dice. Whether or not a person gave birth to a child with a genetic impairment was considered a matter of fate. With the routinization of prenatal genetic screening, wherein prospective parents can learn more genetic information about their fetus, having a child with Down syndrome is now considered a matter of choice. The rhetoric of choice lends itself to a neoliberal framework of personal responsibility. From this perspective, the material hardships that may arise from the personal decision to continue a pregnancy with a fetus with Down syndrome are considered politically unimportant, because parents presumably volunteered for the financial struggles when they knowingly signed up to parent a child with a genetic impairment. In this way, the shift from chance to choice undermines claims to public assistance.

The political implications of this shift cannot be overstated. Dena Davis (2010) captures its corrosive effect on political solidarity. Davis argues that society becomes less willing to pay for the supports and services that people with genetic impairments need to flourish, as genetic impairments come to be seen as "avoidable mistakes" rather than "the luck of the draw." Prospective parents knew what they were signing up for, so to speak, and must therefore take on the consequences of their fully informed, voluntary decision (Davis 2010: 19). Davis (2010: 19–20) candidly admits that the shift from chance to choice even changed the way that she personally views parenthood. "Twenty years ago, seeing a woman in the supermarket with a child who has Down syndrome, my immediate reactions were sympathy and a sense that that woman could be me. Now that testing for Down syndrome is virtually universal in the United States, when I see such a mother and child I am more likely to wonder why she didn't get tested." Hence, the shift from chance to choice has eroded a sense of linked fate or solidarity. Instead of thinking "that woman could be me" and is therefore deserving of support to combat the expenses that follow the whims of the genetic lottery, Davis now thinks in terms of individual choice and personal accountability. This neoliberal framing makes the refusal of prenatal screening technologies seem irresponsible or irrational, and the informed choice voluntarily to raise a child with Down syndrome is reduced to an expensive consumer preference.

Davis is not alone in this way of thinking. The neoliberal logic of personal responsibility has infiltrated bioethical academic discussions. For example, Eric Rakowski (2002: 1398) argues that parents who "intentionally bear children entitled to redress, in the form of additional resources, more expensive education, or special educational opportunities," should be "personally liable for the increased costs associated with their choices." That is, parents should bear the cost of raising and caring for disabled children whom they deliberately chose to have when they could have chosen a different outcome, such as terminating and trying to conceive again. In this way, the choice to carry and raise a disabled child is equated with an expensive lifestyle choice, one that places onus on parents to incur the costs of care on their own.

This individualization of responsibility is not limited to academic debate. In her study of prenatal genetic screening technologies, Jennifer Denbow (2020) importantly analyzes legislative records, including floor debates and committee hearings, in several states that recently enacted so-called prenatal non-discrimination acts. In doing so, she demonstrates how the neoliberal individualization of responsibility has placed the burden for structural economic and political concerns on the shoulders of individual parents while largely ignoring the government's own lack of funding of social services

The Neoliberal Welfare State **137**

for people with disabilities. Denbow provides the following testimony of a mother of a child with Down syndrome, Beth Nodland, who chose to continue a pregnancy following a positive result:

> I want to read to you some direct responses to me that I get on national forums … "The difference with the downs is that it is preventable. The amniocentesis after 35 pretty much eliminates the potential. Yet for the people who refuse abortion [they] should be made responsible for the lifelong up keep of these kids they will bring into the world. Since there is … choice there is no excuse for blatant neglect or [ir]responsibility …" Another one is, "All is well and good for people who can afford to have this type of child, but for the people who do not have the resources the American taxpayer, pays and pays and pays and pays until death do them part …" (quoted in Denbow 2020)

These types of negative public reactions to the choice of knowingly giving birth to a child with Down syndrome are fairly common. In a neoliberal society fixated on slashing social services, people with disabilities are frequently typecast as financially burdensome individuals who use up limited taxpayer dollars. Prospective parents who opt out of testing altogether, or who knowingly bring a genetically impaired child into the world, are then blamed for their decisions and expected to bear all costs by themselves with little regard for the ableist arrangement of affairs that makes raising a disabled child so costly in the first place.

At the same time that parents have been expected to take on more costs on their own, the government has been rebalancing public money away from social policies designed for people with disabilities and toward funding research and the clinical use of commercially driven prenatal genetic screening programs.[21] Several biotech labs have banded together to form the Coalition for Access to Prenatal Screening (CAPS), which lobbies state legislatures and Medicaid commissioners to have their state programs reimburse NIPT. Their efforts have paid off. As of 2021, all but five states and the District of Columbia cover NIPT (twenty states provide Medicaid reimbursement for all women, and twenty-five states cover expenses for "high-risk" women).[22] Many state-run prenatal screening programs, such as the one in California,

---

[21] In 1988, Congress budgeted $3 billion over fifteen years to map and sequence the human genome. These spending priorities signal the state's priorities. As Adrienne Asch (2003: 336) explains: "Instead of developing therapies or treatments for most of the genetic conditions for which the specific gene is known, researchers developed prenatal tests and embryo selection techniques that inform prospective parents about future children, but do nothing for anyone now living with a genetic condition."

[22] For up-to-date information about insurance coverage, see Coalition for Access to Prenatal Screening (2022).

138 Prenatal Genetic Testing, Abortion, and Disability Justice

are explicitly justified in terms of cost containment. According to the logic, spending tax money on prenatal screening services allows individuals to discover and terminate the impairment *in utero*, and, as a result, large savings will be generated by reducing the costs of public services that would otherwise have been used to care for affected individuals down the line.

To be clear, we are not critical of measures to equalize access to healthcare services, but we question whether public financial support for detecting and preventing impairment before birth siphons away resources that would otherwise be spent to improve the social situation of people with genetic impairments who currently exist in our world. We cannot help but ask: do state-supported prenatal genetic screening programs exist to give more women more reproductive choices? Or, as Laura Hershey (1994: 31) questioned decades ago, are government-funded prenatal screening programs "primarily for the benefit of the society unwilling to support disability-related needs?"

From the Limited Neoliberal State to the Supportive State

So far, we have tried to demonstrate how neoliberal social policies constrain women's reproductive options in practice, and how the routinization of prenatal screening and increased rates of selective abortion conversely let the neoliberal state dodge responsibility for attending to citizens' disability-related needs. What is a better alternative to the current state of affairs, and why should we pursue it? In our view, feminist legal scholars are well situated to consider alternatives, since they have long questioned how the costs of care for dependants can be more justly shared so that women do not have to bear the extraordinary burdens of doing it alone, invisibly, and uncompensated in the private sphere. Many have persuasively argued that a differently structured political system that publicly distributes costs related to human development and caregiving—one with paid family-leave policies, for example, or subsidized childcare—might enable a more caring form of liberalism amendable to the pursuit for social justice.

Feminist legal theorists have offered several visions of policy reform grounded in different normative justifications for change. In this section, we compare the work of Martha Fineman and Maxine Eichner in order to endorse the latter. Both Fineman and Eichner pursue the same goal by championing a responsive and supportive state that actively invests in care and human development. However, they ground their arguments in different normative rationales. Fineman advances the idea that caring for children is performing a "public good" that entitles parents to public support.[23] According to this logic, if the benefits of well-nurtured children are public, then some of the costs of childcare should be broadly shared by society. According to our reading, Fineman's call for a responsive state reduces normative considerations to a cost–benefit analysis that does not work well in the case of children with intellectual and developmental disabilities. Eichner, on the other hand, calls for a supportive state that actively values caretaking and human development on the grounds that it follows through on liberalism's commitment to support the dignity and autonomy of its citizens. Even though Eichner only briefly discusses disability, we build from the guiding principles that she develops in order to think about the state's responsibility for ensuring the well-being of disabled citizens and their family members.

To begin, in *The Autonomy Myth: A Theory of Dependency*, Martha Fineman (2004: 35) works from the premise that all humans are vulnerable, experience dependency, and need care at some points in their lives, especially as children, in old age, and when they experience temporary or permanent impairment. Moreover, this inherent need for care gives rise to a secondary form of dependency experienced by caretakers. To the extent that caretakers are precluded from engaging fully in wage labor and social life in order to fulfill their care obligations, they develop a "derivative dependency" caused by their own need for goods and resources (Fineman 2004: 35). She suggests that the dominant liberal ideology of autonomy treats both types of dependency as private matters with which the state has no legitimate concern. Consequently, society is structured as though the need to give and receive care is tangential, rather than central, to political life. In practice, those who bear the caretaking burden for dependants—primarily women in our society—assume the costs of care work to their own detriment (Fineman 2004: 37).

As an alternative, Fineman articulates a theory of collective responsibility for childcare by conceiving of children as public goods. She argues that the state and market rely on family labor by delegating the work of rearing future citizens and workers to mothers. As she explains: "Without aggregate caretaking there could be no society, so we might say that it is caretaking labor that produces and reproduces society. Caretaking labor provides the citizens, the workers, the voters, the consumers, the students, and others who populate society and its institutions" (Fineman 2004: 48). As a result, parents have "a right to be compensated for their services" and their "society-preserving labor" (Fineman 2004: 49). Failure to compensate for childrearing

---

[23] See also Nancy Folbre (1994) and Janet Gornick and Marcia Meyers (2008).

140 Prenatal Genetic Testing, Abortion, and Disability Justice

services would constitute a form of free-riding on the caring labor of families, especially mothers. Hence, measures such as paid parental leave and public childcare subsidies resolve the free-rider problem by reducing the penalties associated with childcare labor, which, as Fineman argues, has broad social benefits.

Fineman's theory is attractive insofar as it explains how public support for children's care is fair to non-parents. Distributing the costs of childrearing broadly among all individuals who pay taxes, rather than expecting parents to bear all the costs of childrearing alone, is politically legitimate, because non-parents would otherwise be free-riding off the labors of those who are raising the next generation of citizens, who will then in turn pay taxes and sustain the survival and well-being of the older generation. She thus distinguishes the choice to parent from an expensive lifestyle choice by drawing attention to the ways in which parenting contributes to the public welfare. In doing so, she draws attention to social interdependence and bolsters claims in favor of increased funding for measures such as public education, paid parental leave, and childcare subsidies.

Yet Fineman's contention that parents are owed compensation because the wider society benefits from their caretaking efforts raises conceptual difficulties in the case of many children with intellectual and developmental disabilities. This theoretical framework cannot easily answer the following questions: Are parents of children with disabilities deserving of the full range of benefits available only if their children can prove their economic worth? Why do we have a collective responsibility to care for disabled children who may never grow up to return the favor?

To step back, some people with intellectual and developmental disabilities like Down syndrome can and do participate in the paid workforce. This has not always been the case. In the past, employment for young adults with intellectual and developmental disabilities was rarely seen as an option, and, to the extent that it was, people with disabilities were placed in sheltered workshops where workers were routinely paid subminimum wage.[24] Thanks to the tireless efforts of disability rights activists who have demanded integration into broader society, paid and productive employment in mainstream jobs with competitive wages is increasingly possible, although still rare. Sadly, owing to pervasive discrimination in education and employment, only 19 percent of working-aged adults with a disability were employed in 2021,

---

[24] See the Section 14(c) provision of the Fair Labor Standards Act (FLSA) for minimum wage exemptions.

The Neoliberal Welfare State **141**

compared to 63 percent of people without disabilities (US Bureau of Labor Statistics 2022b).[25]

That said, even if every possible accommodation was put in place to make community integrated employment a reality—for instance, if anti-discrimination laws were effectively enforced, the physical accessibility of workplaces was improved, and training and vocational rehabilitation programs were adequately funded and accessible to all—some people with intellectual and developmental disabilities may never be capable of engaging in wage labor, paying taxes, or serving as soldiers. Some may not even live long enough to reach adulthood.[26] When children are considered public goods, therefore, what does this mean for people with disabilities who can never contribute to society (at least not in conventional economic ways), even after every possible accommodation is made available to them? Are they a waste of taxpayers' investments? Relatedly, if caretakers deserve subsidies based on the net economic and social benefits that their children bring to society, are parents of children with disabilities owed any public support?

If society's obligation publicly to support care does not arise because well-raised children economically benefit the rest of us, on what grounds is it legitimate to distribute the costs of caring for children with disabilities? Maxine Eichner argues that a liberal state should partially subsidize care responsibilities in order to follow through on one of liberalism's core commitments: promoting personal autonomy and human dignity. In *The Supportive State: Families, Government, and America's Political Ideals*, Eichner (2010: 52) persuasively argues that the liberal state has an active "responsibility to support caretaking and human development." To make her case, she begins by differentiating her strand of liberalism from that of John Rawls. According to her reading, Rawls fails to take the life cycle, human dependency, and the need to give and receive care into account. This glaring omission ignores the reality that most people spend significant periods of their lives dependent on others and in need of care, especially in infancy, old age, and in periods of illness and disability. Eichner argues that liberalism must be amended to acknowledge the reality of human dependency, suggesting that this dependency brings caretaking and human development to the foreground as central political goods.

---

[25] According to Kelsey Bush and Marc Tassé (2017), roughly 16% of working-age adults with Down syndrome reported working in community-based employment for the years 2011–13.

[26] The mortality rate for infants with Down syndrome is over eight times the overall infant mortality rate. During the first year of life, heart and respiratory conditions are the most frequent causes of death in infants with Down syndrome (Goldman, Urbano, and Hodapp 2011).

142 Prenatal Genetic Testing, Abortion, and Disability Justice

Expanding liberalism to accommodate caregiving seriously reorients how dominant liberal values should be conceived. In particular, autonomy cannot be equated with negative rights where the state only protects an individual's freedom to be left alone. According to Eichner, the liberal commitment to non-interference and value neutrality limits the role of the state to an unhealthy degree. Currently, state support is provided only when parents "fail" to provide their children with adequate levels of food and shelter on their own (Eichner 2010: 72). In the absence of active state support, dependency-related care needs too frequently remain unmet, harming the well-being of dependent citizens and undermining their dignity. Moreover, even if care needs are effectively met within the family, caretaking responsibilities disproportionately land on female caregivers, often to their detriment.

Moving beyond a restrained state, while not discarding the liberal commitment to privacy altogether, Eichner argues that liberalism's commitment to ensure that all its citizens have the means and opportunities to live dignified lives can be achieved by making caretaking a first-order good. By reworking Rawls to attend to the inevitability of dependency, Eichner develops the theoretical underpinnings for a supportive state that plays a formative role in fostering human dignity and autonomy. Rather than standing back while citizens exercise their own choices and intervening only to solve conflicts, the supportive state promotes positive rights and creates what Eichner (2010: 49) refers to as "complex systems of nurturance." She explains:

> Incorporating dependency into our understanding of human relations ... transforms the focus of the liberal project: respect for human dignity now demands more than the protection of individual rights and freedoms. It also requires that the state actively support individuals in receiving the caretaking and conditions for human development necessary for them to become responsible, self-directing citizens. This responsibility of the state to support caretaking and human development becomes every bit as fundamental as its responsibility to establish an adequate police force and military in order to safeguard citizens' individual rights. (Eichner 2010: 52)

Eichner envisions the state's responsibility as conjunctive (rather than residual) with that of the family. In her view, the state should play a greater role in regulating laws and structuring institutions to accommodate and value care work rather than in directly providing the care itself, which is best left to the discretion of the family. In her words, families should "bear responsibility for the day-to-day caring for ... children and for meeting

The Neoliberal Welfare State **143**

other dependency needs," while "the state bears the responsibility for structuring societal institutions in ways that help families meet their caretaking needs and promote adequate human development" (Eichner 2010: 11–12). The state and family complement each other. The supportive state concerns itself with the design of social scaffolding that facilitates caretaking (that is, subsidies to make daycare affordable, paid parental leave, a legal cap on mandatory work hours, and making it illegal to fire parents who refuse to work overtime), while parents actually provide hands-on care and make intimate decisions about care arrangements at the ground level of the family unit.

The implications of Eichner's argument for state–family relations are profound. In Eichner's account, the state is not always an impediment to free choice. Rather, it can be a force for good when it protects citizens against the worst abuses of capitalism and other structures of social inequality that diminish opportunities to form and execute choices. "Where early liberals saw the threat to autonomy as coming from the state," Eichner (2010: 64) argues, "much of today's threats of encroachment on decision making come from the market." In order to prevent lives from being completely beholden to market forces, Eichner advocates policies that make work–life balance more manageable. While open to different policy proposals, she insists that the state has a basic obligation to arrange institutions in such a way that families can meet the physical, mental, and emotional needs of children and other dependants while avoiding impoverishment and excessive social and economic hardship.

With these guiding principles in place, we argue that the supportive state model would better promote institutional structures that enable parents of children with disabilities to meet their caretaking obligations and still carry out their other life projects and goals, including work, recreation, and other social activities.

Policy Implications

People with intellectual and developmental disabilities often need community-based long-term supports and services to assist them in a home setting across the life cycle. As this chapter has already shown, the current system is inadequate and disorganized. The tattered state-by-state patchwork is in dire need of a drastic overhaul. Even though the main source of public funding for long-term supports and services has come from Medicaid, the fact of the matter is that it is far from an entitlement, since

Medicaid was designed as a means-tested public assistance program. Unlike Social Security and Medicare, which are social insurance programs funded by payroll taxes, individuals who qualify for Medicaid must usually have low incomes and few assets, although income and asset tests vary from state to state. For many who need long-term supports and services, Medicaid kicks in only at the point of financial ruin. Moreover, eligibility and benefits are specific to each state, which means that families often feel limited in their ability to move across state lines once they have been able to secure services. Moving to a new state means reapplying for benefits, potentially becoming ineligible, going back to the bottom of lengthy waiting lists, and/or losing access to coverage for specific services. In other cases, families desperate for coverage might feel forced to uproot and relocate in search of more generous benefits, with no guarantee that their disabled child will qualify for coverage once they establish residency in a new state.[27] In addition, home- and community-based services are still optional, and, even though waiver programs can rebalance payments away from institutional care, waivers are optional services that are awarded for limited periods with no assurance of reauthorization. The optional nature of home- and community-based services makes them one of the first places state policymakers look to make cuts when faced with budget shortfalls. Medicaid has been a lifeline for thousands of families that have children with Down syndrome and other types of impairments, but ultimately coverage is not stable, universal, or equitable.

In order to guarantee coverage for everyone who needs it and standardize eligibility and benefits across states, we propose turning the current patchwork of scattered programs into a compulsory federal insurance program that provides universal coverage for home- and community-based care. Parents of children with disabilities should have guaranteed access to skilled childcare, respite care, social workers, and case management, among other services. Long-term support in a home setting should be widely accessible and affordable for all in need, for the sake of both those receiving and those providing care. People with disabilities and their families deserve to live within their communities with some measure of dignity. Ideally, the program would operate under a person-centered self-directed services model. Rather than financing a prescribed set of services from the top down, beneficiaries would instead be given an individualized budget (through a cash benefit or some type of voucher system), allowing them to make their own

---

[27] Moving across state lines in the hopes of qualifying for a Medicaid waiver has become so common that such families are now colloquially referred to as "waiver migrants" (Serres and Howatt 2019).

The Neoliberal Welfare State   **145**

spending decisions about which goods and services would make their lives more livable.[28]

Currently, only a handful of countries have adopted a public social insurance approach to long-term care, including Japan, Germany, Luxembourg, Sweden, Denmark, and South Korea. Although these systems differ, they are financed through broad-based social contributions, typically through employee payroll taxes, often matched by employer contributions. Coverage is universal, and participation is mandatory (Feng and Glinskaya 2020; Zeng et al. 2020). Within the US, Washington state passed the first long-term care social-insurance program in 2019, called the Long-Term Care Trust Act. It is funded by a small payroll tax.[29] However, coverage is not universal, since only Washington residents who are 18 or older who have paid payroll taxes for a required amount of time are eligible.[30] In any case, the federal government can find examples at the international and state level when thinking about how to best design its own program.

Recent political efforts have been made to move insurance for long-term supports and services from a public assistance program to a federal social insurance entitlement, but to no avail. In 2010, Congress passed the Community Living Assistance Services and Supports (CLASS) Act as part of the Affordable Care Act, creating a national program of voluntary long-term care insurance. However, the Obama administration never implemented the law and ultimately decided to abandon it in the face of political opposition.[31] Our hope is that one day Congress will resurrect something comparable to the CLASS Act that will be mandatory and provide universal coverage. As Judith Feder (2015) has argued, coverage for long-term care has been the "missing piece" of the Social Security Amendments of 1965. Since that time, Medicaid has essentially stepped in as the primary funding source by default rather than design. It is high time that we think about how to fill this "missing piece" with a more comprehensive public program that benefits all who need it.

Ultimately, improvements to our system of home- and community-based long-term supports and services would have many beneficiaries beyond families of children with disabilities, most notably the elderly. Seniors are the largest consumers of long-term supports and services, and the majority of

---

[28] Wisconsin's "Include, Respect, I Self-Direct" (IRIS) program and California's "Self-Determination Program" (SDP) offer examples of how effectively to implement self-directed community-based long-term supports and services within the Medicaid program.

[29] The benefits will initially be funded with a payroll tax of 0.58 for employees, which begins in 2022 and starts paying benefits in 2025.

[30] The work requirement effectively exempts children and many adults with disabilities who work less than ten hours a week. However, the new law has called for a study of whether to include those who become disabled before they turn 18.

[31] CLASS was formally repealed in the American Taxpayer Relief Act of 2012.

146 Prenatal Genetic Testing, Abortion, and Disability Justice

them would prefer to age in place and live at home rather than be transferred into a nursing home facility (Bennett and Vasold 2018). A more robust federal investment would also benefit paid providers of in-home long-term care, referred to as personal care attendants or home health aides, who are overwhelmingly women of color.[32] Medicaid's low reimbursement rates have created a workforce shortage in this industry. In-home care work has rapidly become the most in-demand and fastest growing occupation in the US largely in response to our growing elderly population. Nevertheless, the median hourly wage for these care workers was $13.02 in 2020, at the poverty line for a family of four (US Bureau of Labor Statistics 2022a). These jobs are so poorly paid that it is hard to keep workers in them.[33] As a result, there are few incentives for home health workers with the requisite training and experience to serve in a home setting instead of taking higher-paying hospital-based jobs (Foster, Agrawal, and Davis 2019: 989). Even when they are available for hire, workers who are exhausted and drained from working long hours or multiple jobs may be more likely to make mistakes or to have lower tolerance for stressful situations. Constant turnover is also frustrating and emotionally taxing. If parents have constantly to train new home health aides, or feel that they cannot entrust their children to skilled and committed personal-care attendants who will provide quality care for the long haul, some find it easier to throw in the towel and provide care themselves. Hence, an overhaul to our home- and community-based long-term care system supports and services is sorely needed for various stakeholders.

Conclusion

Prospective parents who are considering whether or not to use prenatal screening technologies and what to do following a positive result for Down syndrome are doing so in a neoliberal economic context that privatizes responsibility for the care of children with disabilities. Wealthy parents might feel confident enough to choose to carry a fetus with Down syndrome to term without fearing the threat of financial ruin, should they desire to do so, but

---

[32] Home health aides and personal care attendants are disproportionately women of color and immigrants, many of whom have not received a formal education beyond high school (Campbell 2018).

[33] The devaluing of the profession, and the persistent low wages, has deep roots in racism and historical exploitation of Black women's domestic labor. Domestic workers, including home health aides, were excluded from the minimum wage and overtime work protections in the Fair Labor Standards Act (FLSA) that Congress enacted as part of the New Deal in the 1930s. In fact, home health aides were not legally required to be paid the federal minimum wage until 2015. For a deeper discussion of systemic racism and the devaluation of paid domestic care work, see Juan Perea (2011).

poorer ones might see the prospect of having a child with a disability as an unrealistic and unaffordable decision. When government programs and the social safety net are slashed in favor of neoliberal, free-market principles, an attendant consequence is that "it may be poor women of color, not affluent White women, who are most compelled to use prenatal genetic screening technologies" (Roberts and Jesudason 2013: 317). The broader takeaway is that excessive economic pressures constitute a barrier to reproductive autonomy for women living at or near poverty. Of course, no choice is made in isolation, and we all face resource constraints as we make various decisions, but reproductive options made under economic duress give prenatal screening the veneer of choice when in actuality the option to raise a child with Down syndrome with dignity is a class privilege rather than a social right.

A federal long-term care insurance program—one that is universal rather than means-tested—has the potential to redress the financial hardships that are heaped on families of children with disabilities. As a result, the knowledge that there are adequate supports available may enhance the ability of some pregnant women to imagine the possibility of raising a child with Down syndrome without worrying that such a decision might resemble the choice to take a vow of poverty. In this way, the state has a vital role to play in constructing the social scaffolding that provides women with the means to achieve self-determination in reproduction.

References

Alstott, Anne (2015). "Neoliberalism in US Family Law: Negative Liberty and Laissez-Faire Markets in the Minimal State," *Law and Contemporary Problems*, 77/2: 25–42.

Anderson, L., et al. (2018). *Family and Individual Needs for Disability Supports: Community Report 2017*. Minneapolis, MN: Research and Training Center on Community Living, University of Minnesota, http://thearc.org/wp–content/uploads/2019/07/FINDS_report–2017–FINAL–VERSION.pdf.

Asch, Adrienne (2003). "Disability Equality and Prenatal Testing: Contradictory or Compatible?," *Florida State University Law Review*, 30/2: 315–41.

Bagenstos, Samuel (2015). "The Disability Cliff," *Democracy*, 35: 55–67.

Bennett, Joanne, and Kerri Vasold (2018). *2018 Home and Community Preferences: A National Survey of Adults Ages 18-Plus*. Washington: AARP Research, https://www.aarp.org/research/topics/community/info–2018/2018–home–community–preference.html.

Boulet, Sheree L., et al. (2008). "Health Care Expenditures for Infants and Young Children with Down Syndrome in a Privately Insured Population," *Journal of Pediatrics*, 153/2: 241–6.

Brown, Lydia (2018). "Legal Ableism, Interrupted: Developing Tort Law and Policy Alternatives to Wrongful Birth and Wrongful Life Claims," *Disability Studies Quarterly*, 33/2.

Bumiller, Kristin (2013). "Caring for Autism: Toward a More Responsive State," in Joyce Davidson and Michael Orsini (ed), *Worlds of Autism: Across the Spectrum of Neurological Difference*. Minneapolis, MN: University of Minnesota Press, 143–68.

Bush, Kelsey, and Marc Tassé (2017). "Employment and Choice-Making for Adults with Intellectual Disability, Autism, and Down Syndrome," *Research in Developmental Disabilities*, 65: 23–34.

Campbell, Stephen (2018). *US Home Care Workers: Key Facts*. Bronx, NY: PHI, https://phinational.org/resource/u-s-home-care-workers-key-facts-2018/.

Coalition for Access to Prenatal Screening (2022). *Coverage Scorecards*. Washington: Coalition for Access to Prenatal Screening, https://capsprenatal.com/coverage-scorecards/.

Cooper, Melinda (2017). *Family Values: Between Neoliberalism and the New Social Conservatism*. New York: Zone Books.

Daily Mail (2012). "Victory for Couple who Said they 'Would Have Aborted Daughter if they Knew she had Down's Syndrome' as Jury Forces Hospital to Pay $2.9 Million Following Botched Test," March 11, https://www.dailymail.co.uk/news/article-2113342/Deborah-Ariel-Levy-Portland-couple-wins-case-Legacy-Heath-wrongful-birth-daughter-born-Down-syndrome.html.

Davis, Dena (2010). *Genetic Dilemmas: Reproductive Technology, Parental Choices, and Children's Futures*. 2nd edn. Oxford: Oxford University Press.

Denbow, Jennifer (2020). "Prenatal Nondiscrimination Laws: Disability, Social Conservatism, and the Political Economy of Genetic Screening," *Disability Studies Quarterly*, 40/4.

Dixon, Darrin (2008). "Informed Consent or Institutionalized Eugenics? How the Medical Profession Encourages Abortion of Fetuses with Down Syndrome," *Issues in Law and Medicine*, 24/1: 3–59.

Eichner, Maxine (2010). *The Supportive State: Families, Government, and America's Political Ideals*. Oxford: Oxford University Press.

Eichner, Maxine (2017). "The Privatized American Family," *Notre Dame Law Review*, 93/1: 213–66.

Engster, Daniel (2010). "The Place of Parenting within a Liberal Theory of Justice: The Private Parenting Model, Parental Licenses, or Public Parenting Support?" *Social Theory and Practice* 36(2): 233–62.

Engster, Daniel. (2015). *Justice, Care, and the Welfare State*. Oxford: Oxford University Press.

Feder, Judith (2015). "The Missing Piece: Medicare, Medicaid, and Long-Term Care," in Alan Cohen et al. (eds), *Medicare and Medicaid at 50: America's Entitlement Programs in the Age of Affordable Care*. Oxford: Oxford University Press, 253–72.

Feng, Zhanlian, and Elena Glinskaya (2020). "Aiming Higher: Advancing Public Social Insurance for Long-Term Care to Meet the Global Aging Challenge," *International Journal of Health Policy and Management*, 9/8: 356–9.

Fineman, Martha (2004). *The Autonomy Myth: A Theory of Dependency*. New York: New Press.

Folbre, Nancy (1994). "Children as Public Goods," *American Economic Review*, 84/2: 86–90.

Foster, Carolyn, Rishi Agrawal, and Matthew Davis (2019). "Home Health Care for Children with Medical Complexity: Workforce Gaps, Policy, and Future Directions," *Health Affairs*, 38/6: 987–93.

Germany, Nancy Susan (2018). "Disability, Poverty, and the Policy behind the ABLE Act," *NAELA Journal*, 14/2: 81–98.

Goldman, Sharon Ellen, Richard Urbano, and R. M. Hodapp (2011). "Determining the Amount, Timing and Causes of Mortality among Infants with Down Syndrome," *Journal of Intellectual Disability Research*, 55/1: 85–94.

Gornick, Janet, and Marcia Meyers (2008). "Creating Gender Egalitarian Societies: An Agenda for Reform," *Politics and Society*, 36/3: 313–49.

Green, Aimee (2012). "Jury Awards Nearly $3 Million to Portland-Area Couple in 'Wrongful Birth' Lawsuit against Legacy Health," *Oregonian*, March 9, <https://www.oregonlive.com/portland/2012/03/jury_rules_in_portland–area_co.html>

Harbach, Meredith Johnson (2019). "Childcare, Vulnerability, and Resilience," *Yale Law and Policy Review*, 37/2: 459–526.

Harvey, David (2007). *A Brief History of Neoliberalism*. Oxford: Oxford University Press.

Hensel, Wendy (2005). "The Disabling Impact of Wrongful Birth and Wrongful Life Actions," *Harvard Civil Rights–Civil Liberties Law Review*, 40/1: 141–95.

Hershey, Laura (1994). "Choosing Disability," *Ms Magazine* (July–August), 26–32.

Hewitt, Amy (2014). "Embracing Complexity: Community Inclusion, Participation, and Citizenship," *Intellectual and Developmental Disabilities*, 52/6: 475–95.

Himmelstein, David, et al. (2019). "Medical Bankruptcy: Still Common after the Affordable Care Act," *American Journal of Public Health*, 109/3: 431–3.

Jerman, Jenna, Rachel Jones, and Tsuyoshi Onda (2016). *Characteristics of US Abortion Patients in 2014 and Changes since 2008*. New York: Guttmacher Institute, https://www.guttmacher.org/report/characteristics–us–abortion–patients–2014.

Kageleiry, A., et al. (2017). "Out-of-Pocket Medical Costs and Third-Party Healthcare Costs for Children with Down Syndrome," *American Journal of Medical Genetics Part A*, 173: 627–37.

Kaposy, Chris (2018). *Choosing Down Syndrome: Ethics and New Prenatal Testing Technologies*. Cambridge, MA: MIT Press.

Kittay, Eva Feder, with Leo Kittay (2000). "On the Expressivity and Ethics of Selective Abortion for Disability: Conversations with my Son," in Erik Parens and Adrienne Asch (eds), *Prenatal Testing and Disability Rights*. Washington: Georgetown University Press, 165–95.

Laser, Madeline (2018). "A Run for your Money: Are Able Accounts Truly an Innovative, User Friendly Financial Savings Tool for the Broad Spectrum of Disabled Americans," *Touro Law Review*, 34/3: 789–822.

McCabe, Joshua (2018). *The Fiscalization of Social Policy: How Taxpayers Trumped Children in the Fight against Child Poverty*. Oxford: Oxford University Press.

McCluskey, Martha (2003). "Efficiency and Social Citizenship: Challenging the Neoliberal Attack on the Welfare State", *Indiana Law Journal*, 78/2: 783–876.

Mitchell, David, and Sharon Snyder (2015). *The Biopolitics of Disability: Neoliberalism, Ablenationalism, and Peripheral Embodiment*. Ann Arbor, MI: University of Michigan Press.

Mitra, Sophie, et al. (2017). "Extra Costs of Living with a Disability: A Review and Agenda for Research," *Disability and Health Journal*, 10/4: 475–84.

Murdoch, Blake, et al. (2017). "Non-Invasive Prenatal Testing and the Unveiling of an Impaired Translation Process", *Journal of Obstetrics and Gynaecology Canada*, 39/1: 10–17.

Musumeci, Marybeth, and Priya Chidambaram (2019). *Medicaid's Role for Children with Special Health Care Needs: A Look at Eligibility, Services, and Spending*. Washington: Kaiser Family Foundation, http://files.kff.org/attachment/Medicaid's-Role-for-Children-with-Special-Health-Care-Needs-A-Look-at-Eligibility,-Services-and-Spending.

Musumeci, Marybeth, Priya Chidambaram, and Molly O'Malley Watts (2019). *Key Questions about Medicaid Home and Community-Based Services Waiver Waiting Lists*. Washington: Kaiser Family Foundation, https://www.kff.org/medicaid/issue-brief/key-questions-about-medicaid-home-and-community-based-services-waiver-waiting-lists/.

OECD (2021). *Public Spending on Childcare and Early Education*. Paris: OECD Publishing, at https://www.oecd.org/els/soc/PF3_1_Public_spending_on_childcare_and_early_education.pdf.

OECD (2022a). "Child Disability", in *Family Database*. Paris: OECD Publishing, https://www.oecd.org/els/family/CO1%209%20Child%20disability%20FINAL.pdf.

OECD (2022b). *Poverty Rate (indicator)*. Paris: OECD Publishing, https://data.oecd.org/inequality/poverty-rate.htm.

Parish, Susan (2006). "Juggling and Struggling: A Preliminary Work–Life Study of Mothers with Adolescents who have Developmental Disabilities," *Intellectual and Developmental Disabilities*, 44/6: 393–404.

Parish, Susan, et al. (2010). "Economic Implications of Caregiving at Midlife: Comparing Parents with and without Children who have Developmental Disabilities," *Intellectual and Developmental Disabilities*, 42/6: 413–26.

Perea, Juan (2011). "The Echoes of Slavery: Recognizing the Racist Origins of the Agricultural and Domestic Worker Exclusion from the National Labor Relations Act," *Ohio State Law Journal*, 72/1: 95–138.

Pergament, Deborah, and Katie Ilijic (2014). "The Legal Past, Present and Future of Prenatal Genetic Testing: Professional Liability and Other Legal Challenges Affecting Patient Access to Services," *Journal of Clinical Medicine*, 3/4: 1437–65.

Rakowski, Eric (2002). "Who Should Pay for Bad Genes?," *California Law Review*, 90/5: 1345–1413.

Rapp, Rayna (1999). *Testing Women, Testing the Fetus: The Social Impact of Amniocentesis in America*. New York: Routledge.

Rapp, Rayna, and Faye Ginsburg (2001). "Enabling Disability: Rewriting Kinship, Reimagining Citizenship," *Public Culture*, 13/3: 533–56.

Rimmerman, Arie (2015). *Family Policy and Disability*. Cambridge: Cambridge University Press.

Roberts, Dorothy (2005). "Privatization and Punishment in the New Age of Reprogenetics," *Emory Law Journal*, 54/3: 1343–60.

Roberts, Dorothy (2010). "Race and the New Biocitizen," in Ian Whitmarsh and David S. Jones (eds), *What's the Use of Race: Modern Governance and the Biology of Difference*. Cambridge, MA: MIT Press, 259–76.

Roberts, Dorothy (2011). *Fatal Invention: How Science, Politics, and Big Business Re-Create Race in the Twenty-First Century*. New York: New Press.

Roberts, Dorothy, and Sujatha Jesudason (2013). "Movement Intersectionality: The Case of Race, Gender, Disability, and Genetic Technologies," *Du Bois Review: Social Science Research on Race*, 10/2: 313–38.

Romig, Kathleen (2017). *SSI: A Lifeline for Children with Disabilities*. Washington: Center on Budget and Policy Priorities, https://www.cbpp.org/research/social-security/ssi-a-lifeline-for-children-with-disabilities.

Rose, Nikolas (2007). *The Politics of Life Itself: Biomedicine, Power, and Subjectivity in the Twenty-First Century*. Princeton: Princeton University Press.

Rose, Nikolas, and Carlos Novas (2005). "Biological Citizenship," in Aihwa Ong and Stephen Collier (eds), *Global Assemblages: Technology, Politics, Ethics as Anthropological Problems*. London: Blackwell Publishing, 439–63.

Samerski, Silja (2009). "Genetic Counseling and the Fiction of Choice: Taught Self-Determination as a New Technique of Social Engineering," *Signs*, 34/4: 735–61.

Scott, Ellen (2010). "'Feel as if I am the One who is Disabled': The Emotional Impact of Changed Employment Trajectories of Mothers Caring for Children with Disabilities," *Gender and Society*, 24/5: 672–96.

Seavilleklein, Victoria (2009). "Challenging the Rhetoric of Choice in Prenatal Screening," *Bioethics*, 23/1: 68–77.

Serres, Chris, and Glen Howatt (2019). "Minnesota's Arbitrary Aid to People with Disabilities," *Star Tribune*, September 15, https://www.startribune.com/medicaid–waivers–minnesota–disability–county–policies–differ–for–medically–fragile–children/558453052/.

Sheth, Darpana (2006). "Better Off Unborn? An Analysis of Wrongful Birth and Wrongful Life Claims under the Americans with Disabilities Act," *Tennessee Law Review*, 73/4: 641–68.

Social Security Administration (2018). *Number of SSI Program Recipients*. Washington: Social Security Administration, https://www.ssa.gov/oact/ssir/SSI18/IV_B_Recipients.html.

Sonik, Rajan, et al. (2016). "Food Insecurity in US Households that Include Children with Disabilities," *Exceptional Children*, 83/1: 42–57.

Stabile, Mark, and Sara Allin (2012). "The Economic Costs of Childhood Disability," *The Future of Children*, 22/1: 65–96.

Stein, Jillian (2010). "Backdoor Eugenics: The Troubling Implications of Certain Damages Awards in Wrongful Birth and Wrongful Life Claims," *Seton Hall Law Review*, 40/3: 1117–68.

Tabatabai, Ahoo (2020). "Mother of Person: Neoliberalism and Narratives of Parenting Children with Disabilities," *Disability and Society*, 35/1: 111–31.

Thompson, Frank (2012). *Medicaid Politics: Federalism, Policy Durability, and Health Reform*. Washington: Georgetown University Press.

US Bureau of Labor Statistics (2022a). *Occupational Outlook Handbook: Home Health and Personal Care Aides*. Washington: US Bureau of Labor Statistics, https://www.bls.gov/ooh/healthcare/home–health–aides–and–personal–care–aides.htm.

US Bureau of Labor Statistics (2022b). *Persons with a Disability: Labor Force Characteristics Summary*, Washington: US Bureau of Labor Statistics, <https://www.bls.gov/news.release/disabl.nr0.htm>.

US Census Bureau (2020). *Income, Poverty and Health Insurance Coverage in the United States: 2019*. Washington: US Census Bureau, https://www.census.gov/newsroom/press–releases/2020/income–poverty.html.

Wasserman, David (2017). "Justice, Procreation, and the Costs of Having and Raising Disabled Children," in Leslie Francis (ed.), *The Oxford Handbook of Reproductive Ethics*. Oxford: Oxford University Press, 464–77.

Wendell, Susan (1996). *The Rejected Body: Feminist Philosophical Reflections on Disability*. New York: Routledge.

Yakren, Sofia (2018). "'Wrongful Birth' Claims and the Paradox of Parenting a Child with a Disability," *Fordham Law Review*, 87/2: 583–628.

Zeng, Quingjun, et al. (2020). "Comparison of Measurement of Long-Term Care Costs between China and Other Countries: A Systematic Review of the Last Decade," *Healthcare*, 8/2: 1–16.

5

Ableist and Sexist Social Norms

From its first edition in 1946, Dr Benjamin Spock's wildly popular book *The Common Sense Book of Baby and Child Care* was heralded as a revolution in parenting guides. The best-selling book, which sold over fifty million copies, remains the most widely read childcare reference manual ever written. Reassuring and accessible in tone, practically organized, and frequently revised even after the pediatrician's death in 1998, it is credited with bringing about a cultural revolution in parenting practices. Its final section, "Special Problems," offers advice for parents navigating modern challenges such as mothers entering the workforce and parental separation. The penultimate subsection, "The Handicapped Child," encourages parents of children with disabilities to adopt a "sensible attitude" toward impairments and to regard the child with a disability as any other family member. "If the parents accept a handicapped child wholeheartedly and matter-of-factly," Spock (1946: 495) assures, "the brothers and sisters will be apt to also." Throughout, Spock's message is one of adjusted expectations, attentive care, and unconditional acceptance.

The only exception is Down syndrome, or what Spock, using the vernacular of his day, calls "Mongolism."[1] In jarringly darker tones than those employed for cerebral palsy or congenital heart disease, Spock (1946: 502) describes the condition as one in which "the eyes slant upwards like an Oriental's, the face is flattened, the limbs are relaxed and double-jointed … Because of their weak physical condition, these children often die young." After this grim prognosis, Spock (1946: 502–3) offers the following:

> It is usually recommended that the woman who has had a Mongolian baby, and has no other children, try to have another baby before too long, particularly if she is young … If the family can afford to place the Mongolian baby in a special home, it is usually recommended that this be done right after birth. Then the parents will

[1] In his first paper on the subject, published in 1862, John Down himself coined the term "Mongoloid idiot" to describe the condition that now bears his name.

Prenatal Genetic Testing, Abortion, and Disability Justice. Amber Knight and Joshua Miller, Oxford University Press.
© Amber Knight and Joshua Miller (2023). DOI: 10.1093/oso/9780192870957.003.0006

156 Prenatal Genetic Testing, Abortion, and Disability Justice

not become too wrapped up in a child who will never develop very far, and they will have more attention to give to their normal children who need it—either the children that they already have or the ones that they should have afterwards.

Spock's advice is outdated and unprofessional by contemporary standards, and today most parents do not automatically receive medical advice immediately to separate a child with Down syndrome from his or her family by placing the baby in an institution after birth. That said, the condition remains socially stigmatized, and, as a result, many prospective mothers wrestle with fears about social rejection not unlike those their grandmothers faced decades ago (Jain, Thomasma, and Ragas 2002; Huiracocha et al. 2017).

This chapter focuses on social and cultural norms and their impact on reproductive decision-making. Prospective mothers weighing their reproductive options must consider a host of questions about their would-be children that transcend the medical and material, and they often solicit input from their family members, friends, neighbors, and religious communities as they try to picture what their lives might look like as they make difficult decisions following a positive fetal diagnosis. Many prospective parents considering whether or not they want to carry an affected pregnancy to term and/or raise a child with Down syndrome question whether their friend groups and families would greet their decision warmly and value their future child. They might also question whether they could effectively balance their responsibilities for caring for a child who may have heightened care needs with other life projects—including raising other children in the household, maintaining social relationships with partners and friends, and/or pursuing a career—in a non-ideal world that makes the social movements for women's rights and disability justice necessary in the first place. As we will demonstrate, the answers to such questions will tend toward the negative in a society with ableist norms and a stubbornly entrenched sexual division of labor. Ableist and patriarchal social standards in civil society render the experience of mothering a child with a disability more arduous than it needs to be. In confronting the possibility of raising a child with disabilities, then, prospective mothers must make their reproductive decisions within a cultural context that is too often inhospitable to the choice of bringing a disabled child into the world.

This chapter begins from the premise that our cultural norms—that is, our shared social values, attitudes, expectations, and habits—are of enormous political importance. Culture and politics are deeply intertwined. Our cultural values often inform our political priorities, and, conversely, the arrangement of political affairs often legitimates certain types of cultural norms and practices over others. With this mind, this chapter thinks through some the following questions. How might cultural expectations surrounding motherhood and the sexual division of labor affect prospective mothers' reproductive preferences and choices? In addition, how might dominant ideals about "normal" and/or "perfect" babies, cultural attitudes toward people with intellectual and development disabilities, and idealized notions of kinship affect and inform prospective parents' reproductive options? And, as a matter of social justice, what types of cultural reforms would allow women to decide more autonomously whether they want to undergo prenatal testing, terminate a pregnancy following a positive result, carry the fetus to term, raise a child with a disability, or choose adoption?

The analysis proceeds as follows. The first section attends to the unique challenges associated with parenting children with Down syndrome and other types of disabilities. Drawing from empirical feminist scholarship on motherhood and care work, we concentrate on the caregiving costs typically borne by mothers while parenting in an ableist social context, including negative physical and psychological effects, social isolation, and burnout. The next section examines the social and political determinants of these negative outcomes, including ableist social stigmas, cultural constructions of motherhood, and normative conceptions of the family. Here we draw heavily from Eva Kittay's reflections on her experiences of raising a child with a disability, among other parental testimonies, to demonstrate the political harms wrought by certain cultural tropes. The third section offers some potential remedies to the toxic social norms identified in the first two sections. In particular, we encourage citizens to consider the damaging effects of disability-related stereotypes and the ableist marginalization of children with disabilities. Such marginalization may range from passive isolation to aggressive targeting and bullying, but it always has the same effect of creating a world that too often inflicts social mistreatment on children with Down syndrome and their caregivers. In addition, we argue that supporting prospective mothers of children with disabilities requires challenging the pervasive culture of intensive motherhood and mother-blaming that has been thoroughly documented by feminist scholars. Finally, we contend that legal and cultural reforms to normative conceptions of the family can promote women's autonomy by offering a more robust latticework of care networks and social support both for themselves and for their children.

158 Prenatal Genetic Testing, Abortion, and Disability Justice

The Sexual Division of Labor and the Costs of Lifelong Motherhood

Caring for children is frequently joyful but difficult work, and much of that work typically falls to women.[2] Despite rapid gains in labor-force participation over the last fifty years, women still perform the majority of domestic work and childcare in every economically developed country (Coltrane 2000; Gershuny and Sullivan 2003; Craig and Mullan 2011). As a result, women's continued participation in the workforce remains contingent on factors such as the availability of schools, daycare facilities, and other childcare services (Baker, Gruber, and Milligan 2008; Bick 2016). For example, one 2019 study found that mothers are more likely to work part-time or to drop out of the labor force altogether in states with higher childcare costs and shorter school days (Ruppanner, Moller, and Sayer 2019).[3] Many mothers who do pursue full-time employment still dedicate longer hours to childcare in evenings and on weekends than their male partners (Hochschild 1997; Dempsey 2002; Bianchi and Milkie 2010).

Owing to the so-called mommy tax, working mothers also receive lower wages than their childless counterparts (Crittenden 2001). Numerous studies have demonstrated that employers often perceive new mothers as less committed to their jobs, unable to take on extra work, and less flexible with their time than non-mothers, and these attitudes impair career advancement opportunities and earnings over time (Buding 2003; Correll, Benard, and Paik 2007).[4] Employment interruptions and transitions to part-time jobs also create significant wage penalties (Gangl and Ziefle 2009). The amount of income working women lose out on for childbearing and childrearing varies by age and profession, but most estimates are staggering. Not surprisingly, more women in the US workforce are delaying childbirth or forgoing motherhood altogether as a response to wage penalties, limited opportunities for early career advancement, and increasing childcare costs.

In addition to suffering from lost earnings, mothers also experience a leisure gap in the quality and duration of their personal time relative to non-mothers and fathers. Feminist scholars have analyzed the character and

---

[2] In the last decade, men and women have been moving toward a more equal division of paid work and care work than in the past. However, a significant gender gap remains. A Pew study found that "American mothers spend twice as much time with their children as fathers do" (Parker and Wang 2013: 27–8). Furthermore, some data suggest that mothers of children with disabilities shoulder a disproportionate burden of care, even more than in families of "typically" developing children (Cohen and Petrescu-Prahova 2006).

[3] As we explain in the Conclusion, these factors are even more pronounced in the wake of the coronavirus pandemic.

[4] Looking at it from a different angle, Amalia Miller (2011) finds that college-educated women earn an additional 9% more in lifetime wages for every year that they delay having their first child.

Ableist and Sexist Social Norms **159**

quality of women's leisure, especially what Michael Bittman and Judy Wajcman (2000) describe as the "fragmentation" and "contamination" of women's leisure time. While working parents in partnered households report roughly equal time devoted to rest and recreation, the hours of women's leisure are fragmented and broken into smaller parcels (that is, seven minutes here, fifteen there), and their time to relax is often contaminated by multitasking (for example, watching television while folding laundry).[5] These persistently gendered time-use patterns reveal power imbalances within families. Erica Wimbush's observation (1988: 73) nearly forty years ago still rings true for many women today, as the question of leisure "raises issues concerning women's right to time off and to 'a room of one's own' away from the demands of others, a privilege that many men take for granted and are not always willing to relinquish in order to support women's leisure." This body of research clarifies the extent to which the sexual division of labor undermines mothers' abilities to recharge and pursue interests outside work and parenthood.

In short, many American mothers, especially working mothers, are simply exhausted from their parental caregiving commitments. This reality is amplified when mothering a child with a disability. Mothering a child with an intellectual or developmental disability like Down syndrome usually involves caregiving requirements that are distinguished by the intensity and difficulty of the assistance needed and the amount and duration of time devoted to care. Although people's lived experiences raising children with Down syndrome or other types of intellectual and developmental disabilities vary considerably, many parents emphasize the effects of prolonged dependency among their aging children. Indeed, the intensity of caring frequently increases, rather than decreases, over time (McLaughlin et al. 2008). Parents may need to help their children perform instrumental activities of daily living by helping them navigate social situations, make medical decisions, and manage finances, even as they develop into teenagers and adults. Such care extends to bureaucratic elements as well, with mothers fighting insurance companies to procure medical coverage and battling school administrators over educational services.[6] Many mothers effectively act as case managers who coordinate care among various specialists to ensure that their children's needs

---

[5] Other studies show that, while the duration and quality of fathers' leisure time has remained stable over time, the leisure time of working and non-working mothers has fragmented further (Bianchi, Robinson, and Milke 2006: 103).

[6] Janet Read (2000: 65–7) analyzes how mothers frequently serve as mediators between their disabled children and their service providers, finding that mothers must often advocate forcefully for their children in ways that include challenging the authority of physicians, professional caregivers, and social workers who are conditioned to pathologize them. Linda Blum (2007) also describes how mothers often act as "vigilantes" as they battle the educational and medical establishments on behalf of their children with disabilities for the services they need.

are met. In these and manifold other ways, mothers of children with Down syndrome often assume care responsibilities that significantly exceed routine childcare tasks.

These caregiving responsibilities can take their toll. It can be a strenuous full-time job to care for a child with heightened dependency needs, and many mothers subsequently feel depleted from always being on call. Mothers can become so focused on their children that they do not ensure that their own needs are met. Studies have found that primary caregivers to children with disabilities are more likely to experience psychosocial stress, putting them at higher risk for anxiety and clinical depression (Murphy et al. 2007; Plant and Sanders 2007). Moreover, sleep deprivation, a lack of respite hours, and the physical rigors of providing intensive hands-on care can also lead to diminished physical health (Tong et al. 2003; Bourke et al. 2008). Simply put, many mothers of children with disabilities feel pushed to the limit and "at the end of their rope."

Prospective mothers who already have kids in the house and feel beleaguered by childcare responsibilities may have concerns about having more children, especially if the prospective child might potentially need around-the-clock care for the long haul. They might question whether their lives would become consumed by the care for a disabled child, wondering whether they would have to quit their jobs, turn down social invitations, and take time and attention away from their other children to meet their prospective child's heightened care needs. These practical concerns are understandable in a society marked by structural gender inequality in childcare arrangements.

By drawing attention to the costs of caregiving, we do not mean to portray the experience of raising a child with Down syndrome as one of relentless drudgery, distress, sorrow, and hardship. As we acknowledge in Chapter 3, many parents convey the experience of raising a child with Down syndrome as enriching, joyful, and desirable. The point we are trying to make is that the costs of providing care are not necessarily caused by the children themselves but by unjust caregiving arrangements. For example, there is little evidence supporting the widespread belief that raising children with conditions like Down syndrome alone results in higher levels of marital discord or elevated divorce rates (Risdal and Singer 2004; Namkung et al. 2015). Rather, married parents of children with Down syndrome report higher levels of marital strain resulting from factors like care-related financial costs and diminished support from friends and families (Resch et al. 2010). The privatization and feminization of care work, not the child, are the primary sources of strain, which means that these factors can, presumably, be alleviated by changing gender norms and reallocating care duties.

Pernicious Cultural Constructions

In the previous section we made the case that the feminization of care and the sexual division of labor limit women's reproductive choices by denying them an adequate range of options. Pregnant women who feel stuck between a rock and a hard place, unable to imagine how they could possibly manage work–life balance and flourish while raising a child with heightened care needs, may not feel free to make a choice in any meaningful sense. Cultural and linguistic norms can be just as restrictive, as they can distort or warp an individual's preferences and desires. In particular, ableist attitudes, unreasonable cultural expectations about "good mothers" and "perfect babies," and cultural ideals about the nuclear family pose unique challenges to reproductive choice in the new era of genomic medicine.

Ableist Prejudice

First, prospective parents are not immune from ableist socialization and negative cultural messaging about Down syndrome. Cultural attitudes toward people with Down syndrome and related conditions are persistently and discernibly negative (Siperstein, Norins, and Mohler 2007). People with intellectual and developmental disabilities are still the butt of jokes in mainstream Hollywood movies like *Tropic Thunder* (2008). In certain social groups, disparaging language like "retard" and insults about "riding the short bus" are still commonplace. Owing to widespread social stigma, children with intellectual and developmental disabilities are less likely to participate in social activities with peers outside school, and they are more vulnerable to isolation and loneliness than are children without impairments (Solish, Perry, and Minnes 2009; Gilmore and Cuskelly 2014; Lipscomb et al. 2017).

Children with intellectual and developmental disabilities are also more likely to be victims of bullying and social mistreatment (Christensen et al. 2012; Reardanz et al. 2020). For example, in 2019, students on an Indianapolis high-school football team abused and threatened the team manager, Jack, who has Down syndrome. According to the report, a player on the football team took a video of Jack urinating and threatened to post it on social media. Jack told his mother, and the perpetrator was reprimanded by the school. A few weeks later, the same boy who had taken the video threatened to kill Jack and his family if Jack ever told on him again. In the locker room, a different boy on the team then pulled Jack's head to his chest and forced Jack to suck his nipple. Some of the teammates shot a video of this incident too

(Ryckaert 2019). Sadly, this case is not an isolated event. It is representative of a broader pattern of mistreatment made permissible by how people with Down syndrome are devalued in the broader culture.

Prenatal genetic testing gives pregnant women a newfound power to make decisions about the type of children they want to bring into the world, so widespread cultural norms that devalue people with certain genetic characteristics are bound to impact on many people's preferences, even if such biases are implicit or subconscious. While few people may be unwilling to admit that they hold overt biases against people with Down syndrome, the motivation for selective termination can often exemplify what Adrienne Asch and David Wasserman (2005: 181) describe as an "uncritical reliance on a stigma-driven inference from a single feature to hold future life." To be clear, we are not suggesting that all decisions selectively to terminate after a prenatal diagnosis of Down syndrome are driven by prejudice. Our claim is that bias against people with intellectual and developmental disabilities permeates our culture, and reproductive decisions about whether or not to bring a child with Down syndrome into the world, when considered in the aggregate, are not impervious to disparaging social messages.

Even if prospective parents do not themselves harbor any deep-seated prejudice against people with Down syndrome, they may fear the challenges of having to defend their child's existence and advocate for their interests in an ableist society. Eva Kittay (2019: 53) describes how many prospective parents making decisions about prenatal screening and selective abortion question whether they are up to the task of dealing with "punishing attitudes on the part of others." Most prospective parents hope that their future children will experience friendship, love, and acceptance. They want to envision a future where their child will fit in with their peers, neighbors, families, and wider communities, a future where they will hang out with their friends and get invited to birthday parties and school dances. More abstractly, most prospective parents also want civil society fully to respect their child's moral and political equality. Hence, as Kittay (2019: 33) argues, "the fear that our [disabled] child will not be accepted" is powerful, and "the desire for acceptance into a community is hard to abandon." Sometimes pregnant women receive signals of affirmation and acceptance when they share a potential desire to carry a fetus with Down syndrome to term. But the opposite is at least equally common, even from loved ones and trusted friends. The fear of disrespect, and the worry that friends and family will turn away from them or the baby, loom large in many people's minds (Kittay 2019: 44). Few prospective parents have positive examples to look toward in the broader culture as they envision their future and how they hope it will unfold. Understandably, many pregnant women grappling with such difficult decisions may be able to envision only the worst-case scenario of charting a path alone, into an inhospitable unknown.

Findings from social science research corroborate that expectant mothers' decisions are often driven by fears of social rejection. After interviewing pregnant women and parents of children with Down syndrome, Alison Piepmeier (2013) identified factors that people considered as they went through their decision-making process about whether to use prenatal screening and what choice to make based on a positive Down syndrome diagnosis. She found that almost all of the parents and potential parents were eager for community, regardless of the decision they wanted to make (Piepmeier 2013: 178). Unfortunately, some of the women reported that members of their families or broader community, upon hearing the news that they were pregnant with a fetus that had tested positive for Down syndrome, provided "a series of negative narratives … in the face of what they understood to be a tragedy" (Piepmeier 2013: 180). These negative reactions are consequential. A recent survey of women who chose abortion following a Down syndrome diagnosis cited a fear of mistreatment and bullying as one of the most salient reasons to terminate the pregnancy (Lou et al. 2018).

Many prospective parents also express fears about what will happen if their child with Down syndrome outlives them. Like all parents, those raising children with disabilities worry that their children will die before them. Yet many also worry about dying before their children, fearful of how they will fare in an uncaring society without their love and support. Susan Parish, director of the Lurie Institute for Disability Policy at Brandeis University, explains the situation, remarking: "I've worked with several parents who said they've hoped their son or daughter would die before they did because they don't feel there are supports out there" (quoted in Fifield 2016). The rampant sexual violence and physical abuse of people with intellectual and developmental disabilities in congregate settings like group homes casts a long shadow of fear for the future (Fisher et al. 2016; Hughes et al. 2019). Simply put, the indignity of finding a child's death preferable to the dangers that might befall them in an uncaring society is indicative of widescale structural injustice. The imagined prospect of bringing a child into a biased and unwelcoming world—one where merciless taunting, abject isolation, and even physical or sexual violence are far too common—is sufficiently loathsome to give any prospective parent pause for thought.

164 Prenatal Genetic Testing, Abortion, and Disability Justice

"Good Moms" and "Perfect Babies"

In the United States, the cultural construction of ideal motherhood is equal parts canonization and demonization. On the one hand, Americans glorify mothers ("it's the hardest and most important job in the world!"), tasking them with inculcating and safeguarding the nation's moral and physical welfare. On the other hand, mother-blaming is a national pastime of sorts, and people are quick to scapegoat mothers as personally responsible for otherwise systemic problems such as violent crime, drug abuse, and poverty. Misogyny, classism, and racism also shade how Americans think about motherhood and its correlative responsibilities (Roberts 1997; Handler and Hasenfeld 2007; Goodwin 2020).

Feminist scholarship has long considered how ideological constructions of motherhood inform policy debates, shape public attitudes, and impact on women's behavior and sense of self (Douglas and Michaels 2004). Essentially concerned with distinguishing "good" mothers from "bad," maternal ideology regulates women by codifying permissible and impermissible behaviors in the name of fetal health or child welfare. "Good" mothers exude graceful patience and cheerful self-abnegation, subsuming their own interests to those of their children. "Bad" mothers not only form their own discrete interests but pursue them at their children's expense (Malacrida and Boulton 2012). Indeed, the cardinal sin of motherhood is to put oneself first.[7] As Diana Meyers (2004: 257) eloquently explains: "Mothers are culturally represented as self-sacrificial, unconditionally loving, and totally identified with their children—the prototype of a gladly nonautonomous being." Since the emergence of scientific motherhood, which is a movement encouraging mothers to learn the latest childcare research from physicians and psychologists, mothers are now expected to train themselves as "experts" who should predict and respond to all the emotional, cognitive, and physiological needs of their children (Apple 2006). This professionalization of motherhood positions mothers as therapists, pediatricians, and teachers for their children in such a way that the child's needs and interests completely absorb those of the mother.[8]

---

[7] "Intensive mothering" describes an orientation toward childrearing that consumes inordinate time and energy from mothers in the name of children's physical, social, and emotional health. Sharon Hays (1996: 8) identifies three elements of intensive mothering: (1) mothers are central caregivers, even if they are employed outside the home; (2) mothering demands "lavishing copious amounts of time, energy, and material resources on the child," whose needs precede the mother's; and (3) comparing the value of paid work to the unpaid work of motherhood is a non-starter insofar as the two values are incommensurate.

[8] This is not to suggest, however, that women subscribing to the doctrine of medicalized motherhood were empowered to challenge the physician's authority or even to understand themselves as the physician's

Ableist and Sexist Social Norms **165**

Maternal ideology is difficult to ignore and resist. As Sara Goering (2017: 287), an avowed feminist, admits: "It's impossible to achieve, but it has us in its grips." Not only are many mothers gripped by a nagging sense of guilt that they are never doing enough or doing right by their children; maternal ideology also puts women at odds with the demands of modern work life. Some bourgeois white women may indeed have had the material resources and social structures necessary to support motherhood as a totalizing activity. Yet, the majority of women do not have the wherewithal to "have it all": children, a prosperous career, a tranquil marriage, a nurturing home life, and a satisfying sex life. "Having it all" means refusing to make trade-offs in a market-oriented society that demands them. Women who have children are more likely to be perceived as less committed to their careers. Conversely, women who are committed to their careers are perceived as less capable mothers. In sum, the ideology of motherhood sets unattainable standards, encourages mothers to disregard their own desires and interests, creates stumbling blocks for work–family balance, and treats mothers from different races and classes unfairly (Collins 1994; Hays 1996; Goering 2017; Goodwin 2020).

Cultural tropes about motherhood are often intensified when a child is disabled. Mothers of children with disabilities are often publicly portrayed as self-sacrificing "saints" who give love, nurturance, time, money, and energy with unrelenting devotion (Kittay 2019: 45). These cultural messages valorize maternal sacrifice and imply that public support is unnecessary, because the emotional fulfillment of motherhood is its own reward. Again, the work that mothers of children with disabilities perform frequently exceeds routine childcare. Ableism compounds this oppressive construction by setting inherently unachievable standards against which mothers are judged. Insofar as children with disabilities deviate from normative conceptions of acceptable childlike behavior and fail to meet prescribed developmental benchmarks, their mothers are castigated for failing their children, their families, and even their wider communities.

Unreasonable expectations give rise to mother-blaming (Blum 2007; Colker 2015). Barbara Hillyer (1993), whose daughter Jennifer has several impairments, has written extensively about the pernicious effects of mother-blaming in her life. "Assuming that the child's 'treatment' should be the sole or central focus on the mother's life," Hillyer (1993: 88) writes, physicians and other medical professionals often scold and judge mothers of children with

---

equal. Rather, new mothers were encouraged to discount advice offered by traditional support networks—i.e. trusted friends, relatives, and neighbors—and to learn only enough diligently to follow their doctors' advice. See Rima Apple (2006: 12–23).

severe disabilities, describing them in negative terms, including "overanxious, overprotective, out of touch with reality, guilt ridden, arrested in denial, malicious, indifferent, emotionally divorced, lacking in empathy, rejecting, unconcerned, overinvolved, hysterical and/or emotional." Hillyer's analysis (1993: 92) is important, because she suggests that an underlying assumption of maternal omnipotence underpins mother-blaming, as if any mother could be superwoman enough single-handedly to "fix" or "cure" her disabled child. Reflecting on her lived experience, Hillyer (1993: 247) describes the guilt she experienced when she surrendered some of her roles as interpreter, nurse, teacher, and therapist, admitting that she was simply not strong enough simultaneously to fulfill all the roles required to meet her daughter's needs on her own.

Cultural ideals about "normal" or even "perfect" babies are as prevalent as those about "good" or even "saintly" moms. The idea of "normalcy" has developed a strong hold on our collective imagination. For instance, when expectant parents are asked whether they would prefer to have a boy or a girl (a problematic question in and of itself), a common refrain is: "We just hope he or she is healthy—we'll be happy either way so long as the baby has ten fingers and ten toes." The example of ten fingers and ten toes is telling, largely because having digits has little to do with the health status of the fetus and more to do with the desire for a normal, species-typical child.[9] As Eva Kittay (2019) persuasively argues, many prospective parents are conditioned to desire normalcy, not only for themselves but for their children as well. Normalcy is a valuable currency in contemporary culture, largely because people frequently conflate "the good life" with "the normal life." According to Kittay (2019: 57), subsequent fears of abnormality enter into many prospective parents' calculations, and "the fear that a good life cannot be possible for those who fail to fit within the boundaries of normal" drives many to consider selective reproductive procedures to ensure the births of normal children.

For others, perfection is the goal, and new reproductive technologies themselves can heighten pressures to produce "perfect" babies for the sake of the whole. Gail Heidi Landsman (2009: 16) is concerned that we live in a socio-historical context that perpetuates the false assurance that pregnant women can produce "perfect" babies if they just do all the "right things" (that is, take prenatal vitamins, maintain a healthy diet, refrain from alcohol

---

[9] Individuals missing fingers and/or toes from birth rarely suffer physical pain or experience and reduced quality of life on account of the 'missing' digits. One of the co-authors of this book (Amber) was born without five fingers on her left hand. See also Catharine Mills (2015), who examines the term "normal" through a case study of a couple who chose to abort a wanted fetus after an ultrasound revealed that it was missing a hand.

use, and so on). The myth of perfect reproductive control is intimately connected with the increased geneticization and technologization of reproduction. Pregnancy has become increasingly medicalized following scientific advances, which makes it seem as though reproduction is a phenomenon that is under the complete control of human beings and their technologies. The unrealistic expectation that pregnant mothers can overcome the contingencies of the genetic lottery through sheer willpower, responsible decision-making, and the medical management of risk has created a situation where mothers are culturally held liable for birth outcomes. Subsequently, mothers of children with disabilities who fail to produce "perfect" infants frequently feel judged and blamed for the birth of their "damaged" children in American culture (Landsman 2009: 17). Landsman (2009: 153–4) is fearful that new genetic reproductive technologies encourage parents to commodify their children and see them as consumer items that one can pick and choose in the market, thereby licensing others to judge women who seemingly make a "bad" consumer choice such as giving birth to and raising a disabled "lemon." The social pressures to produce perfect babies are all too real in a hyper-competitive, individualistic, and superficial society.

The Idealized Nuclear Family

Cultural expectations surrounding the nuclear family also militate against supporting disabled children and their parents. Even though the traditional, heterosexual, nuclear family makes up only a small proportion of American families today, this idealized family form—immortalized through television shows like *Leave it to Beaver* (1957–63)—continues to have a strong ideological impact in American society and remains the normative standard against which other family forms are appraised.[10] In mainstream usage, the nuclear family implies a two-parent, married, cisgendered, heterosexual couple living with their biological children. In recent decades, however, we have seen an increase in the diversity of family structures in which children grow up. Families are comprised of single parents, two unmarried biological parents, lesbian and gay parents, trans and/or non-binary parents, adoptive and foster parents, blended families formed when parents cohabitate with new partners, childless bonds, and extended families and kinship networks. Despite this reality, dominant portrayals of family life remain steeped in heteronormative and patriarchal social values.

---

[10] For data on family composition, marriage, and cohabitation, see Juliana Menasce Horowitz, Nikki Graf, and Gretchen Livingston (2019).

168 Prenatal Genetic Testing, Abortion, and Disability Justice

Regardless of family composition, the isolated nuclear family is ill-equipped to meet children's and parents' needs. On its own, the private family home lacks the resources to be an effective self-sufficient unit of caregiving. Yet, in a society sorely lacking good childcare options within a globalized and mobile economy that often scatters extended family across the globe, parenting is typically done in relative isolation (Boyd 2010). Despite the wisdom of the old adage that "it takes a village to raise a child," so-called villages can be hard to come by these days. Moreover, if "it takes a village to raise a child," it often takes a village *and* an army of informal caregivers and paid professionals to raise a child with disabilities, including loving friends and family members, physical therapists, occupational therapists, speech therapists, respiratory therapists, nutritionists, and home health aides or personal-care attendants. The need for community support may be more visible when a person is parenting a child with a disability, but, as Alison Piepmeier (2013: 182) counsels, "parenting is never something a person can do entirely alone."

Despite the dire need for an extended network of care and support, many parents of children with disabilities report feeling alone and isolated. Even when friends and family live nearby, the time-consuming task of caring for a child with special needs often entails declining social invitations and losing contact over time (McLaughlin et al. 2008). Writing of his own experience as a father of a daughter with several impairments, Roger Gottlieb (2002) describes the toll that constant and intensive care can take on his relationships. As he explains:

> The ability to have a truly mutual friendship when you are devoting so much time, energy, and emotion to a child is seriously compromised. At the end of a day filled with anxiety and frustration, I often find myself emotionally drained, too filled with my own feelings to listen very well to those of another, or to reach out across a divide in which I literally feel like I live in another country. Our family has often lived at the edge of emotional and physical (not to mention financial) collapse ... Those friends who have stuck with my family have been people who find the relationship rewarding despite a frequent lack of full mutuality. (Gottlieb 2002: 229)

Beyond the practical challenges of maintaining personal relationships, many parents also cite pressures to withdraw from the social world to protect their children with visible disabilities—who may break social norms by grunting, drooling, or talking too loudly—from gawking and other intolerant responses to their child's presence in a public space (Kittay 1999: 166). For some, it can be intimidating to go out to the movies or to eat at a restaurant when strangers might stare or even complain about your child's behavior and presence in a shared space.

In sum, expectant mothers may find the prospect of bringing a disabled child into their lives too overwhelming if they feel they are expected to carry the caregiving load on their own. The experience of raising a child with a disability calls into question the general desirability of bringing up children in an isolated nuclear family. In all family forms, the parent–child relationship is unquestionably enhanced by the availability of support from extended family, neighbors, friends, co-workers, teachers, and a welcoming civil society.

Social and Cultural Change

Social and cultural change is just as important as legislative reform, since symbolic and informal sources of bias are just as real and consequential as legal and material harms. Yet, it is difficult to prescribe cultural change in any detail. Solutions are not as straightforward as proposed policy reforms. As Chris Kaposy (2018: 117) concedes, "it would be impossible to legislate that people with Down syndrome be included in meaningful relationships and other intimate relationships." That said, changes in cultural norms and public consciousness often start with an alternative vision of what a better, more equal society might look like. Strategies and tactics for how to change what *is* into what *ought* to be can then grow out of a well-articulated alternative vision.

Take deinstitutionalization as a prime example. Decades ago, physicians and social workers frequently advised parents to separate their children with disabilities from their families at birth or shortly thereafter, arguing that keeping them at home would be impractical and detrimental to the family. The renowned pediatrician Dr Benjamin Spock (1946: 478), featured at the start of this chapter, once advised that "it is much better for the other children and parents to have him [a disabled infant] cared for elsewhere." Thanks to the tireless efforts of disability rights activists, however, it is no longer widely assumed that people with disabilities should be shut away in institutions or become wards of the state, out of the sight and out of mind. Today, community living has broad-based support, and it is widely accepted that people with disabilities should grow up at home among their parents, siblings, pets, and friends (Llewellyn et al. 1999). Cultural norms and expectations have changed for the better over time.

In this spirit, our first recommended alternative to the status quo involves eliminating pejorative discourse and disparaging media representations of

170 Prenatal Genetic Testing, Abortion, and Disability Justice

people with Down syndrome and other types of intellectual and developmental disabilities. Campaigns to eliminate the use of the word retarded ("the r-word") marks a step in the right direction. People with intellectual and developmental disabilities have advocated for the elimination of the slur since the inception of the US self-advocacy movement in the 1970s (Vanhala 2011). Over the last ten years in the United States, leaders and self-advocates in the "Spread the Word to End the Word" campaign have collected millions of digital and physical pledges to end the r-word. In collaboration with leadership from Special Olympics and Best Buddies, the campaign has grown to reach thousands of schools and raise public consciousness about the value of inclusive language. We hope that these campaigns continue to garner broad-based support.

Moreover, there is a growing recognition that people with Down syndrome deserve to be positively portrayed in popular culture (Thomas 2020). Although positive portrayals of characters with Down syndrome are still too rare, some television shows—including Corky Thatcher on the television show *Life Goes On* (1989–93), Becky Faye Jackson on *Glee* (2009–15), and Ansel Parios on *Stumptown* (2019–20)—have depicted characters with Down syndrome in ways that reject sanitized social stereotypes of them as perpetual children, passive victims, pitiable charity cases, or ever-happy disabled angels. To be sure, representations that give characters with Down syndrome some depth are not perfect. For instance, all of the aforementioned characters are exclusively white. Moreover, popular representations are still full of contradictions and mixed messages, and almost all of them erase or downplay the role that political structures play in creating social disadvantage for people with disabilities. However, positive media content can potentially change public attitudes for the better (Auslander and Gold 1999; Wilkinson and McGill 2008). Media landscapes matter, since they form the terrain in which non-disabled and disabled people alike form their perceptions of disability and difference.

Valuing people with Down syndrome calls for more than better television, however. Encouraged by organizations like the National Down syndrome Advocacy Coalition (NDAC) and the self-advocacy model embraced by the National Down Syndrome Society (NDSS), we call for a greater awareness of people with Down syndrome as fellow citizens with equal rights and moral worth. People with intellectual and developmental disabilities are active citizens with important contributions to make to our society. Insofar as democratic societies derive their normative thrust from recognizing all persons as equals, we must strive for greater civic inclusion and a future where individuals with disabilities are met with respect as citizens.

Ableist and Sexist Social Norms **171**

In addition to changing widespread ableist attitudes, we also embrace a vision for the future wherein society's caregiving arrangements are characterized by a more equitable division of labor. Feminists have been working to realize this vision for decades. In order to reallocate caregiving responsibilities, some aim to redistribute responsibility for care work fairly within and beyond the heterosexual family by challenging the cultural assumption that women should be the primary caregivers for children in the private sphere (Okin 1989; Williams 2000, 2010; Meyers 2004; Tronto 2015). Others have focused on corporate restructuring and "family-friendly" workplace policies that allow employees to balance work and care, including telecommuting, flextime, paid leaves of absence, and so on (Stone 2007; Crouter and Booth 2009; Williams 2010; Blair-Loy et al. 2015). Finally, another approach intersects with the social welfare state scholarship to consider the obligations the state has to provide public support to parents and other caregivers (White 2000; Alstott 2004, 2015; Gornick and Meyers 2008; Eichner 2010; Engster 2015).

We embrace a multipronged approach, believing that cultural change must happen within the family, our workplaces, and the wider culture at large. Here we take the opportunity to confront the dominant cultural notion that being a "good" mother means suppressing all one's own needs and desires. The heightened social demands placed on American mothers have become downright toxic, and the glorification of self-sacrifice is incompatible with gender equality. It is unjust to expect women's lives and identities to collapse completely into their mothering roles. Of course, all children (both disabled and able-bodied alike) are vulnerable and dependent. They inevitably require a great deal of time, attention, and labor to survive, and parents are reasonably expected to attend to their children's emotional and material needs and often place them above their own. It is not an injustice for a parent to feel compelled to buy a sensible, family-friendly vehicle instead of the two-seater sports car. Given the realities of childrearing, therefore, expecting a mother's personal goals and projects to change or to take a back seat from time to time seems unproblematic.

The fact that motherhood is incompatible with women's perfect independence is not cause for alarm, since nobody can or should be unencumbered by the wants and needs of others. As the feminist proponents of relational autonomy featured in Chapter 1 have persuasively shown, we are radically interdependent and affected not just by our own needs and desires but by those of other people. That said, appreciation for the ways in which a mother's life is tied up with that of her children—how the self (mother) and the other (child) are deeply entangled and integrated—does not mean that mothers

172 Prenatal Genetic Testing, Abortion, and Disability Justice

should be expected fully to sacrifice or subordinate the self (Goering 2017). It is one thing to expect parents to factor their children's needs into their own life plans. It is quite another to expect that a mother's individual desires, needs, and life pursuits should always play second fiddle.

The relevant concern, therefore, is with decoupling motherhood from unhealthy expectations of self-sacrifice. We must therefore ask: when do the personal costs of mothering become a source of oppression and indignity? Any attempt to provide uniform guidelines in response to this question is bound to fail. However, we argue that Eva Kittay (1999) offers a useful preliminary standard. Kittay (1999: 66) suggests that a caregiving arrangement is unjust when it becomes "a liability to one's own well-being." "However my needs may be deferred," Kittay (1999: 70) writes, "they cannot be permitted to languish."[11] Although this standard is admittedly vague, egregious violations are obvious. When mothers of children with disabilities have to withdraw from the rest of the social world to fulfill their children's needs, when they are forced to put their career and educational aspirations aside, when they have to drain their savings and retirement accounts or declare bankruptcy to pay for their children's medical bills, when they feel so beleaguered by their care responsibilities that they are at the end of their rope, American culture is clearly expecting them to take on too much on their own.

Hence, it is unjust to exalt motherhood in order to legitimate women's exploitation. Instead of superficial support ("I just don't know she does it!"), we need to recalibrate our cultural expectations and dispel disempowering and restrictive cultural norms that place unrealistic and unattainable expectations squarely on mothers' shoulders. Some examples of pushback are readily available in academia and the wider culture. Within academia, there is a burgeoning literature on feminist mothering.[12] As an early proponent of the term, Andrea O'Reilly (2008: 6) rejects intensive motherhood in favor of feminist mothering practices that empower women, such as combining motherhood with paid employment, performing anti-sexist childrearing, insisting that partners share care labor, engaging in activism, and sustaining life activities outside motherhood. In popular culture, Ayelet Waldman's book *Bad Mother* (2009), a national bestseller, resists the script of maternal

---

[11] Diana Meyers (2004: 52) similarly argues that care work unjustly compromises a caregiver's well-being when "responding to others' needs and fulfilling one's responsibilities to them ... become so consuming that the individual is deprived of any opportunity to pursue personal goals and projects." Likewise, Maxine Eichner (2010: 12) argues that the state has an obligation to facilitate work–family balance in such a way that "family members can, through exercising diligent, but not Herculean, efforts meet the basic physical, mental, and emotional needs of their children and other dependents without being impoverished or having their emotional well-being threatened."

[12] For an overview of the literature on feminist motherhood, see Fiona Green (2020).

Ableist and Sexist Social Norms **173**

perfection and offers a humorous, unedited, entertaining picture of mother-hood as it is practiced in real life. Waldman calls on mothers to deconstruct the notion that motherhood should overshadow everything else in a woman's life. Moreover, mommy blogs—including *Her Bad Mother, Mama's Losin' It, The Good Enuf Mommy, I'm NOT Super Mom*, and *The Anti-June Cleaver*—are sites of resistance that can debunk dominant norms of intensive motherhood that are often perpetuated by white, middle-class, well-educated women who have the resources better to approximate the ideal (Gibson 2019).

The notion that mothers of children with disabilities are saints also needs to be challenged. Sainthood is an unattainable ideal for any mother to live up to, at least technically while still alive. Eva Kittay (2019) explains why this characterization is so harmful. Kittay is no stranger to familiar, well-intentioned, yet deeply problematic expressions such as "You're so brave," "You're such a saint," and "God only gives special children to special parents." These remarks may seem complimentary and supportive, but they ultimately "other" mothers of children with disabilities as people living in a state unthinkable for oneself. Reflecting on her experience raising a daughter, Kittay (2019: 45) discusses how she and her husband resented and resisted these tropes, writing:

> We refused the pity of those who could not understand, and we refused the attempts of others to sanctify us, to call us "remarkable" or "saintly," insisting instead that we were doing only what we assumed a parent normally would do: care for, love, protect, and foster the growth of one's child.

Hence, Kittay does not want to be canonized or sanctified. She sees herself as just an ordinary parent trying to do her best. What she wants is for "others to recognize our wonderful baby and see us as attentive, loving, and wonderful parents" (Kittay 2019: 44). Kathy Radigan (2017) conveyed a similar message in a piece in the *Huffington Post*. Kathy, who also has a daughter with a disability, openly rejects the sainthood label thrust upon her, insisting: "I'm not a saint. Not even close. Nor does my daughter need one. What she does need is her mom. A flawed woman who finds humor in the messes of biblical proportions she confronts almost daily."

Instead of empty platitudes, mothers need genuine support, so that they are no longer held primarily responsible for childcare. In turn, when mothers are able to take a break, it is more likely that they will be able to meet their children's care needs in a dignified manner. As many feminist care theorists have pointed out, a person who cannot attend to her own needs may be unable to provide quality care to others in the long run, or may do so less effectively, if she is exhausted, drained, and burned out (Bubeck 1995: 175; Clement 1996: 47). In fact, data suggest that children with disabilities are more likely to be abused, placed in the foster-care system, or institutionalized when their parents report feeling completely overwhelmed and unsupported (Friedman and Kalichman 2014). While placing more onus on men and extended care networks cannot guarantee that mothers will fulfill their care obligations in ways that enhance the dignity of their children, we can expect that children will be more likely to receive dignified and quality care when their parents are more financially secure, emotionally stable, rested, and content with their own lives. Hence, supporting parents has the potential to promote children's dignity and welfare in the process.

In addition, dispelling the myth that mothers of children with disabilities have to personify saints would go a long way in enhancing women's reproductive autonomy. In a study of women in the US who chose abortion after a diagnosis of a fetal anomaly, one of the women interviewed conveyed a sense of "guilt for not being the kind of person who could parent this particular type of special need" (quoted in Zhang 2020). Aside from the fact that women who choose abortion should never be made to feel guilty or selfish for their personal reproductive decisions, who could possibly feel like the kind of person who could live up to the expectation of becoming some sort of maternal saint with limitless love, nurturance, time, money, and energy, and devotion to her child?

Finally, we recommend embracing a more communal approach to childrearing that spreads the responsibility for childcare beyond the confines of the nuclear family. Two decades ago, Rayna Rapp and Faye Ginsburg (2001: 540–1) called on us to "reimagine the boundaries and capacities of kinship and to recognize the necessity of broader support for caretaking." One way to do so is by reimagining parenting beyond the biological nuclear family.[13] What might this look like? In our view, parenting a child might involve multiple adults (who are not necessarily in a romantic relationship) who are tasked with primary responsibility for the provision of day-to-day care, and it certainly requires higher levels of societal involvement in children's upbringing so that the duties related to bringing up children do not fall disproportionately on mothers and other female caregivers.

The lived experience of Natasha Bakht and Lynda Collins, two women in a non-romantic partnership raising a child with disabilities together, illustrates the type of unconventional care arrangement that we have in mind.

---

[13] Our position also aligns with what Patricia Hill Collins (1994) describes as "other-mothering," and what Eva Kittay (1999) refers to as "distributed mothering."

Natasha and Lynda are friends and colleagues as law professors at the University of Ottawa in Canada. When Natasha was in her mid-30s, she found herself single yet ready to have child. With the support of her family and friends, she used a sperm donor and conceived. In 2010, Natasha gave birth to her son Elaan. Her friend, Lynda, who was also single and thinking that she might like one day to have a child of her own, offered to be Natasha's birth coach. The birth had many complications, and, after several months, Elaan was diagnosed with cerebral palsy, visual impairment, and epilepsy, among other impairments. Natasha struggled to meet Elann's needs on her own. Although it was not their original plan, the two women decided to start raising Elaan in a non-romantic partnership as co-parents. When Elaan was just a year old, Lynda sold her house to move into Natasha's condominium building so that she could help to raise him more conveniently on a daily basis. Lynda and Natasha share all financial, decision-making, and hands-on day-to-day child-rearing responsibilities together. Eventually, they sought to have their parenting arrangement recognized in law. Since they are friends and not conjugal partners, however, Lynda could not apply legally to adopt Elaan. In April 2016, they filed an application with the Superior Court of Justice, Family Court, seeking a declaration of parentage for Lynda. Their case broke new legal ground in Canada when the Court, convinced that it was in Elaan's best interest, declared Lynda a legal parent (Ireton 2017; Bakht and Collins 2018).

In an article that Natasha and Lynda co-wrote together for the *Canadian Journal of Family Law* (2018), they explain how care arrangements for children with disabilities are poorly served by dominant cultural ideals of family found in Western ideology, which elevate and privilege traditional heterosexual nuclear families with biological parents. Reflecting on their family's experience, they observe:

> Often, and particularly in the cases of children born with unanticipated special needs, it takes time and experimentation to determine how best to meet a child's needs and those of her custodial parent. In Elaan's case, we found that his needs were best met through a combination of support from his biological mother, his non-biological mother, extended family, privately-funded care, and state support in the form of in-home assistance and access to a superb special-needs school. All of these pieces were, and are, necessary to ensure his well-being. (Bakht and Collins 2018: 109)

Thus, non-conjugal co-parenting works well for their entire family, and their story successfully demonstrates how family can be culturally and legally decoupled from biology and sexuality. Their example also instructs us to recognize the fact that many people can and should play crucial roles in children's upbringing to the benefit of the entire family unit.

Conclusion

All in all, we suspect that prenatal genetic testing and selective abortion would look very different in a more inclusive cultural context, one that enthusiastically welcomes people with Down syndrome and other types of intellectual and developmental disabilities into its ranks and supports parents in bringing up children. As proponents of the reproductive justice movement featured in Chapter 2 have insisted, social context shapes reproduction, and our social scaffolding and cultural norms open and close particular possibilities to women as they weigh their reproductive options. An oppressive cultural system that disparages people with disabilities, unfairly places primary responsibility for childcare on mothers, and fails to take collective responsibility for the well-being of all of its members can effectively make mothers and the disabled children for whom they care feel like "strangers in their own land," to borrow from Rosemarie Garland-Thomson's apt description (2012: 340) of the social alienation that people with disabilities and their family members too often experience. Reshaping our communal consciousness to embrace people with disabilities, to recognize mothers as well-rounded individuals with their own life projects, and to value diverse family forms can open new horizons for women as they face difficult decisions about their pregnancies.

References

Alstott, Anne (2004). *No Exit: What Parents Owe their Children and what Society Owes Parents*. Oxford: Oxford University Press.

Alstott, Anne (2015). "Neoliberalism in US Family Law: Negative Liberty and Laissez-Faire Markets in the Minimal State," *Law and Contemporary Problems*, 77/2: 25–42.

Apple, Rima (2006). *Perfect Motherhood: Science and Childrearing in America*. New Brunswick, NJ: Rutgers University Press.

Asch, Adrienne, and David Wasserman (2005). "Where Is the Sin in Synecdoche? Prenatal Testing and the Parent–Child Relationship," in David Wasserman, Jerome Bickenbach, and Robert Wachbroit (eds), *Quality of Life and Human Difference:*

Genetic Testing, Health Care, and Disability. Cambridge: Cambridge University Press, 172–216.

Auslander, G., and N. Gold (1999). "Disability Terminology in the Media: A Comparison of Newspaper Reports in Canada and Israel," *Social Science & Medicine*, 48/10: 1395–1405.

Baker, Michael, Jonathan Gruber, and Kevin Milligan (2008). "Universal Child Care, Maternal Labor Supply, and Family Wellbeing," *Journal of Political Economy*, 116/4: 709–45.

Bakht, Natasha, and Lynda Collins (2018). "Are you my Mother? Parentage in a Non-Conjugal Family," *Canadian Journal of Family Law*, 31/1: 105–50.

Bianchi, Suzanne M., and Melissa A. Milkie (2010). "Work and Family Research in the First Decade of the 21st Century," *Journal of Marriage and Family*, 72/3: 705–25.

Bianchi, Suzanne M., John P. Robinson, and Melissa A. Milkie (2006). *The Changing Rhythms of American Family Life.* New York: Russell Sage Foundation.

Bick, Alexander (2016). "The Quantitative Role of Child Care for Female Labor Force Participation and Fertility," *Journal of the European Economic Association*, 14/3: 639–68.

Bittman, Michael, and Judy Wajcman (2000). "The Rush Hour: The Character of Leisure Time and Gender Equity," *Social Forces*, 79/1: 165–89.

Blair–Loy, Mary, et al. (2015). "Stability and Transformation in Gender, Work, and Family: Insights from the Second Shift for the Next Quarter Century," *Community, Work, and Family*, 18/4: 435–54.

Blum, Linda (2007). "Mother Blaming in the Prozac Nation: Raising Kids with Invisible Disabilities," *Gender and Society*, 21/2: 202–26.

Bourke, Jenny, et al. (2008). "Maternal Physical and Mental Health in Children with Down Syndrome," *Journal of Pediatrics*, 153/3: 320–6.

Boyd, Susan (2010). "Autonomy for Mothers? Relational Theory and Parenting Apart," *Feminist Legal Studies*, 18/2: 137–58.

Bubeck, Diemut (1995). *Care, Gender, and Justice.* New York: Oxford University Press.

Buding, Michelle (2003). "Are Women's Employment and Fertility Histories Interdependent? An Examination of Causal Order Using Event History Analysis," *Social Science Research*, 32/3: 376–401.

Christensen, Lisa, et al. (2012). "Bullying Adolescents with Intellectual Disability," *Journal of Mental Health Research in Intellectual Disabilities*, 5/1: 49–65.

Clement, Grace (1996). *Care, Autonomy, and Justice: Feminism and the Ethic of Care.* Boulder, CO: Westview Press.

Cohen, Philip, and Miruna Petrescu–Prahova (2006). "Gendered Living Arrangements among Children with Disabilities," *Journal of Marriage and Family*, 68/3: 630–8.

Colker, Ruth (2015). "Blaming Mothers: A Disability Perspective," *Boston University Law Review*, 95/3: 1205–24.

Collins, Patricia Hill (1994). "Shifting the Center: Race, Class, and Feminist Theorizing on Motherhood," in Donna Bassin, Margaret Honey, and Meryle Mahrer Kaplan (eds), *Representations of Motherhood*. New Haven, CT: Yale University Press, 56–74.

Coltrane, Scott (2000). "Research on Household Labor: Modeling and Measuring the Social Embeddedness of Routine Family Work," *Journal of Marriage and Family*, 62/4: 1208–33.

Correll, Shelley, Stephen Benard, and In Paik (2007). "Getting a Job: Is there a Motherhood Penalty?," *American Journal of Sociology*, 112/5: 1297–1339.

Craig, Lyn, and Killian Mullan (2011). "How Mothers and Fathers Share Childcare: A Cross-National Time Use Comparison," *American Sociological Review*, 76/6: 834–61.

Crittenden, Ann (2001). *The Price of Motherhood: Why the Most Important Job in the World Is Still the Least Valued*. New York: Metropolitan Books.

Crouter, Ann, and Alan Booth (2009) (eds). *Work–Life Policies*. Washington: Urban Institute Press.

Dempsey, Ken (2002). "Who Gets the Best Deal from Marriage: Women or Men?," *Journal of Sociology*, 38/2: 91–110.

Douglas, Susan, and Meredith Michaels (2004). *The Mommy Myth: The Idealization of Motherhood and how it has Undermined Women*. New York: Free Press.

Eichner, Maxine (2010). *The Supportive State: Families, Government, and America's Political Ideals*. Oxford: Oxford University Press.

Engster, Daniel (2015). *Justice, Care, and the Welfare State*. Oxford: Oxford University Press.

Fifield, Jen (2016). "What Happens to Developmentally Disabled as Parents Age, Die?," *PBS News Hour*, August 10, https://www.pbs.org/newshour/health/happens-developmentally-disabled-parents-age-die.

Fisher, Marisa, et al. (2016). "Victimisation and Social Vulnerability of Adults with Intellectual Disability: A Review of Research Extending beyond Wilson and Brewer," *Australian Psychologist*, 51/2: 114–27.

Friedman, Sandra, and Miriam Kalichman (2014). "Out-of-Home Placement for Children and Adolescents with Disabilities," *Pediatrics*, 134/4: 836–46.

Gangl, Markus, and Andrea Ziefle (2009). "Motherhood, Labor Force Behavior, and Women's Careers: An Empirical Assessment of the Wage Penalty for Motherhood in Britain, Germany, and the United States," *Demography*, 46/2: 341–69.

Garland-Thomson, Rosemarie (2012). "The Case for Conserving Disability", *Bioethical Inquiry*, 9/3: 339–55.

Gershuny, Jonathan, and Oriel Sullivan (2003). "Time Use, Gender, and Public Policy Regimes," *Social Politics*, 10/2: 205–28.

Gibson, Charity (2019). "Enacting Motherhood Online: How Facebook and Mommy Blogs Reinforce White Ideologies of the New Momism," *Feminist Encounters: A Journal of Critical Studies in Culture and Politics*, 3/1–2: 1–11.

Gilmore, Linda, and Monica Cuskelly (2014). "Vulnerability to Loneliness in People with Intellectual Disability: An Explanatory Model," *Journal of Policy and Practice in Intellectual Disabilities*, 11/3: 192–9.

Goering, Sara (2017). "Mothers and Others: Relational Autonomy in Parenting," in Leslie Francis (ed.), *The Oxford Handbook of Reproductive Ethics*. Oxford: Oxford University Press, 285–300.

Goodwin, Michele (2020). *Policing the Womb: Invisible Women and the Criminalization of Motherhood*. Cambridge: Cambridge University Press.

Gornick, Janet, and Marcia Meyers (2008). "Creating Gender Egalitarian Societies: An Agenda for Reform," *Politics and Society*, 36/3: 313–49.

Gottlieb, Roger (2002). "The Tasks of Embodied Love: Moral Problems in Caring for Children with Disabilities," *Hypatia: A Journal of Feminist Philosophy*, 17/3: 225–36.

Green, Fiona (2020). "Feminist Mothering," in Lynn O'Brien Hallstein, Andrea O'Reilly and Melinda Vandenbeld Giles (ed.), *Routledge Companion to Motherhood*, New York: Routledge, 36–50.

Handler, Joel, and Yeheskel Hasenfeld (2007). *Blame Welfare, Ignore Poverty and Inequality*. Cambridge: Cambridge University Press.

Hays, Sharon (1996). *The Cultural Contradictions of Motherhood*. New Haven, CT: Yale University Press.

Hillyer, Barbara (1993). *Feminism and Disability*. Norman, OK: University of Oklahoma Press.

Hochschild, Arlie Russell (1997). *The Time Bind: When Work Becomes Home and Home Becomes Work*. New York: Metropolitan Books.

Horowitz, Juliana Menasce, Nikki Graf, and Gretchen Livingston (2019). *Marriage and Cohabitation in the US*. Washington: Pew Research Center, https://www.pewresearch.org/social–trends/2019/11/06/marriage–and–cohabitation–in–the–u–s/.

Hughes, Rosemary B., et al. (2019). "The Relation of Abuse to Physical and Psychological Health in Adults with Developmental Disabilities," *Disability and Health Journal*, 12/2: 227–34.

Huirachocha, Lourdes, et al. (2017). "Parenting Children with Down Syndrome: Societal Influences," *Journal of Child Health Care*, 21/4: 488–97.

Ireton, Julie (2017). "Raising Elaan: Profoundly Disabled Boy's 'Co–Mommas' Make Legal History," *CBS News*, February 21, https://www.cbc.ca/news/canada/ottawa/

180 Prenatal Genetic Testing, Abortion, and Disability Justice

multimedia/raising–elaan–profoundly–disabled–boy–s–co–mommas–make–legal–history–1.3988464.

Jain, Renu, David Thomasma, and Rasa Raga (2002). "Down Syndrome: Still Social Stigma," *American Journal of Perinatology*, 19/2: 99–108.

Kaposy, Chris (2018). *Choosing Down Syndrome: Ethics and New Prenatal Testing Technologies*. Cambridge, MA: MIT Press.

Kittay, Eva Feder (1999). *Love's Labor: Essays on Women, Equality, and Dependency*. New York: Routledge.

Kittay, Eva Feder (2019). *Learning from my Daughter: The Value and Care of Disabled Minds*. Oxford: Oxford University Press.

Landsman, Gail Heidi (2009). *Reconstructing Motherhood and Disability in the Age of "Perfect" Babies*. New York: Routledge.

Lipscomb, Stephen, et al. (2017). "Preparing for Life after High School: The Characteristics and Experiences of Youth in Special Education," in *Findings from the National Longitudinal Transition Study 2012*, ii. *Comparisons across Disability Groups: Full Report*. Washington: US Department of Education, https://files.eric.ed.gov/fulltext/ED573334.pdf.

Llewellyn, Gwynnyth, et al. (1999). "Family Factors Influencing Out-of-Home Placement Decisions," *Journal of Intellectual Disability Research*, 43/3: 219–33.

Lou, Stina, et al. (2018). "Termination of Pregnancy Following a Prenatal Diagnosis of Down Syndrome: A Qualitative Study of the Decision-Making Process of Pregnant Couples," *Acta Obstetricia et Gynecologica Scandinavica*, 97/10: 1228–36.

McLaughlin, Janice, et al. (2008). *Families Raising Disabled Children: Enabling Care and Social Justice*. London: Palgrave MacMillan.

Malacrida, Claudia, and Tiffany Boulton (2012). "Women's Perceptions of Childbirth 'Choices': Competing Discourses of Motherhood, Sexuality, and Selflessness," *Gender and Society*, 26/5: 748–72.

Meyers, Diana Tietjens (2004). *Being Yourself: Essays on Identity, Action, and Social Life*. Lanham, MD: Rowman Littlefield Publishers.

Miller, Amalia R. (2011). "The Effects of Motherhood Timing on Career Path," *Journal of Population Economics*, 24/3: 1071–1100.

Mills, Catherine (2015). "The Case of the Missing Hand: Gender, Disability, and Bodily Norms in Selective Termination," *Hypatia: A Journal of Feminist Philosophy*, 30/1: 82–96.

Murphy, Nancy, et al. (2007). "The Health of Caregivers for Children with Disabilities: Caregiver Perspectives," *Child Care Health and Development*, 33/2: 180–7.

Namkung, Eun Ha, et al. (2015). "The Relative Risk of Divorce in Parents of Children with Developmental Disabilities: Impacts of Lifelong Parenting," *American Journal of Developmental Disability*, 120/6: 514–26.

Okin, Susan Moller (1989). *Justice, Gender, and the Family*. New York: Basic Books.

O'Reilly, Andrea (2008). "'That Is what Feminism Is: The Acting and Living and not Just the Told': Modeling and Mentoring Feminism," in Andrea O'Reilly (ed.), *Feminist Mothering*. Albany, NY: State University of New York Press, 191–204.

Parker, Kim, and Wendy Wang (2013). *Modern Parenthood: Roles of Moms and Dads Converge as they Balance Work and Family*. Washington: Pew Research Center, https://www.pewresearch.org/social-trends/2013/03/14/modern-parenthood-roles-of-moms-and-dads-converge-as-they-balance-work-and-family/.

Piepmeier, Alison (2013). "The Inadequacy of 'Choice': Disability and what's Wrong with Feminist Framings of Reproduction," *Feminist Studies*, 39/1: 159–86.

Plant, Karen, and Mark Sanders (2007). "Predictors of Care-Giver Stress in Families of Preschool-Aged Children with Developmental Disabilities," *Journal of Intellectual Disability Research*, 51/2: 109–24.

Radigan, Kathy (2017). "I'm not a Saint because my Daughter Has Special Needs," *Huffington Post*, October 2, https://www.huffpost.com/entry/im-not-a-saint-because-my-daughter-has-special-needs_b_59d2319be4b034ae778d4c3d.

Rapp, Rayna, and Faye Ginsburg (2001). "Enabling Disability: Rewriting Kinship, Reimagining Citizenship," *Public Culture*, 13/3: 533–56.

Read, Janet (2000). *Disability, the Family and Society: Listening to Mothers*. Buckingham, UK: Open University Press.

Reardanz, Jenna, et al. (2020). "Peer Victimization and Communication Skills in Adolescents with Down Syndrome: Preliminary Findings," *Journal of Autism and Developmental Disorders*, 50/1: 349–55.

Resch, J. Aaron, et al. (2010). "Giving Parents a Voice: A Qualitative Study of the Challenges Experienced by Parents of Children with Disabilities," *Rehabilitation Psychology*, 55/2: 139–50.

Risdal, Don, and George H. S. Singer (2004). "Marital Adjustment in Parents of Children with Disabilities: A Historical Review and Meta-Analysis," *Research and Practice for Persons with Severe Disabilities*, 29/2: 95–103.

Roberts, Dorothy (1997). *Killing the Black Body: Race, Reproduction, and the Meaning of Liberty*. New York: Pantheon Books.

Ruppanner, Leah, Stephanie Moller, and Liana Sayer (2019.). "Expensive Childcare and Short School Days = Lower Maternal Employment and More Time in Childcare? Evidence from the American Time Use Survey," *Socius: Sociological Research for a Dynamic World*, 5: 1–14.

Ryckaert, Vic (2019). "Roncalli Football Players Abused and Threatened Boy with Down Syndrome," *Indiana Star*, November 22, https://www.indystar.com/story/news/crime/2019/11/27/roncalli-football-players-accused-abusing-boy-down-syndrome/4307922002/.

Siperstein, Gary, Jennifer Norins, and Amanda Mohler (2007). "Social Acceptance and Attitude Change," in John Jacobson, James Mulick, and Johannes Rojahn (eds), *Handbook of Intellectual and Developmental Disabilities*. New York: Springer, 133–56.

Solish, Abbie, Adrienne Perry and Patricia Minnes (2009). "Participation of Children with and without Disabilities in Social, Recreational and Leisure Activities," *Journal of Applied Research in Intellectual Disabilities*, 23/3: 226–36.

Spock, Benjamin (1946). *The Common Sense Book of Baby and Child Care*. New York: Duell, Sloan and Pearce.

Stone, Pamela (2007). *Opting Out? Why Women Really Quit Careers and Head Home*. Berkeley and Los Angeles: University of California Press.

Thomas, Gareth (2020). "The Media Love the Artificial Versions of what's Going on: Media (Mis)representations of Down's Syndrome," *British Journal of Sociology*, 72: 693–706.

Tong, Henry, et al. (2003). "Low Back Pain in Adult Female Caregivers of Children with Physical Disabilities," *Archives of Pediatrics and Adolescent Medicine*, 157/11: 1128–33.

Tronto, Joan (2015). *Who Cares? How to Reshape a Democratic Politics*. Ithaca, NY: Cornell University Press.

Vanhala, Lisa (2011). *Making Rights a Reality? Disability Rights Activists and Legal Mobilization*. Oxford: Oxford University Press.

Waldman, Ayelet (2009). *Bad Mother: A Chronicle of Maternal Crimes, Minor Calamities, and Occasional Moments of Grace*. New York: Anchor Books.

White, Julie Anne (2000). *Democracy, Justice, and the Welfare State: Reconstructing Public Care*. University Park, PA: Penn State University Press.

Wilkinson, Penny, and Peter McGill (2008). "Representation of People with Intellectual Disabilities in a British Newspaper in 1983 and 2001," *Journal of Applied Research in Intellectual Disabilities*, 22/1: 65–76.

Williams, Joan (2000). *Unbending Gender: Why Family and Work Conflict and what to Do about It*. Oxford: Oxford University Press.

Williams, Joan (2010). *Reshaping the Work–Family Debate: Why Men and Class Matter*. Cambridge, MA: Harvard University Press.

Wimbush, Erica (1988). "Mothers Meeting," in Erica Wimbush and Margaret Talbot (eds), *Relative Freedoms: Women and Leisure*. Philadelphia: Open University Press, 60–74.

Zhang, Sara (2020). "The Last Children of Down Syndrome," *Atlantic* (December), https://www.theatlantic.com/magazine/archive/2020/12/the-last-children-of-down-syndrome/616928/.

6
Conclusion

The Coronavirus Pandemic and Its Implications

This book was written in the midst of the global coronavirus pandemic and the ensuing economic recession. We have paid close attention to the rapidly evolving political, social, and economic landscape as we have conducted our research, analyzing events as they continue to unfold in real time. Given the unprecedented, world-shattering magnitude of the pandemic, we conclude by grappling with timely questions about how large-scale socioeconomic changes might affect and inform key issues that we have discussed throughout this book, asking: how might socioeconomic developments wrought by the pandemic impact on women's options regarding prenatal genetic testing and selective abortion in the short term? And, what political lessons should we take away from the pandemic for the long run?

To begin, the coronavirus pandemic, which started spreading in the United States in 2020, drastically altered our social world in unforeseen ways. As of May 2022, the World Health Organization (WHO) estimates that the pandemic has been one of the deadliest in recorded history. Over six million people have died from Covid-19 worldwide, with nearly 990,000 recorded deaths in the United States (WHO 2022). Millions more have been infected, with many survivors experiencing prolonged symptoms.[1] The fallout has been felt most acutely by those who have become sick and/or who have lost loved ones. Yet even those who have avoided infection have not been immune from the social disruptions, economic crises, and political strife that have followed in the pandemic's wake. Shelter-in-place orders, school closures, business shutdowns, and mass layoffs have upended people's lives and created newfound challenges (or accelerated and exacerbated existing ones) for nearly everyone.

Despite its global reach, however, the burdens of the pandemic have been anything but universal. The coronavirus crisis, and political responses to

---

[1] These individuals, dubbed "long haulers," comprise roughly 10% of those who have experienced SARS-CoV-2 infection (Greenhalgh et al. 2020).

Prenatal Genetic Testing, Abortion, and Disability Justice. Amber Knight and Joshua Miller, Oxford University Press.
© Amber Knight and Joshua Miller (2023). DOI: 10.1093/oso/9780192870957.003.0007

184 Prenatal Genetic Testing, Abortion, and Disability Justice

it, have compounded existing social inequalities, and the effects have been especially devastating for members of socially marginalized communities. According to the Centers for Disease Control (CDC), Black, Latinx, and Native American communities have experienced significantly higher rates of infection, hospitalization, and death (CDC 2022). People of color have been disproportionately exposed to the virus as low-wage "essential" workers who have been put in a position to risk their health to make a living. Notably, women of color and/or immigrant women, who make up the overwhelming majority of front-line home health aides and personal-care attendants, have been susceptible to contracting the coronavirus from the people for whom they care (that is, children, the elderly, people with disabilities) amidst shortages of personal protective equipment to keep them safe (Shapiro 2020). Once exposed to and infected by the pathogen, people of color are more at risk for severe symptoms and death owing to co-occurring health conditions such as diabetes and heart disease, many of which are themselves the byproduct of structural racism. Existing healthcare disparities then create barriers to accessing affordable and quality healthcare services once someone is ill (Gould and Wilson 2020).

The weight of the economic downturn has been shouldered as unevenly as the burden of disease. Women have been more likely than men to become unemployed during the pandemic, and women of color have experienced the most job losses (Gezici and Ozay 2020). The pandemic has been especially hard on working mothers owing to a lack of childcare options following quarantine measures and daycare closures. The spike in unemployment has resulted in many people losing their work-related health insurance, which translates into reduced access to healthcare, including obstetric and postnatal care (Ramgobin et al. 2021).

As we have argued throughout the book, women's reproductive preferences and options are shaped in part by the broader socioeconomic context in which they are made. The unfortunate reality is that women who have become pregnant during or since the pandemic and are thinking about whether or not they want to bring a fetus with Down syndrome into the world are making difficult decisions during a time that has been particularly harrowing for individuals with disabilities and their families. One study estimates that people with Down syndrome are roughly four times more likely to be hospitalized, and ten times more likely to die from Covid-19, than the general population (Clift et al. 2021). These alarmingly high infection and mortality rates can be partly attributed to physiological variables, including anatomical factors that make people with Down syndrome more prone to severe respiratory illnesses. People with Down syndrome are also more likely to have underlying conditions, such as congenital heart disease and obesity, that increase the likelihood of developing a severe or lethal infection. That said, the most salient risk factors are the byproduct of unjust social and political arrangements, including the continued institutionalization of people with disabilities. Despite the promise of community living embedded in the Americans with Disabilities Act (1990) and the *Olmstead v. L.C.* (1999) ruling, more than 330,000 people with intellectual and developmental disabilities are estimated to live in congregate settings (Larson et al. 2018). The reasons for their continued institutionalization are systemic, including inadequate public funding for home- and community-based services, a shortage of affordable and accessible housing in the community, and Medicaid's institutional bias. The pandemic has revealed the immediate dangers of living in congregate settings. Close quarters, the shared use of essential living spaces, and frequent shift changes among staff have turned institutions into breeding grounds for the virus (Sabatello, Landes, and McDonald 2020). Preliminary studies estimate that roughly one-third of Covid-19 deaths in America have occurred in nursing homes and assisted living facilities (Girvan 2020; Yourish et al. 2020). The astronomical infection and mortality rates in nursing homes and other congregate settings have unveiled the failures of our current care infrastructure for both care recipients and providers alike.

The pandemic also unleashed the depths of ableism within the medical profession. As we discussed in Chapter 3, ableism permeates healthcare institutions. Ableist assumptions about the quality and value of disabled lives came to the fore during the early stages of the pandemic, especially in discussions about the potential need to ration scarce medical equipment for ventilators in instances of critical care. Multiple triage policies that were released to guide providers on rationing care explicitly stated disability as a criterion to deny treatment (Ne'eman 2020; Scully 2020). Moreover, despite the growing knowledge that nursing homes and other institutions had become hotbeds of infection, people with intellectual and developmental disabilities in congregate settings and their support staff did not receive prioritization for vaccines in most states (Landes, Turk, and Ervin 2021).

Relatedly, the politicization of information that we discussed in Chapter 3 came to a head during the pandemic, providing another stark example for the need for government bodies to collect and disseminate accurate, up-to-date, comprehensive information so that people can make informed and autonomous choices about their healthcare. From the outset, US right-wing politicians, including President Trump, and conservative media outlets downplayed the risk of contracting Covid-19 and the likelihood of developing a severe, life-threatening infection. Contrary to advice from public-health experts and the CDC, they also downplayed or dismissed the effectiveness of health-protective behaviors intended to break the chain of transmission, including hand-washing, masking, social distancing, and self-quarantining (Bolsen and Palm 2022). Social media compounded the situation, providing a platform for misinformation campaigns to flourish. Stories that circulated widely on social media included misleading, unvalidated, pseudoscientific claims about transmission (for example, that it spreads through mosquito bites), therapies (for example, that hydroxychloroquine and drinking bleach offer cures), and the potential harms of vaccines (for example, that vaccines cause infertility) (Bolsen and Palm 2022). Misinformation was so rampant that some scholars characterized the politicization of the pandemic as a kind of epidemic in itself, or what some now refer to as a "misinfodemic" (Chou, Gaysynsky, and Vanderpool 2020).

The pandemic also exposed major cracks in other parts of the American social safety net, or lack thereof. As we argued in Chapter 4, our current patchwork of policies and programs to support families of children with disabilities leaves too many financially vulnerable. The pandemic has only worsened the situation. The ensuing recession has put many households in tough financial straits, and the economic toll has negatively impacted on those with limited resources the most, including families with disabled members who disproportionately lived at or near the poverty line before the pandemic even started (Patel et al. 2020). To add insult to injury, the first two rounds of stimulus payments excluded from eligibility adults with disabilities who are considered dependants for tax purposes. These same relief packages also failed to offer dedicated funding for home- and community-based services, which would have helped people with disabilities transition out of the hazardous conditions in congregate settings (Diament 2021). Clearly, government responses to the pandemic were not designed with the needs and interests of people with disabilities in mind.

In addition, the disparaging social attitudes about disability that we addressed in Chapter 5 have been on full display throughout the pandemic as well. As Andrew Pulrang (2020) explains, too many disabled, chronically ill, and elderly people have been portrayed as "acceptable losses" in public discourse. He catalogues how the systemic devaluation of people with disabilities has manifested in the idea that disabled lives are disposable, noting:

> Members of Congress openly argued that high-risk Americans should be willing to die in order to keep the economy humming. The general public was told not to worry about COVID-19 because that would mainly harm people with "pre-existing

> conditions." In fact, COVID skepticism itself is strongly influenced by the idea that the virus is really only a problem for others, namely elderly, chronically ill, and disabled people—as if that makes it less of a problem. (Pulrang 2020)

The stark message that people with disabilities are worth less—that their lives are disposable and their deaths are ungrievable—is degrading and dehumanizing. Moreover, the social expectation that elderly people, people with disabilities, and/or immuno-comprised individuals should willingly sacrifice themselves at the altars of capitalism and/or personal freedom (that is, the "freedom" not to wear a mask) signals a troubling embrace of social Darwinism. Journalist Rachel Charlton-Daily (2022) captures the effect these attitudes have had on the disability community, writing: "For disabled and vulnerable people, the pandemic has been incredibly isolating, not just because we have had to physically isolate, but because we have realized that many consider our safety little more than an inconvenience. Disabled people shouldn't have to convince you their lives are worthy of saving."

Finally, the pandemic has magnified the challenges of raising children with disabilities in isolation from support systems and extended care networks. If social isolation and caregiver burnout were a problem prior to the coronavirus pandemic, as we argued in Chapter 5, social distancing and disrupted services have driven many parents of children with disabilities to the breaking point. To be sure, people's experiences with the pandemic have not been identical. How well families have coped has depended a lot on their resources, both social and financial, and some families have coped well or even thrived with increased time together and a slower pace of life. However, many families who relied on a small army of special-education teachers, therapists, personal-care attendants, and other caregivers to get through the week have been struggling in the prolonged absence of vital in-person services. In addition to working and/or taking on full-time caregiving responsibilities, many parents of children with disabilities have had to step into new roles as special educators, speech therapists, behavioral therapists, and more (Klass 2020). These heightened and competing demands have taken their toll. According to survey data, parents of children with disabilities have experienced higher rates of stress, depression, and anxiety than other parents during the pandemic (Greenberg 2020).

In sum, prospective parents weighing their options following a positive fetal diagnosis of Down syndrome are doing so in a tumultuous time that has been particularly unwelcoming and hostile to people with disabilities and their families. During the pandemic, pregnant women are being told that their prospective children's lives would be expendable collateral damage for those who want life to go back to normal as quickly as possible. Moreover, survey data have also found that financial considerations are already shaping many women's reproductive preferences, as more than one in three American women reported wanting to delay having a child or limit future births in the face of substantial job losses and broad economic uncertainty (Lindberg et al. 2020). We expect the additional financial costs and caregiving responsibilities that are often associated with raising a child with an intellectual and developmental disability to feel extraordinarily intimidating during the worst recession since the Great Depression, especially if strained state budgets jeopardize the meager patchwork of supports and services in place. In the short run, therefore, the pandemic has amplified all the structural constraints—an ableist medical profession, the shortcomings of neoliberal economic policies, and ableist and sexist cultural norms—that we have highlighted in the chapters in Part II of this book.

Even though the human toll from the pandemic has been unimaginably tragic, we are cautiously optimistic about what the future holds. We cannot yet predict the aftermath with any certainty, but the pandemic has the potential to become a catalyst for lasting progressive change. Just as the extreme hardships of the Great Depression called on Americans to lay the foundations for a stronger and more resilient federal government in the form of the New Deal, the coronavirus crisis calls on us to rethink and reorient our relationship to government and each other once again. The pandemic offers the unique opportunity to pause, reflect, re-evaluate our priorities, discuss, and make political decisions about our collective lives.

Recent developments on the ground give us reason to be hopeful. There has been a groundswell of momentum among social justice organizations working in coalition to push for substantial new investments in our social safety net and care infrastructure. Organizations working on behalf of care workers (Caring across Generations and the National Domestic Workers Alliance), the disability community (The Arc), and women's rights organizations committed to work–family balance (MomsRising and the National Partnership for Women and Families) have banded together in the #Care-CantWait coalition to advocate for universal access to paid family leave, affordable and quality childcare, and home- and community-based services for people with disabilities and seniors. Advocates hope that, amid the crisis, the federal government will finally commit to substantial investments in our care infrastructure, and their lobbying efforts appear to be making headway. The Biden administration has made an investment in care a top priority as a pillar of the "build back better" agenda. President Biden's "American Jobs Plan" proposes a $400 billion investment in home- and community-based services for seniors and people with disabilities as part of the "Better Care Better Jobs Act" (Musumeci 2021). While President Biden's plan falls short of the universal long-term care system we championed in Chapter 4, the proposed reforms would be a huge step in the right direction toward the larger goals of eliminating Medicaid's institutional bias, making coverage for long-term home and community-based services mandatory, and paying home health aides and personal-care attendants a living wage.

Building a constituency to demand and implement these changes, and to make them last, will demand a cultural reckoning. Although feminist relational autonomy theorists have long insisted that our political institutions and norms should be designed to accommodate the realities of human vulnerability and interdependence, their message has not been widely adopted in mainstream society. The cult of American individualism has a strong grip on its adherents. That said, the pandemic has laid bare how radically interdependent and vulnerable human beings truly are. If the pandemic has a silver lining, it lies in the potential to jolt Americans into a realization that our fates are linked, and that interdependence, vulnerability, disability, and aging are inevitable aspects of the human condition that should be respected and accommodated in our political institutions. The sooner that the American public comes to terms with human beings' interdependencies, the greater the chances that they will be willing to invest in a more inclusionary and resilient society hospitable to our shared vulnerabilities—and the better off we all will be, especially prospective mothers, who deserve support as they think about what kind of future they want for themselves and their potential children.

References

Bolsen, Toby, and Risa Palm (2022). "Politicization and COVID-19 Vaccine Resistance in the US," *Progress in Molecular Biology and Translational Science*, 188/1: 81–100.

CDC (2022). *Risk for COVID-19 Infection, Hospitalization, and Death by Race/Ethnicity*. Atlanta, GA: Centers for Disease Control and Prevention, https://www.cdc.gov/coronavirus/2019–ncov/covid–data/investigations–discovery/hospitalization–death–by–race–ethnicity.html.

Charlton-Daily, Rachel (2022). "Disabled People Can't Learn to Live with Covid," *Verywell Health*, January 14, https://www.verywellhealth.com/disabled–people–cant–learn–to–live–with–covid–5215746?utm_source=social2&utm_medium=social&utm_campaign=shareurlbuttons&fbclid=IwAR1wfssRgmVFdnTZYHTaQ3EH_ty5_X9qlvBQQxTHVmMTlsgtA8GTNdHjKYA.

190 Prenatal Genetic Testing, Abortion, and Disability Justice

Chou, Wen-Ying, Anna Gaysynsky, and Robin Vanderpool (2020). "The COVID-19 Misinfodemic: Moving beyond Fact Checking," *Health Education and Behavior*, 48/1: 9–13.

Clift, Ashley Kieran, et al. (2021). "COVID-19 Mortality Risk in Down Syndrome: Results from a Cohort Study of 8 Million Adults," *Annals of Internal Medicine*, 174/4: 572–6.

Diament, Michelle (2021). "Advocates: COVID-19 Relief Leaves out People with Disabilities," *Disability Scoop*, January 5, https://www.disabilityscoop.com/2021/01/05/advocates–covid–19–relief–leaves–out–people–with–disabilities/29138/.

Gezici, Armagan, and Ozge Ozay (2020). "How Race and Gender Shape COVID–19 Unemployment Probability," Working paper, https://www.researchgate.net/profile/Armagan–Gezici/publication/343481037_How_Race_and_Gender_Shape_COVID–19_Unemployment_Probability/links/5f3150a192851cd302ed2f e5/How–Race–and–Gender–Shape–COVID–19–Unemployment–Probability. pdf.

Girvan, Gregg (2020). *Nursing Homes and Assisted Living Facilities Account for 38% of COVID-19 Deaths*. Foundation for Research on Equal Opportunity, Austin, TX, https://freopp.org/the–covid–19 nursing–home–crisis–by–the–numbers–3a47433c3f70.

Gould, Elise, and Valerie Wilson (2020). *Black Workers Face Two of the Most Lethal Preexisting Conditions for Coronavirus: Racism and Economic Inequality*, Washington: Economic Policy Institute, https://www.epi.org/publication/black–workers–covid/.

Greenberg, Erica (2020). *Families of Children with Disabilities will Need Support beyond the Pandemic*. Washington: Urban Institute, https://www.urban.org/urban–wire/families–children–disabilities–will–need–support–beyond–pandemic.

Greenhalgh, Trisha, et al. (2020). "Management of Post-Acute COVID-19 in Primary Care," *British Medical Journal*, 370: 1–8.

Klass, Perri (2020). "The Pandemic's Toll on Children with Special Needs and their Parents," *New York Times*, July 27, https://www.nytimes.com/2020/07/27/well/family/children–special–needs–pandemic.html.

Landes, Scott, Margret Turk, and David Ervin (2021). "COVID-19 Case-Fatality Disparities among People with Intellectual and Developmental Disabilities: Evidence from 12 US Jurisdictions," *Disability Health Journal*, 14/4.

Larson, Sheryl, et al. (2018). *In-Home and Residential Long-Term Supports and Services for Persons with Intellectual or Developmental Disabilities: Status and Trends through 2016*. Minneapolis, MN: Institute on Community Integration, University of Minnesota, https://ici.umn.edu/products/1005.

Lindberg, Laura, et al. (2020). *Early Impacts of the COVID-19 Pandemic: Findings from the 2020 Guttmacher Survey of Reproductive Health Experiences*. New York, NY: Guttmacher Institute. Available at: <https://www.guttmacher.org/report/early-impacts-covid-19-pandemic-findings-2020-guttmacher-survey-reproductive-health>.

Musumeci, MaryBeth (2021). *How Could $400 Billion New Federal Dollars Change Medicaid Home and Community-Based Services?* Washington: Kaiser Family Foundation, https://www.kff.org/medicaid/issue-brief/how-could-400-billion-new-federal-dollars-change-medicaid-home-and-community-based-services/.

Ne'eman, Arie (2020). "I Will Not Apologize for my Needs," *New York Times*, March 23, https://www.nytimes.com/2020/03/23/opinion/coronavirus-ventilators-triage-disability.html.

Patel, Jay Anil, et al. (2020). "Poverty, Inequality and COVID-19: The Forgotten Vulnerable," *Public Health*, 183: 110–11.

Pulrang, Andrew (2020). "What I've Learned as a Disabled Person from the COVID-19 Pandemic," *Forbes*, December 28, https://www.forbes.com/sites/andrewpulrang/2021/12/28/what-ive-learned-as-a-disabled-person-from-the-covid-19-pandemic/?sh=1754b08a5e97.

Ramgobin, Devyani, et al. (2021). "Papering over the Cracks: COVID-19's Amplification of the Failures of Employer-Based Health Insurance Coverage," *Journal of Community Hospital Internal Medicine Perspectives*, 11/1: 107–10.

Sabatello, Maya, Scott Landes, and Katherine McDonald (2020). "People with Disabilities in COVID-19: Fixing our Priorities," *American Journal of Bioethics*, 20/7: 187–90.

Scully, Jackie Leach (2020). "Disability, Disablism, and COVID-19 Pandemic Triage," *Bioethical Inquiry*, 17/4: 601–5.

Shapiro, Joseph (2020). "COVID-19 Infections and Deaths Are Higher among those with Intellectual Disabilities," *National Public Radio*, June 9, https://www.npr.org/2020/06/09/872401607/covid-19-infections-and-deaths-are-higher-among-those-with-intellectual-disabili?fbclid=IwAR33qWHWXVrXok9qpnkhicIXRLmZB22qCIhrpFC6o_R4d4vCsITxe7wudi8.

WHO (2022). *WHO Coronavirus (COVID-19) Dashboard*. Geneva: World Health Organization, https://covid19.who.int/table.

Yourish, Karen, et al. (2020). "One-Third of All U.S. Coronavirus Deaths Are Nursing Home Residents or Workers," *New York Times*, May 11, https://www.nytimes.com/interactive/2020/05/09/us/coronavirus-cases-nursing-homes-us.html.

Afterword

Prenatal Genetic Testing and Abortion after *Dobbs*

In June 2022, shortly after we had finished writing this book, the United States Supreme Court overturned decades of legal precedent by ruling that the Constitution does not confer a right to abortion. In *Dobbs* v. *Jackson Women's Health Organization* (2022), the court majority upheld a Mississippi law prohibiting abortion after fifteen weeks of pregnancy, reversing *Roe* v. *Wade*, which for almost half a century had been the law of the land. The reversal was not completely unexpected. As this book has shown, American states have enacted a steady stream of regulations over the last few decades—including waiting period requirements, prohibitions on public funding, and selective abortion bans—to restrict *Roe's* right to abortion and test the limits of *Planned Parenthood* v. *Casey's* undue burden standard. The *Dobbs* decision thus represents the latest step of a decades-long conservative crusade to repeal constitutional protections for abortion.

The implications are profound. We will leave a nuanced explanation of the legal repercussions to constitutional law experts, who will undoubtedly have much to say about *Dobbs's* impact on the scope of rights protected by the Fourteenth Amendment, the doctrine of *stare decisis*, and the legitimacy of the Court, among other topics. Here we want briefly to discuss how the *Dobbs* decision will influence prenatal genetic testing and selective abortion, emphasizing the effects on members of marginalized groups.

As Justice Kavanaugh's concurring opinion notes, the *Dobbs* decision "allows the people and their elected representatives to address the issue" at the state level.[1] With the legal status of abortion left entirely up to state governments, geography will be destiny. Some states will enhance protections for abortion while others will criminalize it, leading to a Balkanization of women's healthcare access across the country. Forecasts differ, but policy experts predict that abortion will remain legal in roughly half of the states across the country, while the rest will impose restrictions or ban it altogether

---

[1] *Dobbs* v. *Jackson Women's Health Organization* 597 U.S. ___ (2022), 5.

Prenatal Genetic Testing, Abortion, and Disability Justice. Amber Knight and Joshua Miller, Oxford University Press.
© Amber Knight and Joshua Miller (2023). DOI: 10.1093/oso/9780192870957.003.0008

(Center for Reproductive Rights 2022; Guttmacher Institute 2022). Moreover, many abortion bans, including statutes already in effect in Missouri and North Dakota, will not include exemptions for rape or incest. Some may not even allow providers to make exceptions to save the mother's life. In these cases, women in the United States will have fewer reproductive options than women in Pakistan or Saudi Arabia, which permit abortion when a mother's health is at stake.

Even though states will decide how to regulate abortion in their respective jurisdictions, legal questions remain about how far the state's interest in protecting "potential life" will extend. It is also unclear how the patchwork of state-by-state rules will affect the availability and usage of various reprogenetic technologies across the country. For instance, will states that ban abortion or set low gestational limits make exceptions for terminating a pregnancy because of "severe fetal abnormality," as Mississippi's Gestational Act does? If so, what counts as "severe"? Conversely, will states that legalize abortion nevertheless pass "prenatal non-discrimination acts" to ban terminations that are pursued because prospective parents do not want to carry a fetus with certain genetic traits? Will states with restrictive abortion laws make exemptions for technologies like preimplantation genetic testing for embryos created through *in vitro* fertilization? Or, will states decide that embryos have "personhood" status and subject these technologies to new regulatory restrictions? Moreover, will state officials dictate what healthcare professionals can say in prenatal genetic counseling sessions? If so, will genetic counselors in states with abortion bans be legally prohibited from discussing termination options in other states? The answers to these questions remain up for debate in this rapidly changing policy landscape, and it is difficult confidently to predict what a post-*Roe* America holds in store for patients and providers alike in different regions of the country.

Nevertheless, we anticipate that the *Dobbs* decision will have disparate effects on women—depending on their place of residence and financial resources—when it comes to their decisions about whether to use non-invasive prenatal testing (NIPT) and what to do upon receipt of results. Pregnant women from privileged backgrounds, even those living in states with abortion bans, may find NIPT more popular than ever. Because it is performed earlier in pregnancy than other screening procedures, NIPT can provide results in a timeframe that would allow women to order abortifacient medications or make a journey across state lines should they desire to terminate a pregnancy affected by Down syndrome or another genetic impairment. We also expect pregnant women who choose to undergo screening to be more likely to decide to abort on the basis of NIPT results alone, prior to diagnostic confirmation, since waiting for amniocentesis or CVS results would make termination practically impossible in many states. Doing so may bring unintended consequences. Though NIPT provides reliable results for Down syndrome, it performs less well for less common and more severe conditions such as Prader-Willi and Angelman syndromes, for which the chance of a false positive result can be as high as 90 percent (Kliff and Bhatia 2021). Consequently, more women who choose to terminate because of fetal genetic impairment may do so earlier based on inaccurate information.

Rates of NIPT use will probably remain relatively unchanged for women living at the social margins, but their options about what to do based on the results of genetic screening will be severely constrained. Women with limited means—who lack cash, reliable transportation, guaranteed time off work, and childcare—will face greater difficulties working around abortion bans should they desire to terminate a pregnancy affected by fetal impairment. Some will resort to self-inducing termination, receive services from unqualified "back-alley" providers, or buy abortion pills online (which may or may not be safe, depending on the source). Abortions procured under unsafe conditions will put women at increased risk of uterine perforation, hemorrhage, infection, and death (Harris and Grossman 2020). In addition, countless pregnant individuals will be forced to carry unwanted or untenable pregnancies to term, thereby experiencing what the Court's dissenting minority in *Dobbs* describes as the "profound loss of autonomy and dignity that coerced pregnancy and birth always impose."[2] Forced pregnancy will be especially precarious for Black women, as they are three times more likely to "die from pregnancy-related causes" than their white counterparts owing to systemic health inequities that make them more likely to have little or no health insurance, experience high-risk pregnancies, and receive discriminatory and/or low-quality obstetric care (Hoyert 2020).

Women from lower-income backgrounds in states that ban abortion will not only find their reproductive choices severely curtailed by *de jure* restrictions on abortion access; they will also continue to face the socioeconomic pressures wrought by the neoliberal policies we have described throughout this book. States like Texas, which currently bans abortion after six weeks of pregnancy without exception for rape or incest, are likely to see sharp increases in birth rates as women without the means to travel out of state or order abortifacient medications have babies. Yet the states that have most aggressively curtailed abortion access are also among those that have demonstrated the least capacity for providing children (with and without

---

[2] *Dobbs v. Jackson Women's Health Organization* 597 U.S. ___ (2022), 40.

disabilities) with safe and supportive environments. Of the states that have banned abortion in the immediate aftermath of *Dobbs*, five were among those that also refused to expand Medicaid under the Affordable Care Act, and three others have subsequently passed further restrictions.[3] These states are also among those with the highest levels of childhood poverty and lowest investments in public education spending. Without realigning investments in public health, childcare, welfare, and education to cohere with enforced motherhood, these states will effectively penalize women for becoming pregnant and then fail to help their families flourish once the children are born. The lack of public support will hit Black families especially hard, since they are more likely to live in households that cannot cover basic living expenses related to food, housing, and transportation (Edwards 2022).

All in all, the setbacks for racial and gender equality cannot be exaggerated. The *Dobbs* decision will all too often have devastating consequences for those in need of abortion services. Personal decisions about reproduction are among the most consequential choices a person can make, and women living in states with abortion bans will be disempowered to make autonomous decisions about their own reproductive healthcare for themselves. Without constitutional protections, women will suffer, since ending *Roe* will not end the need for abortions; it will just shift where they can happen, for whom, and under what conditions.

The end of constitutional abortion rights is a disability justice issue as well. Despite widespread stereotypes that women with disabilities are asexual and/or unfit for parenthood, many disabled women do indeed get pregnant. Like non-disabled women, they also need access to abortion services, especially since certain types of impairments and underlying medical conditions can make pregnancy high risk in ways that restrictive laws tend to disregard. In addition, states without exceptions for rape could put women with disabilities in dire circumstances, as they are three times more likely to experience sexual assault than the non-disabled population (Fisher et al. 2016). People with disabilities also confront additional barriers to accessing abortion services from afar in the face of inaccessible transportation systems. Disabled people live in poverty at twice the rate of people without disabilities, so traveling out of state is a class privilege that many disabled women cannot afford (Drew 2015).

---

[3] States that have both banned abortion and failed to adopt ACA Medicaid expansion are Alabama, Mississippi, South Dakota, Texas, and Wisconsin (Tennessee and Wyoming are expected to ban abortion access soon). States that have both restricted abortion access and failed to adopt ACA Medicaid expansion are Florida, Georgia, and South Carolina.

Moreover, because the loss of bodily autonomy has a deep history in the disability community, many people with disabilities are disinclined to celebrate restrictions on people's rights to make decisions about their own healthcare for themselves, even if they have qualms about the potential eugenic implications of selective abortion. A legal memo signed by nine disability rights organizations warned that overturning *Roe* could strip out a core constitutional basis for protecting the bodily integrity of people with disabilities in a wide variety of contexts, including "the right to accept or refuse care, the right not to be sterilized against one's will, some aspects of the right to keep medical information private, and the right to family living arrangements of one's choice" (Autistic Self-Advocacy Network 2022: 2). Abortion bans will not eliminate ableism, but they may open doors for other laws restricting bodily autonomy.

Thus, given the *Dobbs* decision's negative fallout for members of socially marginalized groups, the need for coalition politics and intersectional solidarity has never been more urgent. Anti-abortion activists and lawmakers are currently strategizing about how to pass state legislation to block the sale of abortion pills, enshrine state-level constitutional abortion bans, and even potentially pass a federal prohibition. The pro-life movement may not have public opinion on its side, but it is a well-funded, well-organized, and politically savvy movement with renewed momentum in the wake of *Roe*'s reversal.[4] A broad-based coalition movement, working together in united opposition, will be necessary to resist the ongoing assault on bodily autonomy and human dignity.

Looking forward, reproductive justice organizations, which are largely founded and run by women of color, have built a strong foundation to lead the way in a post-*Roe* political landscape using tactics not exclusively reliant on state and federal courts. *Roe* may have provided constitutional protections for abortion, but on its own it was never enough. Women of color know this all too well, and reproductive justice organizations have filled in the gaps to empower all people to take control of their own family-planning decisions and reproductive health. Moving forward, they will need more money and a committed network of activists that can organize protests, mobilize voters in states with ballot initiatives to enshrine reproductive freedom in state constitutions, lobby Congress to codify protections for abortion in federal law, repeal the Hyde amendment, raise money for local abortion funds, train providers, counter clinic harassment, and much more. Following *Dobbs*, the

---

[4] According to recent polls, a majority of the American public favours legalizing abortion (Pew Research Center 2022).

References

Autistic Self-Advocacy Network (2022). *Memorandum: Dobbs* v. *Jackson Women's Health Organization and its Implications for Reproductive, Civil, and Disability Rights*. Washington: Autistic Self-Advocacy Network, https://autisticadvocacy.org/wp-content/uploads/2022/06/Dobbs-memo.pdf.

Center for Reproductive Rights (2022). *Which US States are Poised to Ban Abortion?*, https://reproductiverights.org/states-banning-abortion-post-roe/.

Drew, Julia Rivera (2015). "Disability, Poverty, and Material Hardship since the Passage of the ADA," *Disability Studies Quarterly*, 35/3.

Edwards, Khadijah (2022). *Most Black Americans Say they can Meet Basic Needs Financially, but Many Still Experience Economic Insecurity*. Washington: Pew Research Center, https://www.pewresearch.org/fact-tank/2022/02/23/most-black-americans-say-they-can-meet-basic-needs-financially-but-many-still-experience-economic-insecurity/.

Fisher, Marisa, et al. (2016). "Victimisation and Social Vulnerability of Adults with Intellectual Disability: A Review of Research Extending beyond Wilson and Brewer," *Australian Psychologist*, 51/2: 114–27.

Guttmacher Institute (2022). *Abortion Policy in the Absence of* Roe. New York: Guttmacher Institute, https://www.guttmacher.org/state-policy/explore/abortion-policy-absence-roe.

Harris, Lisa, and Daniel Grossman (2020). "Complications of Unsafe and Self-Managed Abortion," *New England Journal of Medicine*, 382/11: 1029–40.

Hoyert, Donna (2020). *Maternal Mortality Rates in the United States, 2020*. Atlanta, GA: Centers for Disease Control and Prevention, https://www.cdc.gov/nchs/data/hestat/maternal-mortality/2020/maternal-mortality-rates-2020.htm.

Kliff, Sarah, and Aatish Bhatia (2021). "When they Warn of Rare Disorders, these Prenatal Tests are Usually Wrong," *New York Times*, January 1, https://www.nytimes.com/2022/01/01/upshot/pregnancy–birth–genetic–testing.html.

Pew Research Center (2022). *America's Abortion Quandary*. Washington: Pew Research Center, https://www.pewresearch.org/religion/2022/05/06/americas-abortion-quandary/.

Index

ableism 90, 92–93, 155–176
  assumptions 185
  biases 21, 23–25, 97–98, 102–104, 111, 112–113
  changing widespread attitudes 171
  cultural constructions 161–169
  and Down syndrome 8
  marginalization of children with disabilities 157
  medical profession 21
  prejudice 161–163
  and sexism 14
  socialization 99–100
  social messaging 25
abortion, selective 1, 4, 5–6, 14
  see also prenatal non-discrimination acts; pro-choice position
  access barriers 26, 65
  bans on 26, 193–197
  criminalizing in cases of fetal genetic impairment 3, 61, 71, 80, 193–194
  culture war, in the United States 1
  and Down syndrome 3, 8
  end of constitutional rights 196
  guilt following 174
  illegal 71–72
  inequalities exposed by *Dobbs v. Jackson* 26
  legal access to 15–16
  legal status 193–194
  motivation for 162
  national debate 2–3
  opponents 79
  and prenatal genetic testing 3, 9, 10–14, 24–25, 68–70, 73–74, 77–78, 176, 183, 193
  right to 15
absence of choices 45
achievement dignity 48
Achieving Better Life Experience (ABLE) 131
ACMG *see* American College of Medical Genetics and Genomics (ACMG)

ACOG *see* American Congress of Obstetricians and Gynecologists (ACOG)
activities of daily living (ADLs) 122–123, 159–160
advanced maternal age
  Down syndrome risk 1–2, 6–7
Affordable Care Act 2, 195–196
agency
  and autonomy 13–14, 36–37
Allen, Amy 12–13
alpha-fetoprotein (AFP) 7
Alstott, Anne 76, 125–126
American College of Medical Genetics and Genomics (ACMG) 1–2
American Congress of Obstetricians and Gynecologists (ACOG) 1–2
Americans with Disabilities Act (1990) 184–185
amniocentesis 5–7
anencephaly 8
aneuploidy 7
anti-abortion movement
  see also pro-life movement
  activism 197
  agenda 3–4, 91
anti-discrimination legislation 8
Arizona 3
Asch, Adrienne 15–18, 101, 102–103, 137–138, 162
Asian Communities for Reproductive Justice 67–68
Association of American Medical Colleges (AAMC) 107–108
authority
  of physician 93–97
autonomia (capacity for self-determination) 40
autonomy 35–55
  and agency 13–14, 36–37
  as an aspirational ideal 38
  bodily 62–63
  conceptual disagreement 22

200 Index

autonomy (*Continued*)
  decision-making 35–36, 41, 50–51,
    95–96, 123–124
  de jure, of women 38
  and dignity 47–49
    of autonomous women 71
  and disability studies 35–36, 43–44
  and feminism 12–13, 35, 38, 42
  full 13–14
  and independence 43
  individual 14–15, 40, 41, 44
  liberal 43–44
  and liberty 37
  masculinist and ableist conceptions of 22
  meaning 39–47
  moral 48
  normative defense of 50–51
  patient *see* patient autonomy
  perfectionist legal framework, favoring 22
  personal 14, 40, 73
  philosophical conceptualization 12
  and politics 22–23, 51–55
    as a practical political ideal 12
  and prenatal genetic screening 39
  prenatal genetic screening
    undermining 102–103
  and privacy 41
  reasons for language of 36–39
  relational *see* relational autonomy
  reproductive *see* reproductive autonomy
  respect for 13–14, 35, 36, 52, 54
    reproductive autonomy 62–63, 71
  and self-determination 40, 43, 64, 80
  and "the social" 46–47
  as a standard 38
  theories 40
  traditional theories 41–42
  value 47–51
  and well-being 54

Baker, Courtney 99
Bakht, Natasha 174–175
Barrett, Amy Coney 9
Beauchamp, Tom
  Principles of Biomedical Ethics 95–96
Beck, Elizabeth 69–70
Bella's Gift (Santorum) 2
Belmont Report (1979) 93
Berlin, Isaiah 37, 50–51
Bérubé, Michael 6, 43–44, 101–102, 106

biases
  ableist 21, 23–25, 97–98, 102–104, 111,
    112–113
  class 74
  in counseling 97–98
  cultural norms 14
  information 97–103
  institutional 131, 184–185
  and Medicaid 131, 188–189
  against people with Down's syndrome 162
  against people with intellectual and
    developmental disabilities 162
  of physicians and healthcare
    professionals 95–96, 100–101
  subconscious 162
  symbolic and informal sources 169
Biden, Joseph 188–189
biocitizenship 133–135
bioethics 10–11, 19, 39, 68, 93
biotechnology 1–2, 5–7, 11–12, 62–63,
    77–78, 133–134, 137–138
Bittman, Michael 158–159
Blum, Linda 159–160
Brock, Dan 69–70
Brosco, Jeffrey 73–74
Brownback, Sam 91
Brownmiller, Susan 65
Buck v. Bell (1925) 68–69
Bumiller, Kristin 129
Bush, Kelsey 140–141
Buss, Sarah 50

Canterbury v. Spence (1972) 94–95
capacity presumption 43–44
capitalism 187
  abuses of 143
  capitalist values, influence on
    reproduction 11
  global 11
CAPS *see* Coalition for Access to Prenatal
    Screening (CAPS)
care
  see also childcare; healthcare system
  Affordable Care Act 2
  feminization of 25
  foster-care 129–130, 173–174
  privatizing 77
  US long-term care system, home- or
    community-based settings 24–26,
    73, 124–125, 145–146, 188–189

Index **201**

#*CareCantWait* coalition 188–189
caregiver rights 76
carrier screening 5–6
case managers, mothers acting as 159–160
CBS
   CBS News 2–3
   Face the Nation 2
Centers for Disease Control (CDC) 183–186
Centers for Medicare and Medicaid Services
   (CMS) 109–110
cfDNA screening 7
Chambers, Clare 12–13
Charlton-Daily, Rachel 187
childbirth, delaying 158
childcare
   affordable 62–63
   children seen as public goods 139–140
   collective responsibility for 76
   costs *see* costs of caring for disabled child
   and costs of lifelong motherhood 158–160
   government costs 126–127
   lack of accessible arrangements 127–128
   privatized 75–77, 126
   responsibilities 160
   skilled 128–129, 144–145
   social expectations as to 66
   state support for 76
   subsidized 138–140
children, commodification 11
Children's Health Insurance (CHIP)
   programs 129–130
Childress, James
   Principles of Biomedical Ethics 95–96
chorionic villus sampling (CVS) 1, 5–7, 121,
   194–195
chromosomal atypicalities 1
civil society 79–81, 156, 162–163, 169
class privilege 146–147, 196
Coalition for Access to Prenatal Screening
   (CAPS) 137–138
collective governance 40
Collins, Lynda 174–175
Collins, Patricia Hill 174
Community Living Assistance Services and
   Supports (CLASS) Act 145
conscience clauses 91, 96–97, 106–109
consent
   informed *see* informed consent
   true 94–95
   voluntary 94

constitutional law 79
Cooley, Carl 104–105
co-optation, feminist fears of 15–16
Cornell, Drucilla 71
costs of caring for disabled child 18–19,
   66, 70, 122–125, 139, 157–158, 160,
   187–188
   financial burden on society 69–70
   foster-care 69–70
   genetic counseling 109–110
   healthcare 39, 69–70, 72, 127
   as lifestyle choice to be borne by parent
      alone 76, 136, 137–138
   lost earnings 158–159
   personal 172
   political 76
   prenatal screening programs 69–70
   screening 69–70, 109–110
   services 130, 137–138
   sharing 138–141
   by the state 126–127
COVID-19 pandemic 25–26, 183–187
credibility excess/deficits 106
cultural norms 5, 21, 25, 53, 62, 156, 162,
   169, 176
   see also social norms
   biased 14
   changing 73
   defining 156–157
   normalcy 80–81
   oppressive 25
   restrictive 172–173
   sexist 187–188
CVS *see* chorionic villus sampling (CVS)

Daniels, Cynthia 113
Davis, Dena 136
Davy, Laura 43
decision-making
   autonomous 35–36, 41, 50–51, 95–96,
      123–124
   capacities 52–54, 112–113
   ethical 11
   following a positive Down syndrome
      diagnosis 123
   free, informed and non-coercive 94–96
   and information 95–96, 101–102, 114
   medical 92–93, 99
   personal 10–11
   power 64

202 Index

decision-making (*Continued*)
  prenatal screening 123
  process 8, 14–15, 90, 163
  reproductive 4–6, 14–15, 26, 81–82,
      100–101, 112–113, 156
  responsible 166–167
  sharing 174–175
  and social class 123
  strategic 78–79
  willfull 40
degrading treatment, prenatal
      non-discrimination acts as 71–72
dehumanization 49–50
deinstitutionalization 169
Denbow, Jennifer 36–38, 136–137
Denmark 145
derivative dependency 139
determinism 13–14
diagnostic tests 5–6, 99–100
  see also prenatal genetic screening/testing
DiGeorge syndrome 7
dignity 47–48
  dignified treatment 70–74
disability
  see also disability rights; disability studies
  feminist disability theorists 15–16
  and impairment 17
  and neoliberal policy 125–133
disability cultural competency 107–108
disability-friendly public policies 20
disability justice 20
disability paradox 103–106
disability rights
  and anti-abortion agenda, advancing 3
disability studies 16–21
  and autonomy 35–36, 43–44
  critical disability studies 4, 35, 55
  and liberalism 41
  medical model 17–18
  social model 17–18
discrimination
  anti-discrimination legislation 8
  pervasive 140–141
  prenatal non-discrimination acts 3–4,
      15–16, 67, 69–70, 72, 136–137, 194
  societal 17–18
  workplace 66
"distributed mothering" 174
DNA

cfDNA (cell-free fetal DNA) 1
  discovery of 25–26
  placental 7
*Dobbs v. Jackson Women's Health
      Organization* (2022) 26, 193–196
doctors *see* physicians
domestic work 158
Down syndrome
  ableist biases 23–24
  and advanced maternal age 1–2, 6–7
  advocacy groups 9
  associated health problems 6–7, 100–101
  biases against people with 162
  care in home setting 24–25
  causes 100–101
  characteristics 100–101, 155
  children outliving parents 163
  clinical history of screening for 7
  common chromosomal disorder 6
  costs to caregivers 24–25
  distinguished from other conditions 8
  fetal diagnoses 6
  forcing women to carry fetuses to
      term 69–70
  and justification of abortion 2–3
  life expectancy 8
  lived experience 8
  mosaic 6–7, 121
  negative and unfounded
      stereotypes 98–99
  perceived as "Mongolism" 155
  physical characteristics 6–7
  positive aspects of bringing up a child
      with 103–104
  quality of life, improvement in 8
  and selective abortion 8
  severity of symptoms 98–99
  termination rates for fetuses with 2–3
  testimonial injustice against
      parents 92–93
  translocation 6–7
  trisomy 6
  types 6
  variation in mental capacities 6–7, 98–99
Down syndrome (trisomy 21) 1
Due Process clause 64–65
Dwight, Valle 98
Dworkin, Gerald 39
Dworkin, Ronald 52

Index **203**

Earle, Sarah 77–78
Earned income Tax Credit 131
Edwards syndrome (trisomy 18) 1
Eichner, Maxine 24–25, 124–125, 138–139, 142–143
  The Supportive State 141
eleutheria (freedom from external constraints) 40
emotion, and rationality 42
English Civil War 40
Engster, Daniel 37–38
epistemic authority 91–92
epistemic humility 107
epistemic injustice 91–92, 105
Epstein, Julia 3
estriol 7
ethics
  decision-making 11
  medical 93
  and political theory 9–12
eugenics 20, 68–70
  strong *vs* weak 68–69
exclusionary policies 17
expressivist objection 16

Fair Labor Standards Act (FLSA) 140–141
"fake news" *see* misinformation/"fake news"
Family and Individual Needs for Disability Supports (FINDS) Survey 127–128, 132
Feder, Judith 145
feminism
  and autonomy 12–13, 35, 38, 42
    dignity of autonomous women 71
  disability theorists 15–16
  early theorizing 64
  fears of co-optation 15–16
  feminist theory 4, 12–16, 35
  Kant, critique of 42
  legal theorists 138–139
  and liberalism 51, 64, 70
  and negative liberty 75
  prenatal testing and state regulation 91–92
  and relational autonomy 38
fetuses with impairments, complexity 6
Fine, Michelle 15–16
Fineman, Martha 138–140
  The Autonomy Myth 139

First Call programs 111
forced pregnancy 195
forced sterilization, state-sanctioned 61, 68–69, 72
Formosa, Paul 48
foster-care 129–130, 173–174
Fraser, Nancy 46–47
freedom
  see also liberty
  and autonomy 37–38
  to be left alone 142
  of choice 45, 64–65
  from external constraints 40
  from government intrusion 76–77
  individual/personal 50–51, 94, 187
  from involuntary sterilization 61
  and negative liberty 37
  from obligation 39
  reproductive 123–124, 197–198
  of the will 39
free market 125
Fricker, Miranda 23–24, 91–93, 105, 106
Friedan, Betty 71
Frye, Marilyn 44–45

Galston, William 53
gametes 5–6
Gammon, Bryan 109–110
Garland-Thomson, Rosemarie 101, 176
gender-neutral language 4–5
Generations Ahead 67–68, 77–78
genetic counseling 23–24, 194
  and healthcare system 91, 104–107, 109–110
genomic medicine 4–5, 23, 74–81
  see also American College of Medical Genetics and Genomics (ACMG)
Getting, Elizabeth 123
Ginsburg, Faye 122–123, 174
"good mothers" 25, 62–63, 73, 161, 164–166
Gottlieb, Roger 168
government regulation
  "pro-choice" defense of 106–114
Great Depression 187–188
Griswold v. Connecticut (1965) 63, 77
gross negligence 109–110
Guterman, Andrea 69–70
Guttmacher Institute 123
Gyngell, Christopher 68–69

204 Index

Habermas, Jürgen 47
habitus 21
harm principle (Mill) 41
Harris v. McRae (1980) 64–65
Hays, Sharon 164
healthcare professionals 23–24, 95–97, 104
  see also physicians
  biases of 95–96, 100–101
  information provided by 102–103
  negative quality-of-life assessments of
    disability 104
  prenatal genetic counseling sessions 194
healthcare system 89–114
  biased and limited information, mis-
    informed choice from 23–24,
    97–103
  and genetic counseling 91, 106–107,
    109–110
  informed consent and physician
    authority 93–97
  "pro-choice" definition of government
    regulation 106–114
  testimonial injustice 23–24, 103–106
health insurance 1–2, 73, 129–130
  Children's Health Insurance (CHIP)
    programs 129–130
  long-term care 147
  public and private 106–107, 109–110
  work-related 184
Hershey, Laura 138
Heyer, Katharina 15
Hillyer, Barbara 165–166
Hirschmann, Nancy 14, 37–38, 45–46,
  54–55
Hitler, Adolf 68–69
Ho, Anita 107
Hobbes, Thomas 41–42
  Leviathan 40
Holmes, Oliver Wendell 68–69
Hong Kong
  non-invasive prenatal testing (NIPT) 1
Hubbard, Ruth 15–16, 18
human chorionic gonadotropin (hCG) 7
humility 107
Hyde Amendment (1977) 64–65, 75, 79–80,
  197–198

Iceland 2–3
IDEA *see* Individuals with Disabilities
  Education Act (IDEA), 1990

ideal motherhood 164
ideology, maternal 165
illegal abortion 72
independence
  and autonomy 43
Indiana 3, 91
individualism
  atomistic individuals 41–42, 44, 51
  individual autonomy 14–15, 40, 41, 44
  individual freedom 50–51, 94, 187
  individual responsibility 10, 18, 19–20,
    76–77, 134, 135–137
  and liberalism 41–42, 44
Individualized Education Program
  (IEP) 131
Individuals with Disabilities Education Act
  (IDEA), 1990 131–132
information
  access to 101–102, 111, 114, 134
  accurate, comprehensive and up-
    to-date 23–24, 90, 91, 111,
    185–186
  balanced 90, 108–111, 114
  biased, limited or incomplete 23–24, 90,
    91–92, 97–103, 112–114
  and decision-making 95–96, 102, 114
  disparities 95
  disseminating/distributing 23–24, 91
  distorted 23–24, 91–92, 95–96
  doctors as gatekeepers of 96
  on fetal health 96–97
  genetic/on Down syndrome 14–15,
    61–62, 71–72, 90, 92–93, 101,
    102–103, 135
  inaccessible 101
  inaccurate 89–90, 194–195
  informed consent 113
  integrity of 111
  lack of 22–23, 112–113
  legislation 90–91, 111–113
  mandated disclosure 114
  manipulating 94–96
  medical/provided by healthcare profes-
    sionals 95–97, 100–103, 106, 113,
    197
  misinformation/"fake news" 90–92,
    97–103, 112, 185–186
  misleading 79, 90, 102–103
  out-of-date 23–24, 92
  politicization of 91–92, 185–186

"post-truth" 91–92
prejudicial 23–24
prenatal screening 96–97, 99–100, 114
presenting 97–98
pro-information movement 90
provision of 20, 22–23, 96–97, 105, 110, 114
and reproductive autonomy 91–92
responsibility of providers of 97
risks of termination 112
sources 95–96, 101–102
standardized 106
stigmatizing 10
supplementary 112
testimonial 101–102, 104–105
unsubstantiated 113
withholding 94–96, 108–109
written, federally-approved 111
information acts 90
informed consent 91–95, 106–107, 112, 113
and physician authority 93–97
instrumental activities of daily living (IADLs) 122–123, 159–160
intellectual and developmental disabilities, people with
see also Down syndrome
associated costs and expenses 127, 187–188
bias against 162
bullying, ridiculing, excluding and disparaging 25, 161–162
caregivers, effect on working hours 127–128
community-based long-term support needs 143–144
compensation issues 140
contributions to society 170
existing infrastructure, exposure by COVID pandemic 25–26
inability of some to work 141
incidence of disability 73–74
institutionalization 184–185
limited support for 20–21, 132–133
media representation 169–170
need to welcome 176
offensive terminology, demands to eliminate 169–170
physical abuse of 163
sexual violence and physical abuse of 163
social isolation of 161

and the state 138–139
variation in lived experience for carers 159–160
workforce participation 140–141
intensive mothering 164
in vitro fertilization (IVF) 5–6, 194

Jackson, Emily 81
Jacobs School of Medicine and Biomedical Sciences, University of Buffalo 107–108
Japan 145
Jarman, Michelle 15–16
Jesudason, Sujatha 3, 15–16, 19–20, 22–23, 62, 77–78
justice, reproductive *see* reproductive justice

Kafer, Alison 15–16
Kant, Immanuel 42, 48
Kaposy, Chris 133, 169
Choosing Down Syndrome 11
Kennedy, Edward 91
Kennedy–Brownback Act 79–80, 106–107, 110, 111–113
Kentucky 3
Kittay, Eva 15–16, 48–50, 73–74, 157, 162–163, 166, 172–173
Kuhse, Helga 49–50

laboratory-developed tests (LDTs) 11–12
labor-force participation, by women 158
Landsman, Gail Heidi 166–167
Leach, Brittany 114
Legacy Health System
Center for Maternal–Fetal Medicine 121
leisure time of women, fragmentation/contamination 158–159
Lettercase National Center for Prenatal and Postnatal Resources 110–111
Levy, Ariel and Deborah 121
liberalism
see also neoliberal welfare state
and autonomy 40–41, 43, 47, 51, 53, 139
and bioethics 93
critiques 41–42
and feminism 51, 64, 70
and individualism 41–42, 44
liberal democracy 10–11, 36, 40
liberal state 54, 62–63, 65, 79–80, 141
mainstream theory 22–23, 36, 41–44, 55

206 Index

liberalism (*Continued*)
  modern 40
  non-interference, commitment to 142
  perfectionist liberal framework 22, 35, 36,
    52, 53–54
  political thought 4, 41, 63, 93
  and privacy 22–23, 142
  and rationality 42
  society 67
  tradition 93
  values 142
liberty
  and agency 36
  and autonomy
    in political theory 36–38, 54–55
    reproductive 66–68, 72–73, 75, 79
  Fourteenth Amendment, protected by 70,
    193
  negative 37–38, 40, 50–51, 54–55, 64–68,
    72–75, 79, 81–82, 125–126
  non-interference, commitment to 64, 75,
    142
  positive 37
life expectancy
  in Down syndrome 8
Littlejohn, Krystale 18
Lo, Dennis 1–2
Locke, John
  Second Treatise of Government 40
Lomasky, Loren 41
Long-Term Care Trust Act (2019) 145
Louisiana 91
low-income backgrounds 77, 195–196
Luxembourg 145
Lynch, Holly 108–109

McCabe, Joshua 131
Mackenzie, Catriona 22, 44, 48, 53
McKinney, Claire 16–17
MacKinnon, Catherine 74
McMahan, Jeff 48–49
malpractice insurance policy 99–100
Marshall, T. H. 74
maternal serum screening 7
MaterniT21 screening procedure 6
means-tested programs 131
Medicaid 11–12, 64–65, 109–110, 130,
  188–189
  benefit for families having children with
    Down's syndrome 143–144

commissioners 137–138
financial assistance, through 129–130,
  143–144
institutional bias 131, 184–185
low reimbursement rates 145–146
waiver programs 130–132, 143–144
medical model 17–18
medical professionals *see* healthcare
  professionals; physicians
Medicare 131
Meyers, Diana 164, 172
mild cognitive impairments 43–44
Mill, John Stuart 41
Miller, David 121–122
Mills, Catherine 21, 166
misinformation/ "fake news" 90–92,
  97–103, 112, 185–186
  see also information
Mississippi
  Gestational Act 194
Missouri 3, 193–194
Mitchell, David 128–129
mommy tax 158
moral theories 10–11
mosaicism, Down syndrome 6–7
mother-blaming 164–166

National Down Advocacy Coalition
  (NDAC) 170
National Down Syndrome Congress 9, 110
National Down Syndrome Society 9, 110,
  170
National Organization for Women 71
National Society of Genetic Counselors
  (NSGC) 110
Nazi medical war crimes 93
Nebraska 91
Nedelsky, Jennifer 41–42
negative liberty and autonomy
  political theory 37–38, 40, 50–51, 54–55
  reproductive autonomy 64–68, 72–75, 79,
    81–82
neo-eugenic thinking 68–69
neoliberal welfare state 19–20, 121–147
  budget reductions 123
  disability and neoliberal policy 125–133
  economic and social pressures 134
  economic policies 21
  limited government 125
  minimal welfare-state provisions 126

neoliberalism as a multifaceted concept 125
policy implications 143–146
pregnant women as neoliberal biocitizens 133–138
and supportive state 138–143
New Deal 188
NIPT *see* non-invasive prenatal testing (NIPT)
Nodland, Beth 136–137
non-directiveness 106–107
non-discrimination acts, prenatal 3
non-invasive prenatal testing (NIPT) 1–2, 5–7, 11–12, 26, 89–90, 137–138, 194–195
North Dakota 3, 193–194
Nozick, Robert 41
nuchal fold 7
nuchal translucency screening 7
nuclear family, idealized 167–169
Nuremberg Code (1949) 93–94
standards 94–95
nurturance, complex systems of 142
Nussbaum, Martha 46–47, 52

Obama, Barack 145
Ohio 3
Okin, Susan Moller 42
Olmstead v. L.C. (1999) 184–185
O'Neill, Onora 64
Oregon
Legacy Health System 121
O'Reilly, Andrea 172–173
Organization for Economic Cooperation and Development (OECD) 126–127
"other-mothering" 174

Palin, Sarah 9
Parens, Erik 17–18
Parish, Susan 163
Patau syndrome (trisomy 13) 1
patient autonomy 91–97, 106–107
see also autonomy; relational autonomy; reproductive autonomy
informed consent 94–95
respecting 94, 108–109
undermining 108–109
people with disabilities, complexity 6
"perfect babies," desire for 25, 62–63, 73, 156–157, 161, 166–167

perfectionist liberal framework 22, 35, 36, 52, 53–54
person-centered self-directed services model 144–145
pervasive reproductive gaze 7
Petchesky, Rosalind Pollack 74
physicians
see also healthcare professionals
authority of 93–97
biases of 95–96, 100–101
doctor–patient relationship 93, 97–98, 100–101
failure to convey information adequately 99–100
paternalism of 94
Piepmeier, Alison 14–16, 19, 163
Planned Parenthood of Southeastern Pennsylvania v. Casey (1992) 70, 112, 114, 193
pluralism 54
political theory 9–12
autonomy in *see* autonomy
concerned with organization and management of society 9–10
and ethics 9–12
politics
see also political theory
and autonomy 51–55
and prenatal testing 10–11
reproductive autonomy and genomic medicine 74–81
pregnancy
commercialization of 11
pregnant women as neoliberal biocitizens 138–143
preimplantation genetic diagnosis (PGD) 5–6
prejudice 105–106
ableist 161–163
prenatal genetic screening/testing 5–6
ableist prejudice 162
and autonomy 39
economic rationale underpinning 19–20
impact on women's reproductive autonomy 6
information 96–97, 99–100
lack of choice, feeling of 97–98
national debate 2–3
normative aim 4
and political economy 124

208 Index

prenatal genetic screening/testing
    (*Continued*)
  programs 20–21
  and reproductive autonomy 22–23, 97–98
  rise of, across Europe 2–3
  routinization of 133
  and selective abortion 9–14, 24–25,
    68–70, 73–74, 77–78, 176, 183, 193
  undermining autonomy 102–103
Prenatally and Postnatally Diagnosed
    Conditions Awareness Act (2008) 91
prenatal non-discrimination acts 3–4,
    15–16, 67, 136–137, 194
  as degrading treatment 69–70, 72
prenatal screening technologies 1–2, 4, 14,
    19–20, 22–23, 39, 62–63, 68, 73,
    81–82, 133, 134–137
  available to all requirement 71–72
  debating use of 146–147
  development and application 77–78
  neo-eugenic thinking 69–70
  political theory 10–12
  refusal of 136
  voluntary 67
prenatal surgical repair 8
privacy 14, 22–23
  and autonomy 37–38, 41, 62–66, 72–74,
    76, 80
  legal 65, 75, 77
  liberal commitment to 142
  negative liberty privacy-centered
    strategy 74
  right to 62–66, 72–74, 77, 80
    constitutional 63
    legal 77
    women 64
pro-choice position 11, 14, 15–16, 64,
    73–74, 76–77
professionalization of motherhood 164
pro-information movement 90
pro-life movement 114, 197
  ideology 23–24
  legislation 79
  organizations 3, 91, 114
  propaganda 92
Pulrang, Andrew 186

Quest Diagnostics 6

racial supremacy, Nazi-like 68–69
Radigan, Kathy 173
Rakowski, Eric 136

Rapp, Rayna 15–16, 68, 122–123, 174
rationality 42
Rawls, John 22, 52, 141–142
Raz, Joseph 22, 50, 54
Read, Janet 159–160
Reagan, Ronald 125–126
Reardon, Marguerite 89–90
relational autonomy 35–36, 38, 44–45, 55,
    62, 80–81, 171–172
  see also autonomy; reproductive autonomy
  aspirational theory of 38
  compared with traditional masculinist
    and ableist conceptions 22
  feminist 189
  and negative liberty 38
  political philosophy 22–23
reproductive autonomy 4–6, 14, 15–16, 39,
    55, 61–82
  see also autonomy; relational autonomy
  denial of as an attack on women's
    dignity 70–71
  dignified treatment 70–74
  disability studies 20–21
  epistemic injustice, restricted by 92
  and existence of prenatal genetic
    screening 22–23
  financial barriers to 24–25
  governmental restraint and active
    support 22–23
  impact of prenatal genetic screening on 6
  information acts enhancing 91
  meaning 22–23, 63–68
  and negative liberty 64–68, 72–75, 79,
    81–82
  normative value 70, 73–74
  politics 74–81
  and prenatal genetic testing 97–98
  rhetoric 21
  social norms 21
  undermining 23–24
  womanhood and motherhood 65
  women of color 67–68, 75, 76–77
reproductive justice 15–16, 22–23, 26, 62,
    67–68, 79–81
  and injustice 77
  movement 62–63, 77, 78–79, 176
  organizations 197–198
  progressive 55, 75
reproductive preferences 13–14, 25,
    156–157, 184–185, 187–188
  and reproductive autonomy 62–63, 65,
    80–81

reproductive rights, as negative rights to
non-interference 64
reprogenetics 5–6, 22–23, 26, 55, 135
and reproductive autonomy 62, 77–78
responsibility
biocivic 134
childcare 160
collective 19–20, 72–73, 138, 139–140,
176
decision-making 166–167
financial 21, 135
individualization of 136–137
information provision 97
moral 10
personal/individual 10, 18, 19–20, 76–77,
134, 135–137
positive 75
primary 5, 18, 61, 125–126, 174, 176
private 19
privatizing 146–147
public 135
redistributing 171
social 74, 135
state 64–65, 138–139, 141, 142–143
Rich, Adrienne 49–50
Rimmerman, Aerie 131
Roberts, Dorothy 10–11, 15–16, 19–23,
37–38, 64–65, 70, 77–78, 133–135
Roberts, M. A. 19
Robinson, Spottswood William III
(Judge) 94–95
Roe v. Wade (1973) 3, 63, 76, 79, 108–109,
193
overturning 197
Rose, Nicholas 133–134
Rosenfeld, Sophia 91–92
Ross, Loretta 22–23
Rothman, Barbara Katz 19–20
Rousseau, Jean-Jacques 42

Samerski, Silja 134
Santorum, Rick 2
Saxton, Marsha 15–16, 77–78, 106
Scanlon, Thomas 49–50
Schroeder, Doris 49–50
screening procedures 5–6
screening technologies 1–2
Seavilleklein, Victoria 123
Sedgewick, Sally 42
selective abortion *see* abortion, selective

self-determination 13–14, 22–23, 147
and autonomy 40, 43, 64, 80
self-governance 37–41, 45–46, 49–50, 53
self-sacrifice 172
self-sufficiency, ideal of 43
Selgelid, Michael 68–69
Sequenom 6
sexism 14
sexual division of labor 158–160
Shakespeare, Tom 10–11, 68–69, 72
Sharp, Keith 77–78
Sheth, Darpana 122–123
Siebers, Tobin 16–17
Simplican, Stacy Clifford 43–44
Singer, Peter 48–50
SisterSong 67–68
Skotko, Brian 102
sleep deprivation 160
SMFM *see* Society for Maternal Fetal
Medicine (SMFM)
Snyder, Sharon 128–129
social alienation 176
social class
see also class privilege
affect on decision-making following positive Down syndrome
diagnosis 123
biases 74
class privilege 146–147, 196
downplaying of class issues by elite
decision-makers 78–79
effect of raising disabled children on the
middle-classes 127–128
and motherhood ideology 165,
172–173
and poverty 128, 131, 196
private health insurance availability 130
tax law favoring the middle-classes and
wealthy 131
"waiver programs" for middle-class
families 130
social constructivism 46–47
socialization 41–42, 44–46
ableist 99–100
better and worse practices 46–47
feminine 45
oppressive 45
restrictive 45
socially marginalized groups 66
social model 17–18

210 Index

social norms 4–5, 46–47, 80–81
  breaking 168–169
  oppressive 21
  sexist 38, 155–176
  shifting 8
  toxic 157
social policies, neoliberal 126–129, 132, 133,
    137–138
  fiscalization of 131
Social Security Administration 129
Social Security Amendments (1965) 145
society, financial burdens on 69–70
Society for Maternal Fetal Medicine
    (SMFM) 1–2
Solinger, Rickie 22–23
Sophocles
  Antigone 40
South Dakota 3
South Korea 145
special needs, children with 19, 72, 133, 168,
    175
  see also Down syndrome; intellectual and
    developmental disabilities, people
    with
special needs trusts (SNTs) 131
spina bifida 8
Spock, Benjamin 155, 169
stare decisis 193
state–family relations 125–126, 143
status dignity 48–49
Stein, Zena 69–70
stem-cell-derived (SCD) gametes 5–6
stereotyping of disabilities/Down syn-
    drome 65, 80–81, 98–99, 157, 170,
    196
Stoljar, Natalie 22, 44, 54
structural inequality 12–14, 62, 75
structural injustice 163
Supplemental Security Income
    (SSI) 129–130, 132
supportive state concept 24–25, 124–125
Susser, Mervyn 69–70
Suter, Sonia 113
Swartz, Martha 99
Sweden 145
synechdocal thinking 101

Tabatabai, Ahoo 126
Tassé, Marc 140–141
Tay-Sachs 8, 122–123

termination
  see also abortion, selective
  benefits recommended by
    physicians 23–24
  choice of 20–21
  for Down syndrome 8, 11
  pressure for 99
  rates, for fetuses with Down
    syndrome 2–3
  risks 112
  seen as only realistic option 24–25
  selecting *see* abortion, selective
  technologies 5–6
testimonial information 101–102, 104–105
testimonial injustice 23–24, 103–106
Texas 195–196
theories
  feminism 35
  feminist 12–16
  moral 10–11
  political 9–12, 35–55
Thomas, Gareth 7, 20
Thompson, Frank 130
transgender rights movement 4–5
translocation, in Down syndrome 6–7
trisomy, in Down syndrome 6
  trisomy 13 1
  trisomy 18 1
  trisomy 21 1, 121
Trump, Donald 185–186
Tuskegee Syphilis Study, US 93

United States
  see also Medicaid; *individual states*
  abortion access, *Dobbs v. Jackson* decision
    affecting 26
  contraceptives, legal restrictions on use
    of 61, 63
  criminalization of abortion 3, 61, 71, 80,
    193–194
  culture war over abortion and women's
    reproductive rights 1
  as a focus of research 5
  forced sterilization, state-sanctioned 61,
    68–69, 72
  Fourteenth Amendment 70, 193
  limited reproductive choices 61
  long-term care system 24–25
  poverty rates 128

prenatal non-discrimination acts *see*
  prenatal non-discrimination acts
prenatal screening, rise of 2–3
restriction of women's reproductive
  options in 14
Roe v. Wade (1973) 3, 63, 76, 79
self-advocacy movement 169–170
termination rates for Down syndrome 90
welfare policy 126–127
wrongful birth lawsuits *see* wrongful birth
  lawsuits, US

value 47–51
Vehmas, Simo 43
Virginia 91

waiver programs
  demonstrations and targeted
    initiatives 130
  Medicaid 130–132, 143–144
  for middle-class families 129–130
  optional nature 143–144
  "waiver migrants" 143–144
Wajcman, Judy 158–159
Waldman, Ayelet
  Bad Mother 172–173
Wall, Steven 50–51
Wasserman, David 101, 162
Wendell, Susan 43
West, Robin 22–23, 75, 76
Will, George 2–3
Wimbush, Erica 158–159
"Woman's Right to Know" Acts 112–114
women of color 145–147, 183–184, 197–198
  reproductive autonomy 67–68, 75, 76–77
World Health Organization (WHO) 183
wrongful birth lawsuits, US 90, 99–100,
  109–110, 121–123

Yakren, Sofia 122–123